Baby Food Matters

Invest in your baby's crucial first 1000 days

Baby Food Matters

what science says about
how to give your child
healthy eating habits for life

DR CLARE LLEWELLYN
DR HAYLEY SYRAD

First published in Great Britain in 2018 by Yellow Kite
An imprint of Hodder & Stoughton
An Hachette UK company

2

Copyright © Dr Clare Llewellyn and Dr Hayley Syrad 2018

External websites are beyond the control of the authors but
all information is correct at the time of writing.

The information in this book is not intended to replace or conflict with the advice given to
you by your GP or other health professionals. All matters regarding your child's health and
diet should be discussed with your GP or other health professional. The author and
publisher disclaim any liability to directly or indirectly from the use of the material in this
book by any person.

Portion size images and guidance: these images and guidance have
been reproduced with the kind permission of the Infant & Toddler Forum.
For further information visit: www.infantandtoddlerforum.org

Tot-it-Up Calculator: developed by the Infant & Toddler Forum, Tot-It-Up
is an interactive tool designed to monitor and assess the food intake and activity levels
of children aged one–four years. It can help parents and carers see whether children are
getting the right balance of foods to help them lead healthy lives, both now and in the future.
Visit: www.infantandtoddlerforum.org/tot-it-up-login

Tables courtesy of First Steps Nutrition.

The right of Dr Clare Llewellyn and Dr Hayley Syrad to be identified
as the Authors of the Work has been asserted by them in accordance
with the Copyright, Designs and Patents Act 1988.

A CIP catalogue record for this title is available from the British Library

Trade Paperback ISBN 978 1 473 66317 6
Ebook ISBN 978 1 473 66318 3

Typeset in Sabon MT by Palimpsest Book Production Ltd, Falkirk, Stirlingshire

Printed and bound by Clays Ltd, St Ives plc

Hodder & Stoughton policy is to use papers that are natural, renewable
and recyclable products and made from wood grown in sustainable forests.
The logging and manufacturing processes are expected to conform to
the environmental regulations of the country of origin.

Contents

Acknowledgements

We would like to dedicate this book to the late Professor Jane Wardle – a world-leading scientist, and our mentor. Jane introduced us to the fascinating world of children's eating behaviours, inspired us and was the brains behind the Gemini twin study. She changed our lives and those of many children and families who have benefited from her decades of research.

Thank you to our families and friends for their unwavering support; words are not enough.

We must, of course, thank Rory Scarfe, for seeing the potential in our research and making this happen – without you there would be no book.

Thank you to Julia Kellaway (the editorial midwife) and Liz Gough (the visionary) – we have loved working with you both, and your guidance and encouragement along the way have been invaluable.

We thank all of the parents who have shared their experiences with us and helped to bring this book alive.

And thank you to our colleagues for advice and information, and to the exceptional scientists that took the time to peer review this book to ensure the content is accurate and representative of the broad scientific consensus on early nutrition and feeding:

Professor Atul Singhal: Great Ormond Street Children's Charity Professor of Paediatric Nutrition at University College London's Institute of Child Health, and Honorary Consultant Paediatrician at Great Ormond Street Hospital.

Dr Alison Fildes: Psychologist and Research Fellow in the School of Psychology at the University of Leeds.

Dr Helen Croker: Research Dietician and Senior Researcher in Great Ormond Street Institute of Child Health, University College London.

Professor Lynne Daniels: Emeritus Professor in the School of Exercise and Nutrition Sciences, Queensland University of Technology, Australia.

Dr Jennifer Fildes: General Practitioner at Fieldhead Surgery, Leeds.

Dr Angela Flynn: Researcher in the Department of Women and Children's Health, School of Life Course Sciences, King's College London.

We would also like to thank Marta Jackowska (mum of Julia, six months) and Susie Meisel (mum of Hannah, six weeks) for reading the manuscript and giving us their feedback from a mum's point of view.

Finally, thank you to First Steps Nutrition and the Infant & Toddler Forum for sharing their fantastic resources with us.

Introduction

You may be expecting a baby, or you may already have a baby or toddler, and are keen to find out how to give him the best possible start in life. But with all the conflicting advice out there about *what* and *how* to feed your child you may be struggling to make sense of it all. This book is here to separate the facts from the fads and tell you everything you need to know about food, feeding and nutrition for the first 1,000 days of your child's life. From pregnancy and milk-feeding to starting solid foods and dealing with the 'terrible twos', *Baby Food Matters* provides you with evidence-based information and practical guidance, from a *scientific* perspective, to help your child establish healthy eating habits *for life*.

As leading scientists in this field, one of our greatest concerns is that much of the advice offered to parents about feeding is based on 'received wisdom', old wives' tales or simply people's opinion. There is no end of books about parenting and feeding, but most are written by authors with no scientific credentials in this area. In fact, when flicking through the many available books and websites, we were surprised to discover that there is virtually no *scientifically based* information for parents on this topic. As a result, some of the advice provided to parents is misguided or, worse, patently wrong. At best, some writers have years of experience but this is very different from having studied the subject scientifically and having a firm understanding of what is and isn't important, and what does and doesn't work when it comes to optimal nutrition and the best feeding strategies. Even some of the government guidance on feeding doesn't stand up to scrutiny and isn't backed up by solid scientific evidence. As scientists, not mums, we are going to try and replace myth with fact, giving you the knowledge and breaking down the science so that you can make your own well-informed decisions about how to feed your child.

Scientists aren't always great at getting research 'out there' into the public domain. Findings tend to be published in scientific journals that either aren't accessible to those who don't pay the hefty subscription fees or are written in such dense scientific language that, even with PhDs in the field, we find some of them challenging to read and understand!

Throughout this book we have used the highest-quality evidence currently available to give you the most up-to-date scientific perspective on every topic we cover. There are some issues on which there isn't yet a scientific consensus, because evidence is lacking, and others that we are more certain about. We are frank about this and give you the low-down on each topic, taking into account everything we know. We have outlined all of the most important scientific findings on eating and feeding during a child's first 1,000 days and have developed guidance and tips based on those findings to help you navigate the most important period of your baby's life.

As a side note, throughout the book we refer to the baby as 'he'. This is not because we are assuming all babies are male, nor is it an attempt to gender-stereotype, but it helps with flow and ensures there is no confusion when we are referring to the mother as 'she'.

Who We Are

We are scientists who have been researching the eating and feeding habits of babies and toddlers for over a decade and we both have a PhD on this topic. Between us, we have read thousands of scientific papers on the subject. But, importantly, we don't just *read* about the science, we actually *do* the science – we have published nearly 100 scientific papers and articles on this topic and are leaders in the field. Our research team at University College London (UCL), led by Clare, is world-renowned for its knowledge in this area. One of our most significant endeavours has been to help set up the largest ever study into the origins of infant and toddler feeding – the Gemini twin study. Gemini has revolutionised our understanding of early eating and feeding behaviour, and has allowed us to make major new discoveries about the importance of early nutrition and feeding for healthy growth and development. (We describe Gemini in detail, and why it is so important and unique, in Chapter 1.) We met while working together on Gemini, and have remained trusted colleagues and firm friends ever since. Throughout *Baby Food Matters* we will offer practical guidance and advice based on this internationally renowned study, as well as a breadth of other high-quality studies that have been undertaken over decades, to make sure the whole picture is represented.

As well as working on Gemini, we both review and evaluate articles for more than 20 scientific journals and have given a number of talks internationally about work in this area. Clare is an editorial board member of three key scientific journals in the field and teaches research methods and statistics on a Master of Science programme at UCL. She also supervises several PhD researchers in this field of research. In short, we know how to sift through evidence, cut out the nonsense and get to the crucial information. In this book, we have done all of that work for you, so you don't have to.

Aside from our scientific background, we have both had very different personal experiences with eating, which were a big impetus behind us writing this book. As a child Clare had 'failure to thrive' and struggled with excessive food fussiness (in fact, at times she had a full-blown phobia of food), which persisted from toddlerhood into early adulthood. She knows first-hand the stress that this causes parents and families, as well as the individual child. We hope that this book will provide information that minimises the chance of this happening to your own child, and that those of you who are currently dealing with a very fussy eater will get the best possible advice on how to deal with it effectively. Hayley, on the other hand, was a model eater growing up and has never had many hang-ups about food. She was always willing to try new foods and, with the odd exception here and there, she always ate what she was given, without overindulging. She puts this down largely to the feeding methods used by her parents during her early years. (You can read about our stories on pages 8 and 14.)

When we provide you with guidance about feeding your child throughout this book, we have never lost sight of our own experiences, which we hope has ensured that the advice we give you is grounded, realistic, empathic and helpful.

PEER REVIEW

'Peer review' is the process whereby scientists' research (scientific papers, articles and books) is sent to other expert scientists in the field for independent assessment. The peer-review process ensures that scientifically based information that is published in the public domain is accurate, of high quality and is presented within the wider context of the field (it doesn't simply present the narrow viewpoint of one or two scientists, but fairly represents the whole field). Many other scientific experts in the field have therefore also contributed to this book and ensured its accuracy.

Why the First 1,000 Days?

The first 1,000 days of your baby's life – from conception to his second birthday – are now considered, without question, to be the most important in his life. It is widely agreed among scientists worldwide that your baby's experiences during his first 1,000 days will have more influence on his future health and happiness than any other time in his life. It is the period during which the foundations are laid for lifelong health, and this is particularly important when it comes to your baby's nutrition. The types of foods your baby receives and the habits he develops have lasting effects.

There is mounting evidence that *what* you feed your baby is likely to have a profound effect not only on his long-term health, but also on his food preferences (the foods he likes and dislikes) for years to come. At the same time, *how* he is fed during this very early period may also play a crucial part in forming his appetite regulation (his ability to control how much he eats) and his relationship with food (for example, his tendency to want to eat in response to stress and sadness, and his fussiness). This is a fantastic opportunity to set your child up for life, and this book will help you to do just that.

The first 1,000 days are a time of extraordinary growth and development, unparalleled by any other period of life. By the time your baby turns one, he will have tripled his birth weight. His brain will also undergo significant development – at birth your baby's brain weighs about 370g, but by the time he is two years old it will weigh over 1kg and will be about 80 per cent of its adult size. All of this growth needs to be fuelled and, for babies, this fuel comes first in the form of milk and then, in time, solid food.

But feeding during the first 1,000 days doesn't come without its challenges. Feeding a newborn baby or a toddler can sometimes be testing, especially if things don't go to plan. Given the importance of feeding during this time, and the lack of scientifically founded, practical guidance for parents, we decided to write this book. We will arm you with all the information and practical tips that you need to give your baby the best possible start in life.

The Book's Philosophy

What your baby eats during his first 1,000 days probably matters more than at any other time in his life. But healthy eating habits are about far more than simply *what* a child eats. Gemini and a wealth of other scientific studies have shown that healthy eating is also about *how* your baby feeds and eats – how much, how often and the relationship he develops with food all really matter. Evidence suggests that *how* your child is fed during his first 1,000 days plays a very important role in shaping his appetite regulation – his ability to eat only as much as he needs, and to view food as fuel rather than comfort, entertainment or even something to be feared. Eating too much or too little of anything isn't healthy, nor is turning to food to control emotions instead of learning how to regulate them using positive strategies. And being excessively fussy about food usually results in a limited dietary repertoire, which can have detrimental effects on health.

It may come as a surprise to many people to discover that our relationship with food is thought to develop soon after we are conceived, through exposure to our mum's diet in the womb.

Important habits then start to develop when we begin milk-feeding on the day we are born, and these become more firmly established during the first 1,000 days of life. But babies also bring their own predispositions to the table (pun intended!). Babies are not all born the same – some babies have hearty appetites from the off, while others have poor appetites. When it comes to feeding, understanding what *type* of eater your baby is and responding appropriately is crucial. But at present there is very little information out there about how to respond to your child's unique eating style.

Understanding the *how* of eating is new, so it is no surprise that there is very little information for parents about the strategies you can use to help your baby or toddler develop good appetite regulation, a healthy relationship with food and healthy food preferences that will persist throughout his life. This is far more than *what* he eats; it's also *how* he interacts with food. This book will provide you with much-needed evidence-based advice about *what* and *how* to feed your child from Day 1.

How the Book is Organised

We have divided the book into four parts that relate to the main stages of nutrition and feeding during the first 1,000 days: Pregnancy and the Early Days (Part 1); Milk-Feeding (Part 2); Introducing Solid Foods (Part 3); and Early Childhood (Part 4). You don't need to read the book all in one go. We have designed it so that you can dip in and out of the chapters that are of the most relevance to you and your child, for the particular stage of feeding that you are at. In each chapter we provide you with the most up-to-date scientific facts about nutrition and feeding, and lots of practical tips to help make sure it goes smoothly.

It isn't possible in one book to cover, in detail, the evidence behind every aspect of early feeding. We have therefore provided a more in-depth discussion of the evidence about topics that have been shrouded in controversy (for example, drinking alcohol in pregnancy), and about topics that we know parents want a lot more information about (for example, the evidence for the benefits of breastfeeding, how to choose formula milk, and the 'when, what and how' of weaning).

Over the course of writing this book we have spoken to dozens of parents who have kindly shared their own experiences of feeding during the first 1,000 days. Some parents have talked about things that went well, while others have shared their difficulties. We hope that these stories will resonate with you and help you to feel supported along the way. As well as providing you with scientifically sound practical guidance wherever we can, we have also included a Useful Resources section (page 367) where you can find information on seeking help and advice if you are struggling at any point. Remember that there is always help available if you are finding things tough during the challenging first couple of years – please don't suffer alone, do ask for help.

Clare's Story: the 'Fussy Eater'

I hope to be able to provide advice, information and comfort to mums with fussy children because I know first-hand how it feels to be an extremely fussy eater. Although I consider myself to be 'normal' now (within most contexts anyhow!), from childhood to early adulthood, I was a highly selective eater. It drove my parents mad and even reduced my mum to tears on occasion. Nothing is ingrained more clearly in my mind than the many confrontational mealtimes that seemed to define much of my early childhood.

Those who have never been fussy eaters themselves often see picky eaters as spoiled children who have been allowed to be difficult, and whose parents have caused them to be the way they are by pandering to their every demand from Day 1. Most parents with a fussy child will be used to the advice of others coming thick and fast (and often uninvited), usually to leave the child to get hungry, because they will eventually cave in and eat when they get hungry enough. They won't. The problem is that excessively fussy children often have a poor appetite and don't get hungry enough to cave in. They can end up losing weight, and the stress around eating only intensifies. Extreme fussiness isn't always a purposeful attempt at control or a manifestation of a difficult personality type. It can indicate anxiety about food or eating and, for some children, even phobia.

As a fussy eater, every mealtime filled me with all-consuming panic. I would often wake in the morning with a sense of total and utter dread about the impending mealtimes. This would persist throughout the day – I could be fixated for hours at school worrying about the evening meal. The problems began when I started solid food. My mum recalls a particular occasion when I was about 16 months old. She had been trying for hours to no avail to get me to eat just a few mouthfuls of beans. Eventually she gave up and, in her exasperation, asked my godmother Susie to come over and help. After an hour she coaxed me into taking a spoonful of three baked beans, whereupon I swiftly fell asleep in my high chair and that was that. On waking a little while later, I spat out the beans that I had been concealing in the side of my mouth. All hope was lost.

My loathing of food was all the more baffling for my parents whose firstborn (my older brother, Chris) was a breeze to feed. Chris, unlike me, enjoyed mealtimes, didn't make much of a fuss and had a hearty appetite. How could things have gone so wrong with me? Differences between siblings are, in fact, pretty common and point very much towards the problem originating in the child rather than the parents.

When I was two years old the problems with my eating really began to escalate, after my mum became seriously ill with pleurisy (a nasty chest infection) and had to be hospitalised for treatment. During this time my brother and I were taken to our grandparents to be cared for. Chris, being three years my senior, understood what the problem was, while I was too young to comprehend what had happened. To a two-year-old child, being suddenly separated from your mum with no plausible explanation is traumatic. After we were reunited, to my mum's dismay I refused to eat. I explained that she had gone away and so I wasn't going to eat and that was that. Despite my mum's attempts to negotiate, I wasn't reasonable and there was no way I was going to play ball, and interactions with food continued to be difficult for many years. Moving to two different countries with extraordinarily different cuisines no doubt aggravated this (Greece and then Dubai), but I was already on a 'difficult eater' trajectory. 'Bits', in particular, had become a serious issue − the idea of consuming orange juice or yoghurt with bits of fruit in it was inconceivable to me, as was mashed potato that hadn't been in a liquidiser for half an hour. These foods and others terrified me and the smallest amount in my mouth would make me gag.

By the time I was five years old I was a highly adept fussy eater who had learned all the tricks in the book for concealing how little I had eaten. I would go to great lengths to get rid of food, or hide it, if Mum left me to it, which she had resorted to in an attempt to minimise mealtime stress. The cliché of 'pushing food around the plate' was my go-to strategy. I remember forcing the food as hard as I could against the perimeter of the orange plastic bowl that I was routinely served my evening meal in. The goal was to create an optical illusion of less food on the plate than there actually was. If I found my efforts unconvincing, I would resort to simply throwing it away. But I was wily and calculating about the tactic; it would be foolish to use the kitchen bin, which could easily give me away, so instead I would flush it down the toilet and make the evidence disappear entirely from view. But I didn't always cover my tracks well and would often find myself on the receiving end of a furious and upset parent who had discovered the remnants of my meal floating in the toilet. Often the safer option was simply to give it to my brother, who was on the other end of the appetite spectrum and happy to eat for two.

When I entered secondary school at the age of 11, I was given a medical examination, which was standard for all new pupils. The school nurse who measured my height and weight was deeply concerned because I had completely dropped off the bottom of the growth chart. I was tiny for my age – both skinny and short. She called my mum and instructed her to take me to the GP immediately. I was diagnosed with 'failure to thrive', as it was called back then – a history of insufficient weight gain over a number of months (probably years by this point) – and I was referred to a paediatric growth specialist. After some discussion of the options, the consultant suggested that I should start receiving human growth hormone in two months' time, should the weight faltering continue. This would be delivered via daily injections. The only thing I feared more in life than food was injections. Oh, the horror! We made a deal that I would be given limited choices of protein, so I had some control over what I ate, or else . . . The threat of injections was all the impetus I needed to try and get my act together and eat enough calories to satisfy the consultant's growth target. I ate a small amount of 'proper food' in the evenings and at weekends when I was under supervision, but I controlled my intake at all other times. I also made every effort to chomp down ginger biscuits and up my milk intake. This strategy worked and I grew more than I had in months – two inches in two months. I succeeded in averting the unthinkable – daily injections. It is interesting to me now looking back that at no point did anyone even so much as broach the question of *why* I didn't want to eat.

By my teenage years I had pretty much reached a place in my life where food anxiety didn't dominate every aspect. And I had my repertoire of foods I would eat quite happily – whether at home or out. But with one caveat: nothing that wasn't simple; an Indian or Chinese restaurant were out of the question (luckily for me there wasn't anything much more exotic than that in the UK in the eighties and nineties). My sustenance came mainly from 'non-food' food: sugary cereals; toast with Nutella; spaghetti with a simple sauce (with no 'bits' or lumps in it) or, even better, from a tin; margherita pizza (as long as it hadn't been contaminated with a basil leaf) or something that deviated from bread, tomato purée and mild cheese; crisps (not the variety made from real potatoes – the maize- or corn-based versions); biscuits; and Marmite sandwiches. 'Proper food' included fish and chips, cheese on toast, eggs and beans on toast. I also developed a penchant for two dishes that our local Italian restaurant served: spaghetti Napoli or Bolognese, which remain my two favourite dishes to this day. Of these foods I would happily eat until I was full. I came a cropper with vegetables (mainly green ones), unprocessed meat and fish, sauces containing unidentifiable items or with a tendency to develop a 'skin', yoghurt (or juice) with bits of fruit in it (this still makes me gag now) and anything with a gelatinous texture. Other than that I was fine!

And so things continued. Eventually I left home at 18 and went to university. I had breakfast and evening meals catered for in my halls of residence but I had about five of these meals in total during my whole first year, preferring instead to hide in my room and eat bowls of cereal or white baguettes with butter and mild Cheddar slices. And I survived on this for a year. I didn't even get ill. But as I entered the second year everything changed – this was a turning point in my life. I moved out of halls and into a house with four of my really good friends. With this move came some anxiety – how would I hide my weird eating behaviour from my house mates? I worried I would be fully exposed. To top it all off, two of my friends were real 'foodies' and they often cooked extravagant meals for the household – me included. This led to a total overhaul in my behaviour. Over the course of a year, I made the transition from a highly selective eater to a relatively 'normal' one. This was driven entirely by social pressure. I was so mortified by my eating habits that I complied with expectations and slowly, meal by meal, made extraordinary progress. By the end of the second year I had had my first curry (admittedly, an unadventurous chicken korma, but nonetheless) and eaten a wider variety of foods than I had eaten in my entire life up to that point.

Things continued to progress and by the time I reached my mid-twenties I considered my eating behaviour to be 'normal'. And now I will eat pretty much anything – okay, maybe not *anything* . . . I turn my nose up at celery, horseradish, mustard, mayonnaise, pre-prepared soggy sandwiches of the type that typically make an appearance at work meetings and conferences (contaminated by slimy lettuce leaves and limp watery tomatoes!), and most Chinese and Japanese food. But I eat my greens and enjoy 'proper' food. By no means would I consider myself 'adventurous' or a 'foodie', but I enjoy meals out with friends and look forward to being cooked for, whether or not I know in advance what might be put in front of me. So, do not lose hope! Children can and do learn to manage their fussy tendencies, and it is possible to get to a place where they are eating a good and varied diet, even if it doesn't include every possible food on the planet.

Life with an excessively fussy child can be stressful – it can ruin holidays, meals out and family time. But people are also quick to point the finger at the parents who are usually blamed for their child's difficulties. I only wish my parents had known then what I know now about problem eating behaviour – where it really comes from and the strategies that we can use to change it. This was an important impetus behind this book for me – to help other parents who are already struggling with a fussy child and to minimise the likelihood that it will happen in the first place.

Hayley's Story: the 'Model Eater'

My childhood eating habits were very different to Clare's. My parents were the envy of friends that had 'fussy eaters' because all of their children (my younger brother Jonathan, my older sister Amy and I) were model eaters. We would eat anything that was put in front of us. For example, at seven years old I ate (and enjoyed) snails in France. Sometimes I can't quite believe I did that, and I am not so sure I would eat them now. Was it that my parents were just lucky to have three children that loved food or was it because of *how* and *what* they fed us when we were younger? I would argue it was a bit of both because we know that some children have a genetic tendency to be fussy (more on this on page 33–4), but we also know that fussiness can be a result of early experience with food (the ethos of this book). Interestingly, some of the tips we provide in this book on how to prevent fussy eating were in fact used by my mum and dad when we were babies; for example, offering vegetables as a first food rather than fruit, and not adding salt or sugar to foods. If I was given fruit during weaning it was fruit that did not contain much sugar, such as puréed cooking apples or plums. My paternal nan tasted my apple purée once when she was feeding me and recoiled, saying that it needed sugar added as it was so tart. My mum had to explain to her that I was quite happy with it as it was and that it didn't need sugar. Sure enough, I ate it without any fuss. My mum believed this was because I didn't know any better and I was used to sugarless foods.

Once I was ready to move on to typical family food, my parents never gave me 'kids' meals' at home or if we ate out. I was given what my parents were eating (cottage pie, fish, mince with vegetables, scrambled eggs) but they did not add salt to the meals during cooking – they added it to their plate once it was served. On another occasion while feeding me, my nan once again tasted the food and said it was bland and needed salt, but my mum insisted that it was not adults' tastes that mattered, but mine. My mum felt that a baby would find plenty of flavour in the food without the need for extra saltiness.

My parents used to home-cook batches of food for me as a baby and would freeze them in portions so that there was always something suitable available for my meals. Not only was this a much cheaper way of doing things than using baby foods off the shelf, but my parents wanted to know what was in the food that I was eating and felt that they could give me much more variety this way. My parents have told me they had no guidance as to *how much* I should eat (we cover portion size in Chapter 11), so I was given what they thought was right as a portion size. Interestingly though, my parents believed that children should eat what they were given – a regime handed down by their parents – so I was often made to clear my plate and not let anything go to waste. This is something I'm sure many of you can relate to, and it's a very difficult habit to get out of, but we do not advocate plate clearing (see Chapter 12 for reasons why).

As a young child I was very occasionally given dessert (rice pudding, stewed fruit and custard) but my parents wanted to try and avoid giving me sugary foods until I was a bit older. I was rarely given snacks but if I was, it was Marmite 'soldiers', home-made cheese straws or fruit, but apparently this was not every day and I didn't make a habit of asking for food between meals. I don't snack much even now and I am pretty good at only eating when I am hungry; I look forward to meals and food tastes so much better to me if I am hungry. But of course, I am human and at times I will eat chocolate if it's offered to me, regardless of whether I am hungry or not!

My eating habits were not totally perfect as a child though; I did go through a stage during early childhood of not eating meat and being faddy about gelatinous substances, such as the jelly on corned beef or the rind of fat on bacon (I still cut this off). And at the age of eight I remember being adamant that I was not eating my maternal nan's cauliflower cheese. Cauliflower cheese was, and still is, one of my favourite dishes, but my nan's sauce really did taste terrible; she had made it using the water from the boiled cauliflower! I was told I would have to sit at the table until I ate it, so I sat there for two hours, on my own, until eventually my nan realised I was not going to eat it and admitted defeat.

There are a few foods today that I am not keen on – namely raw fish, celery and broad beans – but I would say I am quite an adventurous eater and eager to try new foods. I view food as something to be enjoyed, whether it's a fresh salad or chocolate cake, and the key for me has always been to eat a balanced diet and to keep active. I was brought up in an era where you cleared your plate and it is difficult to change the habit of a lifetime, but I have learned how much I can eat without feeling too full and only serve myself that amount.

I have always been fascinated by diet and nutrition. I think that because I have a healthy relationship with food I have been intrigued as to why some people don't. I am passionate about exploring the reasons behind unhealthy eating habits, whether that is excessive fussiness or excessive over- or undereating. Food is such a vital part of our lives, and a person's relationship with food impacts both their physical and mental health. Writing this book has provided me with an opportunity to get the science 'out there' to parents and help instil the best practices to hopefully set many children on the road to healthy eating. That is my mission.

Babies and toddlers bring their own quirks to the table when it comes to food, so parents' feeding experiences are rarely the same, and the challenges they face depend on their own particular child. Some are a nightmare to feed, like Clare, and others a dream, like Hayley. We have written this book to provide you with helpful and practical advice that is relevant to you and your baby, whatever type of feeder he is and for every stage of feeding.

CHAPTER 1

An Appetite for Life

'There is no love sincerer than the love of food'

George Bernard Shaw

You may or may not agree with the above statement – it certainly doesn't resonate with everyone – but no doubt you will have heard some friend or family member make a similar declaration at one time or another, possibly in the midst of a bountiful and glorious feast. But we're not all the same when it comes to food. We all know someone who has very little interest in it; the one who pushes food around the plate and for whom eating is simply a chore. For others, chomping down delicious food is one of the greatest pleasures in life. Just as adults have varying appetites and attitudes towards food, children and babies also differ in their love for (or loathing of) food. Some of you may already have one child who enjoys eating and another for whom mealtimes are a source of enormous stress.

So why do we have such different relationships with food? This is a question that has intrigued researchers for decades and it is relevant today, more than ever before, because of the dramatic rise in obesity as well as the growing concern about eating disorders. There is now burgeoning evidence that your baby's appetite, as well as the foods that he likes and dislikes, are shaped during his first 1,000 days of life – from pregnancy through to around two years of age. And scientists now know quite a lot about how appetite and food preferences develop and the best strategies to use to ensure that babies foster a good relationship with food right from the off. What we know for certain is that *how* a child eats (how he responds to food and interacts with it) is just as important as *what* he eats (the foods he likes and dislikes).

Appetite: How We Eat

'Appetite' is a catch-all word that researchers use to describe how we respond to food and the opportunity to eat. Appetite – what it is and how it is expressed – has been studied for decades. Differences in people's appetites help to explain why some of us are susceptible to gaining too much weight, while others manage to maintain a healthy and stable weight with virtually no effort. So why are we so different, and when does this start happening?

Our understanding of children's appetite was revolutionised in 2001, when Professor Jane Wardle, an eminent behavioural scientist, developed the first comprehensive measure of eating styles in children – the Child Eating Behaviour Questionnaire (CEBQ; see Appendix 1, page 355).[1] This questionnaire enabled researchers to study, for the first time, how much children really differed in their appetite and how appetite related to weight – it allowed us to explore the eating styles of children with underweight, as well as those with obesity. The CEBQ is a questionnaire that you can use to describe how your child behaves in relation to seven different eating styles and it can help to define your child's 'appetite':

1. *Food responsiveness* measures a child's tendency to want to eat when he sees, smells or tastes super delicious foods, even if he isn't hungry; for example, wanting a chocolate bar when he gets to the supermarket checkout and sees a wall of treats.

2. *Enjoyment of food* describes the amount of pleasure a child derives from the experience of eating.

3. *Satiety responsiveness* captures how easily a child fills up once he starts eating, and how long he stays full for before he gets hungry and wants to start eating again.

4. *Slowness in eating* measures how quickly or slowly a child typically finishes a meal or snack.

5. *Emotional overeating* assesses a child's tendency to want to eat more if he has been very upset or cranky.

6. *Emotional undereating* assesses a child's tendency to lose his appetite if he has been very upset or angry.

7. *Food fussiness* measures how fussy or picky a child is when it comes to the types of foods he is willing to eat, and his willingness to try new foods.

The CEBQ led to important discoveries about appetite – children differ enormously in their appetites, and these differences help to explain why some have underweight and others have overweight. But many crucial questions still remained unanswered. We still didn't know whether appetite really *caused* children to develop underweight or overweight, or whether it was actually their weight that caused their appetite to be big or small – the proverbial 'chicken-or-the-egg' problem. And we knew virtually nothing about babies – whether or not babies also showed differences in these eating styles – and where appetite comes from in the first place. This is the nature–nurture question: is our appetite caused by our genes, and therefore already there at birth, or is it shaped by our early experience with feeding?

Twins offer a powerful way of answering these questions. This is because identical twins are 100 per cent genetically the same, while non-identical twins are only about 50 per cent genetically the same, like regular siblings. But importantly, both types of twins share their environments to a very similar extent; they are gestated in the same mother for the same amount of time, grow up in the same family, are exposed to the same parenting policies and so on. This means that researchers can compare how alike the two types of twins are to find out how much genes are involved in shaping a particular characteristic, such as appetite, or the extent to which appetite is learned. If identical twins are more similar than non-identical twins for the trait being studied, genes are important in shaping that trait.

Professor Jane Wardle decided that the best possible way to understand appetite properly was to set up a twin study that measured appetite comprehensively in very large numbers of *babies* right from the beginning of life, and observe their weight gain over subsequent months and years. This would allow us to answer all of the unanswered questions, and more. It also meant developing a new measure of appetite, like the CEBQ, but specifically for very young babies.

In 2007, with financial support from Cancer Research UK, Professor Jane Wardle, Clare Llewellyn and a team of other researchers at UCL established Gemini – the largest study ever undertaken into infant appetite. Since Gemini was set up, we have measured:

- the appetites of more than 4,800 British twin babies during the first few weeks of life when they were still fed only milk, and again when they were toddlers

- their weights and heights every three months since the study began

- everything the children ate and drank for three days when they were toddlers

This comprehensive study has made Gemini one of the richest growth data resources in the world and has created the largest contemporary dietary dataset for toddlers in the whole of the UK. We have used this information to find out:

- if appetite is something that is learned or inherited

- how much babies really differ in their appetites for milk

- how a baby's appetite relates to weight gain

- how a baby's appetite relates to actual food intake

- how a toddler's food intake and eating patterns relate to weight gain

We developed a new measure of appetite for milk-feeding babies (the Baby Eating Behaviour Questionnaire (BEBQ; see Appendix 1, page 352) that allowed us to measure infant appetite in large numbers, in the same way as the CEBQ had allowed us to measure the appetites of large numbers of children.[2] The BEBQ is the first and only comprehensive measure of infant appetite and is used widely in research. It captures four different aspects of a baby's appetite:

1. *Milk responsiveness* indicates a baby's urge to feed when milk is offered, even if they are not hungry, and how demanding they are with regard to being fed.

2. *Enjoyment of feeding* assesses how much pleasure the baby experiences during feeding.

3. *Satiety responsiveness* measures a baby's fullness sensitivity; for example, how easily or quickly he fills up once he starts feeding.

4. *Slowness in feeding* measures a baby's typical feeding speed – whether they guzzle their milk in record time or seem to take for ever.

The wealth of research that has come from Gemini and other studies has transformed our understanding of babies' and children's appetite, and what it means for parents when it comes to feeding them. Alongside other high-quality studies, these findings have formed the basis of much of the advice in this book.

BABIES DIFFER IN THEIR APPETITES FOR MILK

As a result of the BEBQ, we discovered that babies differ enormously when it comes to their appetite for milk. And this is true of both breast- *and* formula-fed babies. Some babies have ravenous appetites, feeding whenever milk is on offer (even if they have just been fed) and emptying a bottle of milk in record time. A few will even guzzle milk so quickly that it comes straight back up. At the other end of the spectrum are the faddy feeders – the babies who can only manage a little bit of milk at a time and seem to take hours over a single feed or even fall asleep on the job. For mums of these babies, feeding can feel like a constant struggle. Yet other babies seem to have their milk intake perfectly in check. In short, babies really vary in their ability to regulate their milk intake according to their needs. This may resonate with you if you currently have a baby who is a nightmare to feed, or if you have a baby who seems to want to feed endlessly!

CHILDREN DIFFER IN HOW THEY RESPOND TO FOOD

Like babies, children also differ a lot in how they respond to food – some love it, others loathe it, and some are in between. You may have already noticed this if you have two children of your own with quite different dispositions towards food. There are distinct eating styles that characterise a poorer or more avid appetite. If your child has a poor appetite, he is likely to show some of the following characteristics, some of which may drive you crazy:

- He may be very 'satiety sensitive', meaning he will fill up very easily once he starts eating and will not be able to eat much in one go. This means that if he has a snack (or even a glass of milk) too close to a meal he might not be able to manage all the food he's offered. He may rarely seem hungry – especially if the available food isn't all that enticing – and is probably far more interested in doing other activities, such as playing on an iPad, than eating his meal.

- He may eat slowly and it can feel like mealtimes take an age, but he likes to take his time and won't be rushed.

- He may be a fusspot – fussier than other children when it comes to food, especially when trying *new* foods. He may not eat certain foods because of their texture; for example, foods with lumps in them (such as yoghurt with bits of fruit in it and some sauces), foods that develop a skin on the top after a while (such as custard or gravy) or slimy foods (such as mushrooms or 'sweet and sour' sauces) – the list is actually endless and may change from day to day! He may also object to foods touching on the plate and may refuse to eat something if it has been 'sullied' by something else, even if he likes the 'something else' on its own (for example, potatoes that have been 'contaminated' with tomato sauce from a side of baked beans, which he apparently likes). He may also declare that he doesn't like a particular food without even having tried it, which of course means he will refuse to taste it.

- After he has been very upset or angry he may completely lose his appetite for a while, so he will eat even less than usual.

If your child has a large and enthusiastic appetite, he will tend to show some of the following behaviours towards food, some of which may prove challenging to manage at times:

- He may be very 'food responsive', and constantly ask for food if treats are on show and he thinks he stands a chance of persuading you! You may be familiar with this scenario: you have gone to the supermarket with good intentions and made it all the way to the checkout only to have to wait there for five minutes while your toddler sits staring at the wall of chocolate bars and sweets . . . pester power kicks in and soon leads to a tantrum if the answer is 'no'. He may also try his luck with seconds, thirds and fourths when the meal you dish up really gets his taste buds going.

- He will really enjoy snacks and meals, and probably makes this shamelessly obvious. For him eating is pure pleasure. In general, this makes mealtimes easy insofar as he is an adventurous little eater who is interested in new types of foods and willing to give anything a go.

- He eats very quickly. Sometimes it seems as though he has inhaled the meal that you just spent hours preparing. There's no pushing his food around the plate, he just dives straight in.

- Not even emotional upset is enough to put him off his food. In fact, sometimes he even eats more than usual when he's upset. Because he loves food and it brings him a lot of pleasure, it's something that makes him feel better when he's upset.

Of course, children don't necessarily fit neatly into one category. In fact, it isn't uncommon for some children to have a hearty appetite when it comes to unhealthy foods – sweets, crisps, cakes and ice cream, for example – but to be incredibly fussy when it comes to other foods (usually the ones you would most like him to eat, such as vegetables). You may be thinking this about your own child. Unfortunately, most children prefer unhealthy foods to healthier ones – this is a parent's perpetual challenge, especially given the access to these foods that children have today. But in general, children with a big or poor appetite tend to demonstrate distinct eating behaviours such as the ones we have just described. What type of eater do you think your baby or child is? Have a go at completing the BEBQ (for babies up to 6 months) or the CEBQ (for children over 12 months) in Appendix 1 (pages 352 and 355) to find out.

The fact that children vary so much in their appetites means that each child brings unique challenges to you as a parent when it comes to feeding them. If you have a child with a poor appetite who hardly eats anything, mealtimes can feel like a battle of wills, and a long, drawn-out and stressful chore. If you have a child with a hearty appetite, mealtimes can be a pleasure, but dealing with his constant requests for food can be equally as testing. There can be no 'one-size-fits-all' advice about feeding your child – it depends entirely on the type of eater your child is, and your feeding strategy needs to be tailored to suit him and his particular quirks. This is the purpose of this book – to provide you with information about the many different eating styles of babies and children, and to help you make sure you respond to your own baby's or child's appetite using the most appropriate feeding strategies.

APPETITE PERSISTS THROUGHOUT CHILDHOOD

Research that measured the appetites of 428 British children when they were 4 and again when they were 11 years old showed that appetite is a fairly stable trait that persists throughout your child's development.[3] If you have a toddler with a poor appetite, he is likely to become a child who isn't particularly interested in food, and finds activities other than eating more enticing. If you have an eager eater, on the other hand, he will probably grow into a child with a very hearty appetite who loves food and derives a great deal of pleasure from eating.

But, this does not mean that your child's appetite can't be changed. A landmark study called NOURISH has shown that parents who feed their babies and toddlers using certain strategies (called 'responsive feeding' – see Chapter 6 for more on this) can have an important and lasting impact on their child's developing appetite.[4] So, although a toddler who has a tiny appetite is unlikely to grow into a child with a large and voracious one, the way that you feed him can make an important difference to his relationship with food, the foods he will eat and his ability to eat enough. The same is true for a toddler with a large and voracious one, which can be tempered with the right feeding strategies. A word, in particular, about food fussiness . . . We know from research that fussiness seems to follow a pattern in your child's development – it tends to emerge during toddlerhood, increase during the preschool years and gradually diminish during later childhood (although in rare instances it can persist into adulthood).[5] So, don't worry if your child has suddenly become fussy, when yesterday he seemed fine. This is very common and is a normal part of development for many children, but that doesn't mean that it isn't stressful (!). In fact, dealing with fussiness can be one of the most stressful aspects of feeding. The good news is that it's usually just a phase that your child will eventually grow out of and throughout this book we have some great strategies for you to use to help him overcome this.

APPETITE HAS AN IMPACT ON WEIGHT

Research has shown that your child's appetite is one of the most important influences on his early growth. Gemini allowed us to examine in detail for the first time the relationship between a baby's appetite during the first few months of life and his subsequent weight gain. Babies who are more responsive to milk, derive greater pleasure from feeding, feed quickly and are less sensitive to their fullness signals tend to be more prone to overfeeding. These babies grow more quickly and are at greater risk of excessive weight gain. Babies with poorer appetites are more likely to underfeed, grow more slowly and are at greater risk of weight faltering (meaning insufficient weight gain over a period of a few weeks or months); although weight faltering in the UK is actually very rare – see page 95.

When we compared the weight gain of pairs of twins with very different appetites, we found that the twins with the heartier appetites grew much faster than their co-twins with poorer appetites from birth to toddlerhood.[6] By the time they were toddlers there was a 1kg difference in weight between twin pairs who had very different early appetites. This might not sound like a lot, but the average weight at 15 months was about 10kg, so a 1kg difference is a 10 per cent difference in body weight. In adult terms, this is the equivalent to being 10 versus 11st, or 60 versus 66kg. This is a big weight difference. You would certainly notice if you gained or lost 10 per cent of your body weight, and the chances are so would your friends and family.

This study was groundbreaking because it showed for the first time that early appetite plays a crucial role in how much weight babies gain – it helps to explain why some babies have rapid weight gain, while others have weight faltering. Another study in Singapore replicated our finding in a sample of unrelated babies;[7] and a wealth of studies have shown, pretty much without exception, that toddlers and older children with a more avid appetite carry more body fat and are more likely to develop overweight or obesity, while those with a poorer appetite carry less body fat and are more likely to develop underweight or have weight faltering.[8]

We now know that optimal early weight gain is very important for your baby's later health (see Chapter 3), so finding that appetite plays such an important part in this process highlights the need to help your baby develop good appetite regulation right from the beginning of life. That is the main aim of this book. Throughout each stage of feeding we will give you practical strategies so you can support your baby in developing good appetite regulation right from Day 1.

You can imagine how being a food-responsive child who really enjoys food can easily lead to overeating in the context of the modern food environment. Children are bombarded with food cues throughout the day via the relentless onslaught of food advertising – for sugary and fatty food mind you, not for healthy food. The largest study of television food advertising to children in the UK recorded 5,000 hours of commercial programming on 14 channels popular with children and families in 2008.[9] Of all adverts 12.8 per cent were for food and drinks, but adverts for non-core foods (unnecessary foods high in fat, sugar and salt) vastly outnumbered those for core nutritious foods (foods required daily to ensure optimal nutrition) by 56 per cent compared to 18.1 per cent. This may not seem like a big deal for a young child who doesn't yet have the independence to go out and buy the foods that he sees and then eat them, but a review of 18 experimental studies examining how much people eat after watching adverts (either on the television or on the Internet), found that children eat more at a meal following exposure to food adverts.[10] This is because watching food adverts is thought to make food-responsive children want to eat, simply by looking at the food. But the modern 'obesogenic' environment isn't just restricted to the television or Internet; it is virtually impossible to walk down a high street without seeing or smelling food as you go about your business. If your child is food responsive, these food cues will make him want to eat. In fact, in Gemini we found that toddlers who were more food responsive ate more often throughout the day.[11]

Children with weaker fullness sensitivity (satiety) are also vulnerable to the modern food environment because they have a tendency to carry on eating, as long as there is still food to eat. In Gemini we also found that toddlers who were less sensitive to their satiety consumed a larger amount of food every time they ate.[12] Larger portions of food than are needed can therefore prove particularly problematic for these children, in terms of encouraging overeating. Portion sizes have gone up – even in recipe books – and foods are often heavily marketed with incentives for buying larger quantities ('Do you want to supersize that?', '3 for the price of 2', etc.). Children who are less sensitive to feelings of fullness have a tendency to eat too much if portions are bigger or if they are distracted during eating, such as eating in front of the television or playing with an iPad at the table. This is the sort of information we feel is very important for parents to know and is where this book comes in. We know that your child's unique appetite needs to be taken into account when feeding him. Throughout this book we provide practical advice and tips about *how* to deal with food cues and make sure that portion sizes are appropriate. The challenges that a parent faces with a faddy eater are completely different to the ones related to a relentlessly hungry child. But there are ways to deal with all types of babies and children, to ensure that they neither under- nor overeat. The key to making sure you get it right is *responsive feeding* and we will explain exactly how to do this for each stage.

WHERE DOES APPETITE COME FROM?

This is the age-old question of whether appetite is caused by our genes (nature) or our early feeding experiences (nurture), and is a pretty important one for you as a parent. If your baby's appetite is largely shaped by his early feeding experiences, the onus is on you to make sure you get it right. If your baby's genes are important in shaping his appetite, it's more about understanding what type of appetite your baby is born with and making sure you respond to him appropriately.

There is actually pretty widespread (and largely unsupported) belief among researchers, as well as health professionals, that all babies are born with a natural ability to regulate their milk intake perfectly (they will take only as much milk as they need). In practice this means they are able to feed whenever they are hungry and stop as soon as they are full. The prevailing view is that your baby's appetite regulation is developed through a process of learning, and that you are the main shaper. The theory is that if your baby's signals of hunger and fullness are consistently met by you with a prompt, developmentally appropriate feeding response, he will quickly learn how to regulate his milk intake according to his needs. This is thought to be the pathway through which appetite regulation is developed and optimised. However, this view puts a huge amount of responsibility for a baby's appetite regulation onto you. And anyhow, is it really the case that all babies are born with the potential for perfect appetite control and it is only compromised if interfered with by you? This implies that all babies are born on a level playing field and that appetite regulation is largely learned.

We were able to answer the nature–nurture question for the first time in Gemini because we studied twins. We found that identical twin pairs were far more alike than non-identical twin pairs for all aspects of their appetite. [13] This indicated that a lot of the differences between babies' appetites for milk are, in fact, down to their genes. This discovery is new, and came as quite a surprise to many researchers and health professionals, although it makes sense given that we know that appetite is actually largely controlled by biology. Two systems in our brain control how hungry or full we feel: the 'homeostatic system', controlled mainly by part of the brain called the hypothalamus, and how rewarding and pleasurable we find food, and the 'hedonic system', controlled mainly by the mesolimbic pathway which produces dopamine. Several appetite hormones, such as ghrelin (the 'hunger hormone') and leptin (the 'satiety hormone'), control our appetites by regulating these systems in the brain. [14] Scientists have also found that the genes that influence our satiety sensitivity and food responsiveness are most highly expressed in areas of the brain that control our appetite. [15] The fact that your baby's genes influence his appetite so strongly has big implications for you as a parent. You need to get to know the appetite he is born with, and respond appropriately.

In Gemini, we also looked at the nature and nurture of food fussiness, emotional overeating and emotional undereating in *toddlerhood*. It may provide some comfort to you if you have a fussy toddler to discover that fussiness actually has a pretty strong genetic basis – it's not your fault! If you have a fussy toddler you may feel judged or guilty about his eating difficulties. Understanding that he has a genetic predisposition towards this might help you to go easier on yourself. Some toddlers are just prone to being a lot more finicky than others.

But when it comes to toddlers eating more or less in response to emotion, genes are *unimportant*.[16] Instead, it is a baby's early experiences that shape this. We also now know that parents play quite an important role in nurturing this behaviour. With researchers from Norway we used a large ongoing study of 1,000 families with very young children to show that a young child who is offered food in order to soothe him when he is upset is more likely to learn to turn to food to control his emotions when he is older.[17] It is important to find alternative strategies to comfort a baby or toddler who is upset, rather than use milk or food. We will explain how you do this in the chapters that follow.

So, if genes are at the root of most aspects of a baby's appetite, does this mean it can't be changed? No. It is a common misconception that if something has a strong genetic basis, it can't be modified. This absolutely isn't the case. Your baby's genes are *not* his destiny when it comes to his appetite. A strong genetic influence on your baby's appetite means that he is born with a *disposition* to have a more avid appetite or to be a more difficult feeder. But the extent to which his genes will have an impact is dependent on his early nutritional and feeding experiences. For example, people with a strong genetic predisposition to lung cancer are very unlikely to get it if they don't smoke. Your baby's genes set his appetite *potential*, but his early environmental experiences can act as a volume control. The appetite-control systems in the brain start to develop in utero and continue to do so during the first few weeks and months after he is born. We know that during this time, his nutritional and feeding experiences can influence his appetite importantly, and for the rest of his life. This means that mum's nutrition during pregnancy, and your baby's early nutrition and feeding experiences matter. *What* your baby is fed (breast milk versus formula milk, and his first foods) and *how* he is fed (your feeding strategies) can, in fact, have a really big impact on his early appetite regulation and relationship with food. What all this really means for you, as a parent, is that it is crucial for you to understand your baby's appetite and to develop strategies that are tailored to his unique eating styles. Understanding your baby's appetite, and responding to him appropriately, is a fundamental part of supporting him in developing healthy eating habits for life. This book will provide you with scientifically based advice about how best to achieve this.

Food Preferences: What We Eat

'What is food to one man is bitter poison to others.'

Lucretius c.99–55 BC

How your baby responds to food – how much and how often he wants to eat – will drive his weight gain, but *what* he eats is important too. Nobody needs to be convinced that diet matters – 'we are what we eat', after all. A bad diet is probably responsible for about 10 per cent of the entire world's ill health,[18] and research indicates that your baby's nutrition during his first 1,000 days may matter more than at any other time in his life.[19] Your baby's early diet will determine not only his health and development now, but also how he fares well into his adult life. In particular, the first two years are unprecedented in terms of brain development and optimal nutrition is vital for this.[20] But your baby's early nutrition and growth can also 'programme' his later health, impacting importantly on his risk of developing obesity and metabolic diseases, such as heart disease and type 2 diabetes.[21] So, making sure his nutrition is optimal during this developmental window of opportunity will give him the best possible start in life.

It's all very well knowing this, but getting your child to *actually eat* a healthy diet is quite a different matter, as any parent will know. Our food preferences – the foods that we like or dislike – determine *what* we actually eat or avoid. And this is probably even truer for young children than it is for adults. If a baby or toddler doesn't like something, they're simply not going to eat it. And it's unlikely that you're going to be able to negotiate with him, given that babies and toddlers lack the cognitive ability to understand the health benefits of eating something they don't like. So the real question is: how can you get your baby or toddler to like healthy foods? If you get this cracked, he will eat them. Our aim in this book is to do just that: help you crack it! And we have a number of tricks up our sleeves to help you.

The main hurdle that you will come up against is that the foods that babies and toddlers naturally tend to dislike the most are the healthy ones that you will want him to eat – the prime example being vegetables and, in particular, the green, bitter-tasting ones, such as spinach. Things also get a bit trickier with little ones because studies have shown that babies and children have a much greater liking for sweetness than adults do – the sweeter the better.[22] Very few babies or toddlers would turn their nose up at a piece of chocolate or a spoonful of ice cream, no matter how faddy they might be. In fact, you may have looked on in wonder at the sheer amount of sugary food a young child will put away at a birthday party, given the chance! These taste dispositions make sense in terms of evolution – liking sweet foods and disliking bitter foods are traits that help vulnerable babies and toddlers survive. Sweet foods contain sugar, and therefore calories, which they need to fuel their growth, so it's good for them to gravitate towards these foods. On the other hand, foods containing harmful toxins taste bitter, which signals that something is unsafe to eat, so disliking these tastes helps to protect them from harm. These traits can prove challenging when it comes to encouraging your baby and toddler to like and eat healthier foods. But, fear not, there are lots of things that you can do to help your child develop healthy food preferences. For example, when you move your baby on from milk to solid food, start off with giving him the bitter-tasting vegetables – it is his first experience of food and he doesn't yet know that chocolate exists! (See pages 243–6 and 260–1 for more tips like this to get your little one eating vegetables.) We will take you through strategies such as this throughout the book.

There are also developmental changes in babies' and toddlers' willingness to *try* certain foods. In general, babies are much more willing to try new foods – flavours and textures – and accept them, than toddlers. At around 20 months of age they become much more wary about eating foods they don't recognise – in fact, they can be put off by even small changes in appearance, from packaging to differences in preparation. This developmental phase is called 'neophobia' – refusing any new or unfamiliar food usually based on sight – and is pretty common in most toddlers and young children between about 20 months and six years of age.[23] This explains why some toddlers reject a food that they apparently liked only the day before. What this means for a parent is that it will usually take much more effort to get a toddler or young child to try a new food and to like it, than a young baby. Babies are most open to new flavours around the time of weaning.

But age may be an even bigger deal when it comes to *texture*. Babies who have not experienced different textures during their first year of life find new foods difficult to accept after this point. This can persist into later childhood and beyond. These babies are less likely to accept foods that aren't smooth in texture – those that require lots of chewing and are harder to swallow, such as fruit, vegetables and protein foods. It also impacts on their speech development.

This means that the greater the variety of foods your baby tries early on during weaning the better. But even so, you can expect things to become a little more challenging during the second year. It may help to know that this is a natural part of your baby's development and there are still tricks that you can use to encourage him to try new things. One of the main ways he learns which foods are safe to eat is by looking to you – he wants you to test-drive them first and check they're okay. You may already be aware that your child copies you, and other adults, a lot of the time. The same applies with eating; if he sees you eating something he is more likely to eat it as well. This is called 'vicarious learning' (see page 267). So, if you want your baby to try a new food, the best way you can encourage this is to eat it yourself, in front of him, without making a fuss. Better still; give the impression that you are thoroughly enjoying it. Being a role model yourself and using others as role models, works well, as does rewarding your child for trying healthy foods with *non-food* rewards, so he learns that this is a good thing to do (see page 313). In fact, there are a whole host of tricks that you can use to help things go smoothly, and this book is packed full of them.

Given that there are general tendencies that we observe across all babies and toddlers, we may assume that what we like to eat is written into our genes and that all babies and toddlers like and dislike the same foods, but actually there are big differences between the food preferences of any two babies or toddlers of the same age. They may all have a *general tendency* to like sweet foods and dislike bitter ones, but this is true for some children more than others. You may even have noticed differences between your own children – one might have no issue at all with eating spinach, while the other one will refuse to eat anything that has even been touched by it on the plate. And the extraordinary thing is that each baby's food preferences show remarkable stability, persisting from infancy all the way into adulthood. This raises the question of where they come from in the first place – nature or nurture? We have been able to answer this question using Gemini.

WHERE DO FOOD PREFERENCES COME FROM?

When the Gemini twins were three years old we asked their parents to tell us how much they liked 114 foods, so that we could carry out the largest study to date on the nature and nurture of toddlers' preferences for key food groups: vegetables, fruit, protein (such as meat and fish), dairy (such as cheese and yoghurt), starch (such as bread and pasta) and 'junk food' (foods high in sugar and/or fat, such as chocolate and ice cream).[24]

We found that genes play a part in shaping toddlers' food preferences; but genes are more important for toddlers' liking of vegetables, fruit and protein, than they are for liking of junk food, dairy and starchy foods. This was an important finding that helped us to understand a bit more about fussy eating, because for fussy children, the biggest problem foods are vegetables, then fruit, then animal-based protein foods (meat and fish) – in that order. They have no issue with eating fatty, sugary foods, carbohydrates (such as bread and pasta) and dairy foods (unless we're talking about yoghurt with bits of slimy fruit in it). You may have noticed this with your own child if he is fussy – no encouragement is needed at all to get him to eat a biscuit, but persuading him to try some green beans is a whole different kettle of fish. This is because many of the genes that cause a child to be fussy are *the same* as the genes that cause him to dislike vegetables and fruit (but they don't cause him to dislike junk foods, dairy or starches). It seems that all of this is 'part and parcel' of an underlying food-avoidance trait – you might think of them as the 'yucky' genes. This clustering of fussiness and dislike for these types of foods may reflect some kind of hypervigilance among these children, given that protein foods are the main source of bacteria that cause serious illness, and vegetables and fruit sometimes contain toxins that can be poisonous. A hypervigilant child is fearful of anything that might cause him harm, including food.

For parents, this means that it can be a bit trickier to get your child to eat these foods, because, to some extent, you are battling their biology. But genes are not the full story, and you *can* get your child to eat these types of foods; it just takes a bit more effort. Importantly, Gemini also showed us that nurture (early experiences with food, such as first weaning foods, the foods that they see you and others eat, your attitudes towards food, etc.) is at least as important as genes for children's liking or disliking of *every* type of food – including vegetables, fruit and protein. In fact, early experiences are actually by far the most important reason why some toddlers have a penchant for junk food – a taste for these foods is largely learned, not inherited. This means there is a lot of opportunity for you as a parent to shape your child's food preferences, and make sure he is as healthy as possible.

CAN I TEACH MY BABY TO LIKE HEALTHY FOOD?

Yes. Two key processes are involved in children learning to like certain foods: familiarity and feeling sure that a food is safe.[25]

One of the most powerful ways to get babies and children to like a food is through repeated exposure to it – they need to actually taste it and become familiar with its texture. Exposure to different flavours and textures is the journey to familiarity, and therefore to liking. A recent discovery that shocked many people was that this process probably begins in the womb: a mother's amniotic fluid is flavoured with her own diet, the baby swallows it, and in this process he is exposed to whatever tastes are in there.[26] So, in fact, your baby is swimming in a sea of flavours right from the beginning of his life. His taste buds start to develop at only 13–15 weeks, and by the third trimester he breathes and swallows about a litre of amniotic fluid every day. Experimental studies have shown that flavours such as garlic, aniseed and carrot can make their way into the amniotic fluid and flavour it for the baby (see page 52).[27] The changing flavour of amniotic fluid might also explain the rather intriguing finding that babies whose mums experienced severe vomiting during pregnancy (hyperemesis gravidarum) seem to prefer saltier foods – the theory being that Mum's amniotic fluid was probably a bit saltier because she was dehydrated.[28]

Exposure to flavours continues on the day your baby is born, when he starts milk-feeding. If he is breastfed he continues to enjoy your diet, which also flavours your breast milk. If he is formula-fed he will learn to like the flavour of his main type of formula milk, and will be predisposed to like the distinct flavours in that particular formula as an older child as well.[29] Through the process of weaning, your baby's food preferences will be shaped further by the foods that he gets exposed to. His first foods may be particularly important in terms of his willingness to eat certain foods. Giving him plenty of vegetables during this early process is likely to encourage him to eat them later. However, fussy eating and refusal of certain foods is pretty commonplace among toddlers. For many parents, mealtimes mean tantrums, and knowing how to deal with a child who flatly refuses to eat anything other than their favourite foods can be challenging. In Part 3 we will provide you with detailed guidance about *what* solid food to introduce during weaning and *how* to introduce it because we know from research that these strategies may help to prevent fussiness.

THE BOTTOM LINE

- Babies and toddlers are not all the same when it comes to milk and food.

- Some babies and toddlers are less sensitive to their fullness; they have a little bit too much each time they eat. These babies and toddlers are more susceptible to overeating if portion sizes are too large – be it milk in a bottle or food on a plate.

- Some babies and toddlers react more strongly to milk and food; wanting to eat (or overeat!) when they see, smell or taste delicious food; they are susceptible to overeating because they are always hungry and will eat at any opportunity.

- Toddlers with poor appetites and little interest in food tend to be faddy eaters who are prone to being fussy and often dislike vegetables, fruit and protein foods; they are more susceptible to poor dietary quality.

- Differences in appetite are probably one of the most important reasons why some babies gain weight too rapidly and others too slowly.

- When it comes to feeding your baby, it's all about under-standing what type of eater he is and making sure you respond to his unique appetite.

- Your baby's food preferences can be influenced by his early experiences – and when we say early, we mean when he is still in the womb!

- Exposure is crucial. Your baby will eat what he knows. He will start to enjoy mum's diet during pregnancy and breastfeeding, because it will flavour your amniotic fluid and breast milk. Weaning then shapes his food preferences, and the first foods you offer are key.

The chapters that follow will equip you with evidence-based tips about how to manage every type of eater, and how to help your baby develop healthy food preferences that will endure for years.

PART 1

Pregnancy and the Early Days

If you are expecting a baby, you may have discovered that there is a lot of conflicting advice out there about what to eat and drink, and how much exercise to do during pregnancy. If this is your first child, the experience of being pregnant will be completely new, and you may be looking for sound advice about how to have a healthy pregnancy, and what to do when your baby arrives. With newborns in particular, the guidance on how often babies should be weighed and what healthy weight gain looks like can be confusing – not to mention growth charts!

We now know that Mum's nutrition and weight gain during pregnancy have an impact not only on her own health but also on her baby's long-term health.[30] With that in mind, we provide you with facts and practical advice about how to eat healthily and exercise safely during pregnancy, and the benefits of this for you and your baby (Chapter 2). We also know that babies' early growth has an important influence on their future health – well into adult life. So it's important to keep an eye on this. But some mums are unsure about how to monitor their baby's weight gain and what to look out for. In Chapter 3 we explain exactly what healthy weight gain looks like during the first two years of life, how to spot weight gain that is too fast or too slow and why early weight gain is important for a baby's health now and in the future.

CHAPTER 2

Pregnancy: The First 270 Days

Pregnancy marks the first 270 days of your child's life. It can be exciting but also quite daunting, and you are likely to have some apprehension and many questions . . .

Will I have cravings?
Will I feel sick?
What should I be eating?
Can I exercise while I am pregnant?
How much weight am I going to put on?

In this chapter we equip you with advice on nutrition during pregnancy, and offer information on healthy weight gain, which matters both for you and your baby. There are a lot of different guidelines on nutrition in pregnancy – we have looked at all of these and summarised the most important evidence-based advice that is relevant for pregnant mums in the UK. We also give you ideas for how to eat healthily even if you feel sick and have cravings. We don't intend for this chapter to be 'preachy' or judgemental; we simply want to give you the guidelines and the reasons behind them so that you can make up your own mind about what is right for you. We hope that you will come away from this chapter feeling a little less daunted and more confident that you have all the information you need for a healthy pregnancy.

Why Your Eating Matters

You will probably already know that healthy eating during pregnancy is vital for the growth and development of your baby. Energy (calories) and nutrients are needed to meet your needs, as well as the needs of your growing baby. A poor diet in pregnancy is linked to poor outcomes for Mum, such as gestational diabetes (pregnancy-induced diabetes that can cause complications for Mum and baby such as premature labour and birth, and pre-eclampsia), iron deficiency anaemia and pre-eclampsia (when blood flow to the placenta is low so the baby doesn't get enough oxygen and nutrients) – and for baby, such as low or high birth weight, neural-tube defects (such as spina bifida) and stunted or accelerated growth.[31] Many people are also surprised to discover that a mother's diet during pregnancy may also influence her unborn baby's appetite and food preferences, which, in turn, affects their baby's risk of obesity and future health; so it's a good idea to pay attention to your diet during pregnancy, as far as you can.

PROGRAMMING OF APPETITE

Your baby's appetite regulation starts to develop during gestation and continues to mature during the first few weeks and months after birth. Appetite regulation (hunger and satiety, as well as food responsiveness) is largely controlled by the brain and, in particular, a structure called the 'hypothalamus'. A baby's early nutritional experience in the womb can affect the development of his appetite regulation very profoundly. Mums who are under- or over-nourished during pregnancy tend to have babies that are small or large for their gestational age respectively.[32] Being born too small or too big puts a baby at greater risk of a number of diseases later in life (see Chapter 3 for more on this), and there is growing evidence that the appetite pathways in the brains of babies who are born both small and big have been disrupted during their early foetal growth, such that they are predisposed to overeat and to prefer foods that are high in sugar and fat.[33]

Both over- and under-nutrition appear to result in permanent alteration to the same neural circuits controlling appetite and a key appetite hormone – leptin – seems to be involved. Leptin is made by fat cells (the more fat we carry, the more leptin we have) and plays a fundamental role in regulating our hunger and satiety in the brain. It is often called the 'satiety hormone' because the more of it we have, the less hungry we feel, and vice versa. Research has suggested that babies who are born small, to mothers who had poor nutrition during pregnancy, are born with very low levels of leptin, so are very hungry, and they also have a permanent increase in their appetite via changes to their hypothalamus, making them susceptible to overeating.[34] These developmental changes are thought to occur because the body is predicting a famine when the baby is born, so an avid appetite would provide a survival advantage in an environment where food is scarce. It is this increased appetite that drives rapid early growth for babies who are born small (called 'catch-up' growth). The problem is that if a baby who is born small enters an environment that is, in fact, rich in food (and not a famine), the result is an increased risk of obesity. For babies born very large, the reason for their increased appetite seems to be that their hypothalamus is somehow resistant to the effects of leptin – they have high amounts of it (as would be expected, given the increased amount of fat), but it doesn't have the appetite-dampening effect on the hypothalamus that it should have. It isn't clear at the moment why this occurs, or even if it has any particular survival advantage, but it appears to increase the risk of obesity.

PROGRAMMING OF FOOD PREFERENCES

There is research to show that the flavour and smell of foods and drinks from Mum's diet during pregnancy makes its way into her amniotic fluid. In one study involving pregnant women, half were given a capsule to swallow which contained garlic and the other half were given a placebo capsule. The odour of the amniotic fluid in women who had the garlic capsules was judged by a sensory panel of adults to be stronger than that of the women consuming the placebo capsules.[35] Experimental studies have shown that exposure to certain foods in the womb may increase babies' acceptance and enjoyment of those foods.[36]

With this in mind, if you have a healthy diet containing lots of fruit and vegetables during pregnancy, your baby may be more likely to accept and like these healthy foods. Of course, eating healthily is far easier said than done if you have terrible nausea. A friend of ours ate nothing but peanut butter on toast and seeds for the first 17 weeks of both her pregnancies because she felt so horrendously ill. Vegetables and fruit may be the last thing you feel like eating when you feel sick, but do try and incorporate some into your diet during pregnancy – even if it's in the form of soup or a pasta sauce. Good nutrition during these nine months will benefit both you and your baby.

WEIGHT GAIN DURING PREGNANCY

'You're going to put on weight and that's a fact, so there's no point in getting anxious about it.'

Carla (30 weeks pregnant)

During pregnancy consuming a healthy diet is important to ensure that your baby is well nourished, so that he develops normally and has a healthy birth weight. But in the UK, there is currently no guidance on appropriate weight gain during pregnancy (at the time of writing this book), so it's difficult to know how much is the right amount and it will vary for different women. In general, those with underweight should be gaining more than those with overweight when they start their pregnancy; but you should *not try to lose weight during pregnancy*.

The baby, placenta and amniotic fluid account for about 35 per cent of weight gain.[37] Other increases in weight come from increased maternal blood volume, breast-tissue development and increased fat – women store an additional 2–5kg fat in order to prepare for breastfeeding (extra energy reserves are required in order to produce the milk). About 50 per cent of women are thought to gain too much weight during pregnancy, based on American guidelines, and this can lead to problems for both Mum and baby, including:

- non-elective Caesarean delivery

- postpartum weight retention (not losing the weight you gained after pregnancy)

- being born large for gestational age (above the 90th centile) or macrosomic (birth weight greater than 4kg)

- childhood overweight or obesity[38]

It's therefore a good idea to try not to gain excessive amounts of weight during your pregnancy (although this is easier said than done). Excessive gestational weight gain is usually due to eating too much overall and, in particular, eating too many foods high in fat and sugar. So making sure you eat well and are physically active, are the important things to focus on during your pregnancy; these should be the aim rather than a specific amount of weight gain. This is important whether you have underweight, overweight or a healthy weight.

Nutrition During Pregnancy

Healthy eating during pregnancy is about eating a balanced diet with a wide variety of foods to ensure you have a good store of nutrients to meet the demands of your baby, and keep you healthy. It's also about eating the right amount.

ENERGY

There is a widely held belief that pregnant women should, or need to, 'eat for two'. And some women nearly double their calorie intake.[39]

'I am growing another person so I need to eat more.'

Julie (32 weeks pregnant)

However, contrary to this popular belief, women don't need any additional calories at the beginning of pregnancy. The International Federation of Gynecology and Obstetrics (FIGO) recommends that pregnant women should focus on eating well, rather than eating more.[40] An increase in energy intake is not needed until the third trimester of pregnancy, and even then this is only an extra 200 calories per day (the equivalent of half an avocado or two slices of wholemeal toast).[41] The increase is needed to make up for the energy used to grow and maintain the baby, the placenta and the mother's tissues, and to make milk.

FATS

Fats have structural and metabolic functions in the body and are a source of essential fatty acids, which the body cannot make. Fat also helps the body absorb nutrients such as vitamins A, D and E. Fat that you consume that is not used by your body will be stored as body fat. During pregnancy, total fat intake should represent 15–30 per cent of your overall energy intake to prevent excessive weight gain. This is actually no different to standard advice for all adults. There are also 'good' and 'bad' fats (see page 284 for more on this). Saturated fat is an unhealthy fat so should also be limited. It is found in animal-derived fats, such as butter and cream. Processed foods, such as chocolate, crisps, biscuits, pastries, ice cream and cakes, are often high in saturated fat (see page 284).

Polyunsaturated fatty acids (PUFAs) are a much healthier alternative and are important for the development of your baby's brain and eyes, so it is important to make sure you include some of these in your diet (in small amounts). They can be found in oily fish (though avoid fish that contain mercury, such as swordfish and shark), some vegetable oils (such as flaxseed oil) and some nuts and seeds (such as walnuts and flaxseeds).

CARBOHYDRATES

Carbohydrates provide fuel for the body and help organs and muscles to function properly. They should be the largest source of energy during pregnancy because they are broken down into simple sugars which pass easily across the placenta and provide energy to you and your growing baby. Try to choose carbohydrates that have a low glycaemic index (GI), which means that your blood-sugar levels will rise slowly after eating them. 'Low-GI' foods typically have a GI of 55 or less and include foods such as soya products, beans, whole fruit (not fruit juice), milk, pasta, grainy bread, porridge and lentils. If possible, opt for *wholegrain* varieties of foods rather than refined ones. These foods are more slowly digested, absorbed and metabolised and cause a lower and slower rise in blood glucose. This means you are less likely to experience sudden rises or dips in your blood-sugar level (called glycaemic control) which is important for the healthy growth and development of your baby. A diet containing low-GI foods during pregnancy reduces your risk of having a big baby and improves glucose levels.[42] Low-GI foods will also mean that you feel fuller for longer (see page 323 for more information on this).

PROTEIN

Proteins are one of the building blocks of body tissue, so more are needed in pregnancy. Most British adults get plenty of protein so you shouldn't worry overly but it's important to ensure you include protein in your diet during pregnancy. Good sources include lean meat, fish, chicken, eggs and dairy. If you are vegetarian, include some legumes (for example, lentils and beans), soya foods (for example, tofu and edamame beans), nuts, seeds and nut butters.

FIBRE

There are two types of fibre – soluble and insoluble. Soluble fibre dissolves in water and makes bowel movements easier, helping to prevent constipation. It is found in grains (such as oats and barley), fruit (such as bananas and apples), beans and pulses (such as baked beans and chickpeas) and root vegetables (such as carrots and potatoes). Insoluble fibre does not dissolve in water; it passes through your intestines without being broken down and helps other foods move through your digestive system more easily. This keeps your bowels healthy. It is found in high-fibre breakfast cereals, wholemeal bread, pasta and brown rice, nuts and seeds.

Constipation is quite common during pregnancy because of an increase in the hormone progesterone which relaxes smooth muscle in your body and makes food pass through your intestines more slowly. Increasing your fibre intake, drinking plenty of fluids and doing some gentle exercise can help with this. There is also some evidence to suggest that fibre might also reduce the risk of gestational diabetes and pre-eclampsia.[43] All adults in the UK are recommended to eat around 30g fibre per day, with no specific increase during pregnancy.[44]

FOLIC ACID (FOLATE)

Folic acid (folate in its natural form) is a B vitamin which is vital for the formation of red blood cells. It is particularly important before and during the first few weeks of pregnancy. Babies rapidly develop spine and nerve cells in the early stages of pregnancy and inadequate folic acid at this time increases the risk of the baby developing a neural-tube defect, such as spina bifida. Folic acid may also help to prevent cleft lip and palate. Therefore, the

National Institute for Health and Care Excellence (NICE) has recommended that all women should take a supplement of 400mcg (micrograms) folic acid a day when planning a pregnancy, or as soon as they find out they are pregnant, and should take it for at least the first 12 weeks of pregnancy.[45]

In later pregnancy, folic acid prevents a particular type of anaemia. So it's important to eat foods naturally rich in this vitamin, and foods that have been fortified with folic acid, such as some breads and breakfast cereals. Folic acid is destroyed by heat, so if you cook foods high in folic acid, the folic acid will be lost. Good food sources of folic acid include:

- spinach

- kale

- cabbage

- broccoli

- beans and legumes (for example, peas and chickpeas)

- yeast and beef extracts

- oranges and orange juice

- wheat bran and other wholegrain foods

- wholegrain cereals

VITAMIN B12

Vitamin B12 helps to keep the body's nerve and blood cells healthy and helps make DNA. It is found in animal products such as fish, meat, poultry, eggs, milk and milk products. Women can become deficient in vitamin B12 if they do not consume animal-based foods, so if you follow a vegetarian or vegan diet FIGO recommend taking at least 2.4mcg vitamin B12 supplements per day before and during pregnancy.[46]

VITAMIN D

Vitamin D is essential for healthy bones, teeth and muscles. During pregnancy vitamin D is important for the development of a baby's bones and immune and nervous systems. Lack of vitamin D during pregnancy can affect how much vitamin D your baby stores for the first months of his life. Although vitamin D is found in some foods (such as red meat, egg yolks and oily fish), it is in such small amounts that it is virtually impossible to get enough of it through diet alone. Most of our vitamin D actually comes from the sun; our skin makes it when exposed to sunlight. But in the UK we don't get enough sunlight during the winter months to make adequate amounts, and given the public health advice to wear sunscreen and stay out of the sun during the summer, UK adults tend to be deficient in vitamin D. Those with darker skin or who cover up completely when outside, may be particularly short of it. Babies born to mothers that are vitamin D deficient are more likely to have low birth weight and are at higher risk of developing allergies during childhood.[47] (See page 254 for more information on allergies.) Since 2016, the UK adult population, including pregnant women, have been recommended to take a 10mcg vitamin D supplement daily, although FIGO suggests that higher doses between 25mcg and 50mcg are beneficial and not harmful.[48]

VEGETARIANS/VEGANS

If you are a vegan or vegetarian you may already be aware that many of the essential nutrients, such as iron, calcium, vitamin B12 and vitamin D, are found in animal-based products (such as red meat, fish, milk and eggs). It's possible to get the nutrients you and your baby need without eating animal-based food sources but you may need to eat fortified foods and take supplements just to make sure. It's a good idea to speak to your midwife or GP so that they can help establish what you need. Below are some good sources of nutrients if you follow a vegetarian or vegan diet:

- Protein: legumes, soya foods, nuts, seeds and nut butters.
- Iron: fortified breakfast cereal with added iron, wholegrain bread and other grains (for example, brown rice, oats and wheat), legumes (such as lentils and chickpeas), tofu and other soya foods, green vegetables, dried fruit (such as apricots) and eggs (for vegetarians).
- Calcium: calcium-fortified almond or soya milk, breakfast cereals, white beans, tahini and calcium-set tofu, almonds or sesame seeds, kale, broccoli and pak choi.
- Vitamin D: fortified plant milks and cereals, and eggs (for vegetarians).
- Vitamin B12: unsweetened soya milk, fortified breakfast cereal and yeast extract (such as Marmite).

VITAMIN C

Vitamin C is another important nutrient during pregnancy as it is needed by the body to make collagen, a protein that makes up cartilage, tendons, bones and skin. During pregnancy vitamin C requirements are increased by about 10mg (milligrams), so it's a good idea to make sure you eat some foods rich in vitamin C, including citrus fruits, green vegetables (such as broccoli and kale) and cereals fortified with it.

VITAMIN A

Vitamin A plays a crucial role in maintaining healthy vision and the immune system. It comes in two forms:

1. Retinol, found in meat, fish, dairy foods and eggs.

2. Beta-carotene, found in fruit (for example, apricots) and vegetables (for example, carrots, green vegetables such as broccoli and kale, and sweet potato) that the body then converts into vitamin A.

There is a risk of abnormal development of a baby's eyes, skull, lungs and heart if Mum has too much or not enough vitamin A.[49] Be careful about eating liver which contains high amounts of vitamin A. Many foods are now fortified with preformed vitamin A and, as a result, pregnant women should avoid multivitamin or prenatal supplements (for example, fish oil) that contain more than 1,500mcg vitamin A.

IRON

Your body uses iron to make haemoglobin, a substance in red blood cells that transports oxygen throughout your body. During pregnancy, your body produces more blood to support the placenta and to supply oxygen to your baby, so the demand for iron goes up to keep up with the increase in blood supply. This increase in blood means that without enough iron your organs and tissues will not get enough oxygen, and this can increase the risk of low birth weight and preterm delivery, both of which are linked to stunted growth in later life[50] (your child being shorter). It is therefore a good idea to make sure you include some iron-rich foods in your diet, such as lean red meat, poultry, pulses, dark green vegetables and fortified foods (such as cereals and breads). Certain substances make it harder for your body to absorb iron, including: tannins (found in tea); calcium (found in milk); polyphenols (found in coffee); and phytates and oxalates (found in wheat bran and pulses). So try to avoid drinking tea and coffee at the same time as eating iron-rich foods. Generally you shouldn't need to take a supplement because your body will adapt to pregnancy to reserve iron levels, but if your iron levels become too low you may be advised by your GP or midwife to take a supplement.

CALCIUM

Calcium helps keep bones healthy. Although calcium needs are increased during pregnancy, the body adapts to ensure more calcium is absorbed. Calcium can be found in dairy products such as milk, cheese and yoghurt, and eating these foods regularly during pregnancy will ensure you get enough. Non-dairy sources of calcium include: spinach, tofu, peas, beans and lentils, oranges and egg yolk.[51] If you only eat plant foods, choose soy products and other non-dairy drinks that are calcium enriched.

IODINE

Iodine helps make thyroid hormones and plays a role in regulating metabolism. It is also important for healthy brain development and insufficient iodine in pregnancy is the main cause of mental retardation worldwide. There is some evidence that British pregnant women are mildly deficient and this is linked with slightly lower IQ and reading ability.[52] Pregnant women are recommended to have 220mcg iodine a day[53], although it should be possible for most to get this from their diet and supplementation isn't recomended in the UK. The main source of iodine in the UK is dairy products but it can also be found in fish and seafood. It is also important not to have too much iodine. Intakes should not exceed 940mcg a day. Some types of seaweed have very high concentrations of iodine and are not recommended. If you are vegan, it's best to seek advice about sources of iodine during your pregnancy.[54]

ZINC

Zinc plays a role in enzyme and insulin production, and it helps to form a baby's organs, skeleton, nerves and circulatory system. It is found in meat, fish, eggs, milk, pulses, nuts and most cereals. There is no need to take a supplement.[55]

> **SUPPLEMENTS**
>
> Only supplements of folic acid and vitamin D are recommended in pregnancy and, as mentioned on page 81, vitamin B12 is recommended for vegetarian or vegan women. No other supplements are required if you are eating a heathy, balanced diet. Healthy Start – a welfare food scheme in the UK – provides food and nutrition support, as well as supplements, to young and low-income women (see page 286 for more on this).

Healthy Eating During Pregnancy

You don't need to go on a special or unusual diet to get all the nutrients you and your baby need during pregnancy; it's about making sure you eat a *balanced* diet, although this can be tough if you are feeling sick, exhausted, fighting cravings and trying to juggle lots of things in your life to prepare for your new arrival.

First Steps Nutrition Trust (www.firststepsnutrition.org) is a British independent public-health nutrition charity providing evidence-based and independent (not supported by industry) information about nutrition during pregnancy and the early years (0–5 years). Their freely available booklet 'Eating Well for a Healthy Pregnancy: A Practical Guide' is excellent, and includes detailed information about nutrition in pregnancy, alongside affordable meal plans (eating healthily for £4 a day) and recipes. In line with the government's Eatwell Guide,[56] they suggest that meals and snacks should be based mainly around two food groups which should each make up more than one third of all the food you eat each day during your pregnancy:

- Starchy foods, such as bread, pasta, rice, potatoes, breakfast cereals and noodles: aim for wholegrain low-GI options, such as whole oats, brown or basmati rice, wholegrain bread, new baby potatoes and wholewheat pasta (see page 323). These are a good source of energy and a range of nutrients such as fibre, iron, calcium and B vitamins.

- Fruit and vegetables: aim to eat at least five portions of these every day (one portion is about 80g), which include fresh, frozen, tinned, dried or juiced in water. Bear in mind that dried fruit and fruit juice contain a lot of free sugars which are sugars added to foods, and those found naturally in honey, syrups and unsweetened fruit juices, so try not to have too many of these during your pregnancy to optimise glycaemic control (your blood-sugar level) and have them with a meal (the high vitamin C content in most fruit juices has the added benefit of supporting the absorption of iron from non-meat sources). Fruit and vegetables are a great source of vitamins, minerals and fibre.

Two other food groups are also important and should be eaten regularly during pregnancy:

- Dairy and alternatives: these include milk, cheese and yoghurt. Aim to eat these foods every day in moderate amounts, and choose lower-fat and lower-sugar options where possible.

- Protein foods, such as meat, fish, poultry, eggs, beans, pulses and nuts: try to eat more beans and pulses, choose lean meats and avoid adding extra fat when cooking, and aim for at least two portions of fish per week, including *oily* fish such as salmon, fresh tuna, mackerel or sardines (but do not have more than two portions of oily fish per week).

Try to limit the amount of food you eat that's high in fat and/ or sugar, and salt. Foods high in fat and/or sugar will displace those that are nutrient dense and make it difficult for you to get all the nutrients you need for your pregnancy without eating too many calories. Try also to opt for foods low in saturated fat and, where possible, opt for polyunsaturated fats instead.

- You should aim to have less than 30g (around seven sugar cubes) of 'free sugars' every day.[57] Sugars found naturally in whole fruits, vegetables, grains and cereals are not 'free sugars', so these are fine. Food labels usually only describe total sugars, so it can be difficult to know how many free sugars are in a food (see page 290 for more on this). As a guide, most desserts (cakes, biscuits, chocolate) contain free sugars, as does 100 per cent fruit juice. If you have sugar in your tea or coffee, pregnancy is a great time to try and give it up by gradually reducing the amount you add each day.

- Try to eat less fat overall, and less saturated fat. You can reduce your saturated-fat intake by: cutting the fat off meat and buying lean cuts of meat; grilling, baking or poaching foods rather than frying them; taking the skin off poultry meat; opting for lower-fat dairy products, such as semi-skimmed milk and low-fat yoghurt; using less spread on bread; having fewer processed foods such as cakes, biscuits, fried snacks and takeaways.

- Aim to have no more than 5g[58] salt (about 1 teaspoon) per day. Most of the salt we eat is from processed food, so if you limit these you will probably cut down on your salt intake.

Foods containing a lot of salt include: smoked fish and meats; ham and bacon; savoury snacks (for example, crisps); cheese; bread; some breakfast cereals; and takeaways.

FOOD SAFETY

During pregnancy it is very important to be aware of food hygiene to avoid the risk of food poisoning, which can be harmful to you and your baby. It will also be particularly unpleasant while you are pregnant, especially if you are already suffering from sickness or nausea. Some cases of food poisoning can be very dangerous for your baby, such as listeria, which can be found in uncooked meats and unpasteurised cheeses.

- Wash all fruit, vegetables and salad (even pre-packaged salad) as soil can contain a parasite (toxoplasma) that causes an infection (toxoplasmosis) and harms unborn babies. It can lead to miscarriage, stillbirth or damage to the baby's brain or other organs such as the eyes.[59]

- Wash all surfaces, utensils and your hands after preparing raw foods such as meat, poultry and fish and keep raw foods separate from ready-to-eat food to avoid contamination and food-poisoning germs, such as salmonella, campylobacter and E. coli O157.

- Use a separate knife and chopping board for raw meats.

- Cook all meat thoroughly so that there is no trace of blood or pink meat, especially poultry, pork, sausages and minced meat.

FOODS TO AVOID

There are certain foods you should limit or not eat while pregnant because they can cause harm to your baby. For example, according to Public Health England (PHE), in the UK there are approximately 200 cases of listeriosis per year, with 12 per cent of these among pregnant women.[60] So, it is pretty rare, but can have serious consequences if you are pregnant, with miscarriage occurring in 20 per cent of cases.[61] Below is a list of foods to be avoided:

- Soft cheeses with mould-ripened white rinds, such as Camembert, Brie or some goats' cheese, or soft blue cheeses, such as Gorgonzola and Roquefort. Thorough cooking should kill any bacteria though so these are fine to eat if they are cooked such as baked Brie or Camembert. Hard cheeses such as Parmesan and Cheddar are fine, as are other soft cheeses that have been pasteurised, such as cottage cheese, feta, mozzarella, ricotta, cream cheese, halloumi and processed cheeses, such as cheese spreads. Bear in mind, however, that soft cheeses are less acidic than hard cheeses and contain more moisture, so they can be an ideal environment for harmful bacteria, such as listeria, to grow in. Make sure you store them carefully in the fridge once they have been opened and don't eat them past the 'use by' date.

- Unpasteurised milk or foods made from them.

- Pâté (any type, including vegetable) as it can contain listeria. Liver pâté also contains high levels of vitamin A which can harm your baby (see page 61).

- Raw eggs and food containing raw or partially cooked eggs, such as home-made mayonnaise, hollandaise or Béarnaise sauce, Caesar salad dressing or tiramisu, should be avoided.

Home-made ice cream is okay if you use a pasteurised egg substitute or an egg-free recipe. Only eat eggs that have been cooked until both the white and yolk are solid. This is to avoid the risk of salmonella, which causes a type of food poisoning leading to diarrhoea and vomiting. However, if eggs have the British Lion logo stamped on their shell they have been produced under the British Lion Code of Practice and are safe to eat during pregnancy even if they are raw or only partially cooked.[62]

- Raw and undercooked meats as there is a risk of toxoplasmosis (see page 67). All meats must be cooked all the way through so that there is no pink meat or pink juice as uncooked meat can carry harmful bacteria and lead to food poisoning. This even includes the meats that would normally be fine to eat slightly pink, such as a steak. Some cold meats, such as salami, chorizo, Parma ham and pepperoni, are cured (preserved through ageing, drying, canning, salting, brining or smoking) rather than cooked and may contain toxoplasma. Freezing cured meats for at least four days or cooking them will kill most parasites and the meats will be safer to eat. Pre-packaged cooked meats such as ham and corned beef are safe to eat.

- Shark, swordfish and marlin (if you are partial to eating these!), and limit the amount of tuna you eat to no more than two steaks (weighing about 140g cooked or 170g raw) or four medium-sized tins (about 140g drained weight per tin) per week. This is because of the high levels of mercury in these fish. Mercury can harm a baby's developing nervous system and maternal exposure has been linked to lower intelligence and impaired language, attention and memory in children. High levels can cause mental retardation.[63]

- Raw shellfish, such as oysters, as they can be contaminated with harmful bacteria and viruses that could cause food poisoning, which can be particularly unpleasant during pregnancy. Cooked shellfish, such as mussels, lobster, prawns and crab, and white fish, such as cod, and smoked fish, such as smoked salmon, are safe to eat during pregnancy.

- Caffeine should be limited as it can result in babies having low birth weight and can cause miscarriage.[64] A large review of 53 studies found that an increase of 100mg caffeine was associated with increased risk of miscarriage, stillbirth, preterm delivery, low birth weight and of babies being small for gestational age. You should therefore have no more than 200mg caffeine per day which is approximately two mugs of instant coffee or tea or one mug of filter coffee. Also be aware that some sugar-sweetened beverages such as cola contain caffeine.

If you would like more information about food safety in pregnancy, see the 'foods to avoid in pregnancy' section of NHS Choices.

Alcohol

Drinking alcohol in pregnancy is a controversial topic that has received no end of media attention over the years. You may be wondering what the evidence really says, and whether or not you should have anything alcoholic to drink at all. Or you may feel worried if you didn't know you were pregnant in the first few weeks during which you were still drinking, and are wondering if this is likely to have caused your baby any harm.

There is clear evidence that chronic (very regular) heavy drinking in pregnancy increases the risk of miscarriage, still birth and foetal alcohol syndrome (FAS). FAS can include a range of developmental problems, such as: learning difficulties; physical disabilities (movement and coordination problems called cerebral palsy); mood, attention and behavioural problems (such as autism and attention deficit hyperactivity disorder); problems with the liver, kidney, heart or other organs; hearing and vision problems; poor growth (small birth weight, slow growth and shorter height in adulthood); small head size and distinctive facial features.[65] What is less clear is whether there is any harm from low or moderate amounts of drinking. In other words, is there any level of alcohol that is safe to drink in pregnancy? A comprehensive high-quality review of the evidence concluded that there is no strong evidence for any developmental problems from low amounts of alcohol in pregnancy.[66] However, there is some evidence of increased risk of preterm birth and behavioural problems (such as hyperactivity and inattention) from moderate levels of drinking. The review defined 'moderate' as drinking 30–40ml or more per occasion (4 to 5 units, or 2 to 2.5 standard glasses of wine), or 70ml or more per week (about 9 units, or 4 to 5 standard glasses of wine). So, the evidence suggests that light drinking is unlikely to be harmful to your growing baby, but moderate or heavy drinking is a bad idea.

However, none of the studies have been designed in such a way that it is possible to know for certain if drinking any alcohol during pregnancy is safe. Many studies have relied on women reporting their alcohol consumption retrospectively after pregnancy, which makes the information unreliable because of the difficulty of remembering accurately. It is also possible that women who drink in pregnancy and those who abstain completely are different in important ways that also affect their health. For example, the extent to which they follow all sorts of health advice; education; and other pressures on their lives. The only way to study this fairly would be to randomly allocate women to drink or not to drink in pregnancy, and compare the outcomes (a randomised controlled trial), but we can't do this type of study because it would be unethical. This means we can't be sure if there is any level of alcohol which is really safe to drink, particularly during the first trimester when foetal development is probably most adversely affected. Alcohol passes through your blood into the placenta, so if you drink, your baby does too. But it is certainly not going to harm your baby if you *don't* drink. This is the reason why the chief medical officers in the UK and the RCOG recommend that it is probably safest to stop drinking alcohol altogether when you're pregnant.[67] If you do drink, limit yourself to no more than one or two units of alcohol, once or twice a week, but it's probably best to abstain during the first trimester when your baby's development is most likely to be affected adversely by drinking. At the same time, try not to feel overly worried if you didn't know that you were pregnant and were still drinking regularly. The likelihood is that everything will be fine. But aim to stop as soon as you find out you are pregnant.

One unit is 10ml – or 8g – of pure alcohol and is the equivalent of:

- a single 25ml measure of spirit, such as vodka at 40 per cent ABV
- a third of a pint of beer
- half a standard glass (175ml) of wine at 12 per cent ABV.[68]

It can be very difficult to give up habits that have taken years to acquire; for example, if it has become routine to share a bottle of wine over dinner on a Friday night. If you are finding it hard to cut down, there's a lot of support out there to help you (call Drinkline on 03001231110 or visit www.nhs.uk to find local alcohol support services). It may prove very difficult to do, but both you and your baby will benefit enormously if you manage it, so it's worth a try.

Achieving a Healthy Diet

It's one thing knowing what a healthy, balanced diet is during pregnancy, but it's quite another to actually make sure you achieve it. It can be challenging, especially when there are lots of other things to think about during this time, or if you are experiencing cravings and sickness. There are a few strategies that research has shown to be helpful in achieving a healthy diet, including during pregnancy: setting healthy food goals; having structured meal plans; and monitoring your dietary intake.[69]

SETTING FOOD GOALS

Goal-setting is an important part of making sure you actually do something, so this is a fantastic way to try and make small, healthy changes to your eating habits when you're pregnant. It involves a four-step process:

1. Recognise a need for change. For example, increasing the amount of fresh fruit and vegetables you eat during pregnancy.

2. Establish a goal. For example, eat five portions of fruit and vegetables per day.

3. Adopt a goal-directed activity and monitor it. For example, instead of eating a bag of crisps as a mid-morning snack have carrot sticks with hummus, and monitor your food intake using an app.

4. Reward your goal if you achieve it. For example, put 20p into a jar each day if you eat five fruits and vegetables. (A few examples of other non-food related rewards include: an evening out; a new piece of clothing; a new baby gift; a spa treatment; or a trip to the hairdresser.) Try not to use food as a reward, for example, a bar of chocolate as a treat.

The key to goal-setting is to make them SMART (Specific, Measurable, Achievable, Realistic and Timely):

- Specific: for example, specifying that you want to eat three vegetables and two pieces of fruit each day.

- Measurable: you must be able to measure your goals, for example by tracking your fruit and vegetable intake in a life-style app.

- Achievable: the goal you set for yourself must be achievable or you are setting yourself up for failure. If you currently only eat one portion of fruit or vegetables per day, aim to start increasing this to two or three, and gradually increase your intake.

- Realistic: if your goal is not realistic, for example going to the gym every day before work if you are so tired you are already struggling to get out of bed when your alarm usually goes off, then it will not be achievable.

- Timely: you need to set a timeframe for your goal so that you have a fixed time limit in which to reach your goal. With pregnancy this is perfect because you have nine months set out for you. But you can also set shorter time periods than this. For example, over the next week aim to eat one extra piece of fruit each day as your mid-morning snack.

STRUCTURED MEAL PLANS AND BREAKFAST EVERY DAY

Planning and structuring meals will not only help to ensure that you obtain essential nutrients and food groups for you and your baby, but it can also make life easier because your meals are planned from day to day or week to week. Try to plan lunch and dinner for four to five days of the week and, when you do the weekly shop, stick as close to the ingredients you need as you can. Planning meals in advance reduces the number of decisions required when it comes to food choices, and this may help you make sure you don't eat unnecessary unhealthy snacks or foods. Shopping online can also save you time, and means you don't have to lug bags all the way home if you do a big weekly shop.

Try to establish a routine of eating breakfast every day. If you miss breakfast you may be tempted to snack mid-morning on high-fat, high-salt and high-sugar foods, which means missing out on the nutrients that most breakfast foods provide, such as fibre, iron and zinc. As well as breakfast, try to eat three meals per day with healthy snacks in between (see page 78 for ideas for healthy snacks). This will help to keep your hunger at bay.

DAILY MONITORING OF DIETARY INTAKE

Monitoring the food you eat helps you keep track of the food groups and nutrients you are consuming. There is now a huge range of apps available for smartphone devices that will track your daily intake over the course of a day, and some that are specifically designed for use during pregnancy. Research suggests that monitoring your dietary intake can help prevent excessive weight gain, and it is thought that this is because it increases people's awareness of their behaviour and the circumstances that surround their eating behaviours.[70] However, bear in mind that many of these apps focus on calorie counting which we do not advocate during pregnancy, as dieting is not recommended. In addition, some apps are badly regulated and are of poor quality so make sure you go for one from a reputable organisation.

SICKNESS AND CRAVINGS

Nausea and/or vomiting, especially during the first trimester, occur in more than half of pregnant women.[71] They can occur at any time of the day – not just in the morning. Triggers such as food smells, perfume and cigarette smoke can cause these. The cause of nausea and/or vomiting in pregnancy is poorly understood, although the consensus is that it is caused by biological changes relating to pregnancy (such as hormones). Some researchers have suggested that it has a protective function in making sure harmful foods or substances are avoided or expelled from the body. There is some evidence to support this theory; for example, symptoms are strongest during the first trimester when your baby's development is most susceptible to harm.[72] Nevertheless, the symptoms can be very difficult to cope with, especially if they are severe. So what can you do to alleviate them? There is some evidence to suggest that ginger might be an effective treatment for nausea during pregnancy,[73] but this is inconsistent. In fact, there is a lack of well-designed studies into dietary strategies to help with this. If you are struggling with nausea and/or vomiting, then it might be worth trying some lemon and ginger tea. First Steps Nutrition suggests three other tips:

1. Have small bland or dry snacks regularly (for example, dry toast or rice cakes).

2. Have a dry snack on waking.

3. Avoid fatty or spicy foods, or foods with strong smells.

The British Nutrition Foundation also has a very useful online resource which provides advice on how to cope with sickness during pregnancy (see www.nutrition.org.uk).

As well as sickness, some women experience strong aversions to foods, such as tea, coffee and fried foods.[74] Intense cravings, or strong urges for foods, also often occur during pregnancy.[75] It is thought that between 50 and 90 per cent of women experience cravings during pregnancy. Cravings for high-fat, high-sugar foods (for example, sweets, desserts and chocolates) during pregnancy may result in increased overall calorie intake, and, in turn, this can lead to excessive gestational weight gain (see page 53). One study found that the only thing that predicted excess gestational weight gain among African-American women was food cravings.[76] This is a relatively understudied area so it is not entirely clear what causes strong urges (or aversions) for specific foods during pregnancy, but it has been suggested that hormonal fluctuations or the nutritional needs of mother and baby may play a role, or that it is an adaptive mechanism to protect the baby from toxins – hence the commonly reported aversions to meat, fish, caffein- ated drinks and alcohol. Regardless of the cause of cravings, you will know if you have had them that they are very difficult to resist! Try your best to opt for healthy-snacks (see below for some healthy-snack ideas) if you can.

'When I was pregnant with Rhys I put on 6st 7lb. I had a very sweet tooth and craved cream cakes and Weetabix! With Amelia I loved avocado, tuna and lemon and was a pretty good eater. Perhaps I was more careful because of the first time. I felt good and only put on 2st 11lb.'

Phoebe, mum of Rhys (12 years) and Amelia (6 years)

HEALTHY SNACK IDEAS

- Fresh fruit
- Carrot, celery and cucumber sticks with hummus
- Plain yoghurt
- A small low fat cream cheese and tomato sandwich
- Boiled egg
- Crackers with cottage cheese
- A handful of unsalted mixed nuts
- Rice cakes with hummus
- Pitta bread with guacamole dip
- A small slice of malt loaf with a thin amount of low-fat spread
- A small bowl of wholegrain cereal with semi-skimmed milk
- A slice of wholemeal toast with a thin scrape of yeast extract (for example, Marmite)

PHYSICAL ACTIVITY

It comes as a surprise to many expectant mums to discover that not only is it safe to exercise in pregnancy, but it is recommended. It will help support healthy weight gain in pregnancy, as well as prepare you for the birth.

'I was paranoid about exercise so I stopped playing netball and stopped Pilates. I was worried about falling over and that something would happen. I didn't want to risk it.'

Evie (26 weeks pregnant)

Exercise is regarded as a safe way to maintain health and vitality during pregnancy, and there are *no known risks to the baby or mother* in most circumstances. During pregnancy you need to prepare yourself for labour – think of it as training for a marathon! Physical activity can help you ensure that you are fit and healthy before you give birth. The Physical Activity and Pregnancy Study, led by Oxford University, carried out the highest quality review to date of the evidence for the benefits of exercise in pregnancy. There was clear evidence for less gestational weight gain and lower risk of caesarean section. There was also some evidence that it reduces your likelihood of developing gestational diabetes and hypertensive disorders, such as high blood pressure. Importantly, there was no evidence of any harm to Mum or baby, suggesting that it is safe to exercise in pregnancy.[77]

The National Institute of Health and Care Excellence (NICE) recommends moderate physical activity during pregnancy (activity that makes you breathe faster, but still allows you to hold a conversation). If you have a low level of activity before pregnancy, it is recommended that when you are pregnant you start with 15 minutes of light-intensity activity (such as walking) three times per week, increasing to 30 minutes daily. All pregnant women should aim for 150 minutes of exercise per week during pregnancy, and do aerobic exercise – for example, using a treadmill or bicycle, and light to moderate strength-conditioning exercise, such as 8–12 repetitions of muscle strengthening activities that involve all the main muscle groups twice a week (for example, lunges and squats).[78] They have produced a brilliant physical activity infographic that can be viewed online.[79] It is advised that pregnant women should minimise activities that risk loss of balance and trauma, such as skiing and contact sports, but other activities are fine. Many local sport centres and gyms hold fitness classes specifically designed for pregnant women, such as prenatal yoga, aqua aerobics and Zumba. These help to keep you physically active, can be a lot of fun and are a great way to meet other expectant mums.

EXERCISE TIPS[80]

- Exercise daily: even if this is only 30 minutes of walking. Every little helps.
- Do not exercise in hot weather.
- Drink plenty of water.
- Ensure you inform any exercise-class instructors that you are pregnant.
- Swimming is a great low-intensity exercise during pregnancy.
- Always warm up before exercise to gradually increase your heart rate and circulation; this will loosen your joints, increase blood flow to your muscles and help prevent injuries.
- Always cool down after exercise, for example, by brisk walking, as this brings your heart rate and breathing back to normal, removes lactic acid which can build up in your muscles and reduces muscle spasm, cramping and soreness. Be cautious of exercise such as horse riding, skiing or cycling – there is a risk of falling and injuring yourself and your baby.
- Avoid exercises in which you lie flat on your back for extended periods of time – the weight of your bump presses on the main blood vessel that brings blood back to your heart and can make you faint.
- Avoid contact sports such as kickboxing or squash as physical injury could hurt you and your baby.
- Avoid scuba diving as this can cause depression sickness and gas embolism (gas bubbles in the bloodstream).
- Avoid exercise at heights of 2,500m above sea level or higher. Your baby is at risk of altitude sickness.

THE BOTTOM LINE

- Excessive weight gain during pregnancy is linked to poorer outcomes for both Mum and baby. A balanced diet and physical activity are both key to achieving healthy weight gain.

- Do not eat for two: only 200kcal extra per day are needed during the last trimester.

- Eat a healthy, balanced diet rich in starchy carbohydrates and fruit and vegetables.

- All women should take supplements of 400mcg folic acid and 10mcg vitamin D daily during pregnancy.

- Vegetarian or vegan women should take 2.4mcg vitamin B12 during pregnancy.

- Consume iron-rich foods such as green vegetables and lean red meat.

- Do not take vitamin A supplements.

- Limit alcohol and caffeine.

- A good way to make sure you eat well and get enough exercise during pregnancy is to set yourself goals.

- Try to incorporate 150 minutes of exercise into your week.

- Be aware of food hygiene and avoid certain foods during pregnancy to minimise the risk of food poisoning.

CHAPTER 3

Your Baby's Early Growth

Concern about your baby's growth is a natural part of being a parent. Many parents are uncertain about how much weight gain is too much or too little (especially if your baby is breastfed and you can't 'see' how much milk he is taking), when it really becomes a problem, and how to read and interpret growth charts. We have known for decades that poor foetal growth in pregnancy and insufficient weight gain in the first few months after birth can cause health problems for children later on. And, in recent years, the spotlight has also turned on excessive weight gain. It is now well established that *both* a healthy birth weight *and* optimal early weight gain in the first two years after birth set the stage for lifelong health. Growth is also a good barometer for your baby's general health – lack of, or excessive weight gain, can sometimes indicate that your baby has an underlying health problem that is causing the slow/rapid weight gain. It's therefore useful to keep an eye on your baby's weight gain during the early weeks and months after birth.

Your baby will grow extraordinarily quickly during his first year of life, which means he needs to eat an awful lot of calories (mainly in the form of milk) to fuel his growth. This is why feeding can feel like an endless activity during the early weeks and months. By one year of age, your baby's growth will have slowed down considerably.

Your baby's weight gain will be far from constant as he will grow at very different rates during certain developmental phases. The usual growth pattern is for your baby to lose weight initially after birth, but to regain his birth weight by two to three weeks of age. After this he will gain weight very quickly, with the fastest weight gain of all at about six weeks of age (called 'peak weight velocity'), after which his rate of weight gain will slow to a plateau at around six months.[81] Weight gain from six months will be much steadier. You will also notice that your baby's weight will increase a lot more than his length during the first year. On average, at one year of age he will have increased his weight by a whopping 300 per cent, but will have grown in length by only 50 per cent. This is why one-year-old babies look squat, chubby and adorable!

This complex early growth pattern means that the only way to check if your baby's weight is healthy at any one time is to compare it *over time* to that of other babies of exactly the same age and sex, and to look at his weight in the context of his previous weight gain. This is what the growth chart in your Personal Child Health Record (PCHR) book is for – to see your baby's weight (and length) *in context*.

How to Interpret a Growth Chart

Those of you who have had your baby will have been given a PCHR. This includes a growth chart that can be used to monitor your baby's weight and length gain over his first few months and years. Interpreting your baby's weight and length gain using the chart can be tricky, so it's good to be armed with information about what it is, and how and why it was developed. Growth charts are developed by measuring the weights (and other things, such as length and head circumference) of a very large number of male and female babies and children, at all different ages. This provides a reference against which the weights of other babies can be compared. The measured weights of all the babies of the same age and sex are organised into 100 bands called 'centiles'. These centiles tell you the proportion of babies' weights that fell at or below the weight of a particular centile, in the sample that was measured. There are equivalent centile charts for length as well as head circumference.

So, when you plot your baby's weight and find his centile, this tells you where his weight sits *relative to all of the babies in the sample* that were measured. The 50th centile weight is the average – half of babies in the sample had a higher weight and half a lower weight. The 50th centile is not 'normal' weight, just average. This means that around half of the babies in the sample had a healthy weight that was above or below average. The 95th centile indicates that 5 per cent of babies in the sample had a higher weight than this, but 95 per cent had a lower weight. The 5th centile is at the other end of the spectrum – 5 babies in every 100, based on the sample, would have a *healthy weight* lower than this weight but most babies (95 per cent) had a higher weight. This means that for some babies having a weight at the 5th or 95th centile is likely to be *perfectly healthy*, especially if they are also around the same centile for length, have always been around these centiles and have shorter or taller than average parents respectively.

THE UK-WHO GROWTH CHART

Since 2009 in England (and 2010 in Scotland), the chart included in the PCHR is the UK-WHO growth chart, developed for babies and young children from two weeks of age to four years. The sample of babies used to develop these charts were from six countries (Brazil, Ghana, India, Norway, Oman and the US) and they were healthy, full-term and breastfed, so they represent the *optimal growth pattern* for all babies – how babies *ought* to grow under the best possible conditions. These growth charts have therefore become the standard against which all babies should be compared, whatever their ethnicity and whether or not they are breast- or formula-fed.

A baby's weight gain during the first two weeks is hugely variable so, on the 0–1 year chart, there are no centiles between birth and two weeks of age as some degree of weight loss is common after birth. The most important thing during this period is to make sure that your baby regains his birth weight. During this period your midwife will be regularly weighing your baby so they will be able to advise you if he is following a healthy weight trajectory. After these two weeks, you will see nine centile lines on the chart. The lowest centile line (0.4th) represents the lowest threshold below which only 1/240 healthy children will fall, followed by the 2nd, 9th, 25th, 50th, 75th, 91st, 98th and 99.6th.

For premature babies born between 32 and 36 weeks their weight centile needs to be adjusted for their gestational age until they are 12 months old. For very premature babies (born between 23 and 31 weeks), their weight needs to be adjusted for their gestational age until they are two years old. Your health professional will help you with this.

WEIGHT, LENGTH, HEIGHT AND BODY MASS INDEX

Growth is about far more than just weight gain – it is length gain as well. However, your baby's weight is the main measurement that will be taken during his first two years of life to monitor his growth, simply because it can be measured easily and reliably; much more so than his length. Length and height are not quite the same – because length is measured lying down, and height standing up, height will always be slightly less than length as gravity compresses the spine slightly. But in reality, they don't differ that much. Your baby's height will not be routinely measured before he's two years old because it's too difficult to measure it reliably in children younger than this (most toddlers less than two years old – and even those over the age of two – are too wriggly!). So, prior to the age of two, your baby's length will be measured instead, though measuring his length accurately is still a challenge. How frequently your baby's length is measured will depend on the practices within your local area. It is often the case that your baby's length will not be measured unless there is a concern about his weight. The growth chart shows length centiles up to two years of age, and then switches to height centiles at two years. At this point the centiles suddenly shift down slightly, because height is a little less than length.

When your baby is two to two-and-a-half years old you will be invited for their final early years review (although this is not compulsory), which will usually be done by a health visitor (or occasionally a nursery nurse). This can be done at home, a baby clinic or a children's centre, or even at your GP surgery. The review will cover lots of aspects of your baby's development, including his growth. His height as well as his weight will be measured and used to calculate his body mass index (BMI). BMI is a ratio of weight to the square of height – your baby's weight taking into account how tall he is – and is a crude measure of his body fat. It is calculated using a simple equation:

weight (in kilograms) / height squared (in metres)

Your child's BMI centile will then be calculated using the UK-WHO BMI chart and will give an indication of his relative body fat compared to other children. The PCHR doesn't include a BMI centile chart, only weight and length/height charts, but you can calculate your child's BMI centile using the NHS online calculator by entering his weight, height, sex, date of measurements and date of birth.[82] The BMI centiles can be used to classify two-year-old children as underweight (less than the 2nd centile), healthy weight (between the 2nd centile and the 91st centile), overweight (above the 91st centile) and very overweight (above the 98th centile).

HOW OFTEN TO WEIGH YOUR BABY AND WHAT TO LOOK OUT FOR

Growth rates (especially weight gain per week) are incredibly variable from week to week for an individual baby. They also vary enormously between babies, even siblings. It is very important not to compare and make judgements about your baby's growth based on the weight gain of babies of other family members or friends, even if they are the same age. Your baby's growth will depend on a lot of things, including the height and weight of parents and other family members. Weight gain is not a competition and greater weekly weight gain is not a valid sign of a healthy baby 'doing well' or one baby doing better than another.

Babies' weights are like adults' weights in that they can fluctuate during the day depending on whether or not they have just been fed or if they have just done a wee or a poo. It's therefore a good idea to try and weigh your baby under the same conditions each time, for example, just before a feed or straight after changing his nappy (a full nappy can account for quite a lot of weight!). Always weigh your baby without his nappy and with no clothes on. This isn't always the most pleasant experience for a baby, so be sure to keep him warm before and afterwards. The weighing scales you use can also make a difference to the weight. Home weighing scales designed for adults are not always accurate and don't usually have small enough units for you to be able to see small increments in your baby's weight gain (it can also be tricky keeping your baby on them!) so we wouldn't recommend using them. It is much better to weigh your baby using a baby scale if you have one or wait for a health professional to weigh him for you.

Routine weighing during infancy

The UK had a strong tradition of weighing babies during the first two years of life. This ensured that if there were any problems with a baby's growth they would be picked up early, so that Mum and baby could be supported to get him back on track. This monitoring system was a fundamental part of our child health system for many years, and the envy of many countries worldwide, but today due to funding cuts, weighing your baby will largely be left to you to organise. However, you will usually be offered five routine health and development reviews in the first two to two-and-a-half years, during which your baby will be weighed (among other things)[83]:

- soon after birth

- at one to two weeks

- at six to eight weeks (two months)

- at nine months to one year

- at two to two-and-a-half years

These health reviews are not compulsory and will usually be done by your midwife or health visitor at home, your GP surgery, a baby clinic or children's centre (depending on the area in which you live). We would recommend that you take advantage of the health and development reviews offered to you, and that you have your baby weighed in between these more detailed reviews as well. For guidance on how regularly to have your baby weighed see pages 90–91.

Weight during the first two weeks after birth
Your baby will be monitored by your midwife during the first two weeks after birth, and as part of this his weight will be measured to make sure that feeding has been established and is going well. This usually happens the day after you have been discharged from hospital, at 5 days and again at 10 days (although the exact timing can vary). This will either be at your home or in the clinic, depending on where you would like to be seen. You don't need to organise this yourself, the appointments will be made for you. The weight checks during the first two or three weeks are taken very seriously, and it's important to do these. It is normal for your baby to lose some weight (up to 10 per cent but no more) during the first few days after birth, because his body fluid changes. But weight loss usually stops after the first three or four days, and he should have regained the weight by the time he is three weeks old. Your midwife will let you know if she is worried about your baby's weight gain and will support you in making sure he gets back on track.

At about three weeks of age, the health visitor takes over from your midwife, and may weigh your baby to check that his weight is back to where it was at birth. Most babies (80 per cent) have regained their birth weight by two weeks of age, and very few (3–7 per cent) have lost 10 per cent of their birth weight or more by two weeks of age.

The usual cause of weight loss during these first few days and weeks is that your baby isn't feeding properly. A study of 26 infants who lost more than 10 per cent of their birth weight found no underlying medical problems, suggesting that it was feeding problems that were the most likely cause.[84] In particular, breastfeeding can be tricky to get right when you first start and a common challenge is the baby's attachment and positioning at the breast. Your midwife will check this. If you are struggling to breastfeed on your own, then do tell your midwife and badger them to make sure you get the help and support that you need at this very early stage. There is also plenty of help in the community (see page 132). This can make the difference between you carrying on or giving up.

The following are signs that your baby isn't feeding properly during the first few days and weeks:

- He is producing fewer than 5 wet nappies per 24-hour period (from Day 5 onwards) – if he is producing fewer than this he may be dehydrated (in the first 48 hours, he is likely to have only two or three wet nappies). A wet nappy should contain the equivalent of 2–4 tablespoons of water.

- He may appear listless and docile when awake (rather than alert), or restless, unsettled and irritable.

Weight from three weeks to two/two-and-a-half years
We recommend that you continue to have your baby weighed regularly during the first two years to ensure he is on a healthy weight trajectory. You can do this in addition to the other routine health and development reviews. For example, you could have him weighed once or twice in between the 2-months and 1-year reviews and once or twice in between the 1-year and 2-year

reviews. You can either contact your health visitor to come to your home, take your baby to a baby clinic or visit your GP. Do bear in mind that it is important *not to weigh your baby too frequently* because weights measured too closely together can be misleading and can lead to unnecessary concern. For this reason, the Department of Health recommends that babies should be weighed *no more than*:

- once a month from 2 weeks to 6 months of age

- once every 2 months from 6 to 12 months of age

- once every 3 months from 12 months of age[85]

It is common for healthy babies to move up and down the centile chart quite a bit in their first six weeks, so don't feel alarmed if your baby isn't tracking steadily during this early period. In particular, if your baby was born big he may fall slightly (called 'catch-down' growth), and if he was born small he may move upwards (called 'catch-up' growth), before settling. After six weeks there is less movement and your baby's centile position will usually become a bit more stable, although a big drop in his weight after minor illnesses is common and nothing to worry about, as long as when he regains the weight he goes back to his 'usual' centile, which normally happens within two to three weeks. It is only *persistent* and *substantial* changes in weight that should concern you (after *repeated measurements* consistently show downward or upward crossing of centiles), so don't panic if on one occasion your baby's weight has moved up or down.

Rapid Weight Gain

Rapid weight gain is gaining too much weight too quickly. It can compromise your baby's health so is worth looking out for. Your baby would be considered to have rapid weight gain if he crosses *more than two major centile spaces upwards*, regardless of what centile he started on. Because the greater concern historically has always been weight faltering (insufficient weight gain), there are still no official guidelines in the UK on rapid infant weight gain in the first two years. UK policies and culture around early-life nutrition haven't really moved on since times of food insecurity – such as post-war Britain – when weight faltering was much more prevalent. For this reason, your health visitor might not mention rapid weight gain, and if he or she does, they may not provide any suggestions about what you can do about it. In the subsequent chapters we provide strategies to support your baby in developing good appetite regulation, and help him to grow at a healthy rate and not too quickly.

HOW COMMON IS RAPID WEIGHT GAIN?

Rapid weight gain in infancy is common in the UK – about one quarter of babies (27.5 per cent) have rapid weight gain.[86]

WHY IS RAPID WEIGHT GAIN A PROBLEM?

Rapid weight gain in infancy has been linked to metabolic diseases in adulthood including obesity, cardiovascular disease and type 2 diabetes. One study found that babies with rapid growth were nearly four times more likely to have obesity as children than babies staying on the same centile. Rapid early growth even predicted adult obesity as late as 66 years of age. Importantly, the effect of rapid growth on obesity is the same for breastfed and formula-fed babies, boys and girls, and for those born with a large, small or healthy birth weight.[87] As well as increased risk for obesity, babies who grow very quickly tend to gain fat around their middle and are less sensitive to the effects of insulin during the first three years of life, which is an important marker of metabolic health and is involved in the development of type 2 diabetes and cardiovascular disease.[88] Rapid growth in the first few months after birth also promotes earlier puberty, which may seem unimportant in itself, but it is related to reproductive cancers, metabolic diseases and all-cause mortality (dying from any cause).[89] Optimal growth during the first 1,000 days is therefore an important part of your baby's later health, and is something to keep an eye on.

WHAT CAUSES RAPID WEIGHT GAIN, AND WHAT CAN YOU DO IF IT HAPPENS TO YOUR BABY?

Babies with rapid growth tend to have larger appetites and high demands around feeding. Part of your baby's appetite is due to his genes (genes influence his appetite and therefore his weight gain)[90], but *how* your baby is fed can also influence his appetite and his response to milk and food. Babies' appetites and relationships with food develop through a complex interplay between their own genetic predispositions and their early experiences with milk, food, feeding and eating. Some of this is due to your baby's genes, but *what* and *how* he is fed can also affect his milk and food intake. Throughout this book, we have provided detailed guidance about *what* and *how* to feed your baby if he has a large appetite, to ensure that you support his appetite regulation and give him the best possible chance of having healthy growth (see pages 232–3). If your baby is experiencing rapid growth, it's worth making sure you are not encouraging him to overfeed (see page 196).

WHAT ABOUT 'CATCH-UP GROWTH'?

Many babies who are born small for gestational age experience 'catch-up growth' in the first 6–12 months of life, which is gaining weight (or length) at a faster rate than babies born with a healthy birth weight. It is a form of rapid growth, but is important for survival and the prevention of infection, stunting and other developmental problems, such as lower IQ. If catch-up growth doesn't occur during this early window, about half of the babies will be shorter as adults than expected if they had not been born small for their gestational age.[91] So, if your baby was born small, it is likely that he will have faster growth so that he can 'catch up' and reach a healthy weight. However, it can sometimes be excessive, and if this happens your health professional may flag this to you. The strategies that we suggest in the subsequent chapters of this book for *how* and *what* to feed your baby will help you to support him in developing good appetite regulation and a healthy relationship with food, whether he was born with a low, normal or high birth weight.

Weight Faltering

Weight faltering (which used to be called 'failure to thrive') is when your baby is gaining weight more slowly than he should, which can compromise his health and development.[92] This is what most parents (and health professionals) worry about during their baby's first two years. There isn't an overall accepted definition, but most health professionals become concerned if your baby's age- and sex-adjusted weight crosses a certain number of major centile spaces (the lines printed on the growth chart) downwards, depending on how big or small he was to start with.[93] When it comes to deciding how many centile spaces a baby needs to cross before anyone should be concerned, it depends on which centile the baby was on before the weight problems started. There should be less allowance for babies already on a low centile (downward crossing of only one centile should be a red flag for a baby who is already small) and more leeway for babies already on a high centile (a big baby can cross several centiles downwards before anyone needs to worry too much). The 2017 guidelines from the National Institute of Health and Care Excellence (NICE) therefore suggest the following criteria[94]:

- For babies born below the 9th centile: a fall through only *one* centile space is sufficient to warrant concern and close monitoring.

- For babies born between the 9th and 91st centiles: a fall through at least *two* centile spaces is required before weight faltering is a concern.

- For babies born above the 91st centile: a fall through *three* centile spaces or more is necessary before there should be any concern about weight faltering.

If you or your health professional are concerned, your baby's length (or height if they are two years old or older) should also be measured.[95] If your baby has *both* a low weight centile *and* a low length centile, this can indicate *growth faltering*, which usually means that he is not consuming enough calories. However, a low length or height centile can also reflect your baby's genetic predisposition to be of a shorter stature. If you and your partner are short, then it is likely that your baby will be short too (his adult height will typically be an average of both parents). If you are both pretty tall and your baby's length is low, this is more concerning. If your health professional is worried, then your baby's weight may be monitored more regularly. Bear in mind that, in general, it is babies and children who are already of a *very low* weight (below the 0.4th centile) or BMI (below the 2nd centile) that need to be monitored very carefully. Those with low weight/length/BMI *as well as* weight faltering (crossing two centile spaces downwards) need to be assessed.

If your baby has weight faltering, your health visitor or GP may suggest some feeding strategies to help get him back on track. In the chapters that follow we provide tips on how to feed your baby if he has a poor appetite for milk or difficulty eating solid food, to make sure that he is getting enough (see pages 233 and 338). Your baby is considered to have 'recovered' when he goes back to within one to two centile spaces of his previous position, which can take several months.

HOW COMMON IS WEIGHT FALTERING?

Weight faltering in infancy is *rare* in affluent countries such as the UK, and tends to be mild when it does occur, so try not to feel overly anxious about this happening to your baby. After the first four months, only 0.5 per cent of babies in the UK (1 in 200) are considered cause for concern (an average baby crossing two centile spaces)[96]. This means that the babies with rapid growth outnumber those with weight faltering by about 55 to 1 (27.5 per cent versus 0.5 per cent).

WHY IS WEIGHT FALTERING A PROBLEM?

Health professionals take weight faltering seriously because if it is *prolonged* and *severe* it can cause developmental problems. Many studies of babies and children have reported that *severe* weight faltering is linked to:[97]

- IQ deficits of 3–5 points (this is a very small impact)

- reduced academic performance

- stunting (being shorter)

- smaller head size

- lower immunity and increased infection

- gastrointestinal problems

- heart problems

However, as we have said, in the UK weight faltering is rare and is usually mild in comparison to the more severe cases that are seen in developing countries in which many of these studies are undertaken. Early treatment and recovery can reverse the problems with immunity and gastrointestinal and heart problems, although children are often still shorter and have a slightly lower IQ and academic performance.[98]

WHAT CAUSES WEIGHT FALTERING, AND WHAT CAN YOU DO IF IT HAPPENS TO YOUR BABY?

Many years ago weight faltering was called 'the maternal deprivation syndrome' and was believed to be caused by emotional and physical neglect of the child.[99] In fact, it is only in rare cases that weight faltering is caused by parental neglect, mental-health problems or addiction (about 5 per cent of weight faltering cases).[100] Most children with weight faltering *are not neglected*. Nor is it related to poverty in the UK, which is probably due to our welfare system that protects families with young children. It is also rare for it to be caused by an underlying disease – diagnosed diseases have only been found to cause about 5–10 per cent of cases in the UK.[101] It is especially unlikely that there is an underlying disease if your baby or child seems otherwise well in every other respect. So what does cause poor weight gain?

What we have learned over the last 30 years is that weight faltering has a *predominantly nutritional cause* – it most often happens because your baby or toddler isn't consuming as many calories as he needs. This accounts for 90 per cent of cases.[102] There is increasing evidence that poor weight gain is related to your baby's appetite and feeding and eating behaviour.[103] In many cases children with weight faltering have a poor appetite, this can lead to difficult mealtimes, increasingly stressful interactions and spiralling difficulties with feeding and eating. If your baby is a difficult feeder, there are lots of strategies that you can use to make sure you support him in getting the nutrition that he needs (see pages 233–5).

Birth Weight

Your baby's early growth is important during his first few months of life, but his weight at birth matters too. Birth weight is thought to indicate the quality of his nutrition during pregnancy. If your baby has a low birth weight (less than 2.5kg/5lb 8oz) he may have had under-nutrition in pregnancy, but there are ethnic differences in birth weight too and many South Asian babies are born small, which is probably genetic. If your baby has a high birth weight (more than 4kg/8lb 13oz), called macrosomia ('large body' in Greek), he may have had over-nutrition. But because boys are born slightly heavier than girls, and gestational age influences birth weight enormously – a baby born at 40 weeks will have a higher birth weight than a baby born at 37 weeks – both of these are taken into account when classifying your baby as having a low or high birth weight. Being born 'small for gestational age' (SGA) is usually considered to be a birth weight in the lowest 9 per cent of babies of the same gestational age and sex (*below* the 10th centile) and 'large for gestational age' (LGA) is a birth weight in the highest 9 per cent (*above* the 90th centile).

In the most recent national UK data the average birth weight was 3.7kg/7lb 7oz (boys: 3.4kg/7lb 9oz; girls: 3.3kg/7lb 5oz).[104] Eleven per cent of babies were born with a high birth weight and 7 per cent with a low birth weight. More girls than boys are born SGA, and more boys than girls are born LGA. In spite of many alarming press headlines about birth weight increasing[105], this simply isn't supported by research. In fact, in the UK, the average birth weight has been *decreasing* (as it has in many other countries as well, including Canada, France, Denmark, Korea, Japan and China). This is partly because length of gestation has decreased due to more medical interventions such as inducement, and very premature babies are more likely to survive. These factors bring the average birth weight down. In addition, in the UK since 2000 the number of babies who are born SGA has increased, and the number born LGA has decreased, suggesting that foetal growth has actually slowed down over recent years.[106]

WHY IS A LOW OR HIGH BIRTH WEIGHT A PROBLEM?

The largest and most comprehensive review ever undertaken into birth weight and later health was published in 2016.[107] This review found convincing evidence for a link between birth weight and a range of health outcomes:

- low birth weight and increased risk for all-cause mortality (dying from any cause)

- SGA and childhood stunting

- higher birth weight and better bone health in the hip (higher bone mineral concentration), and lower risk for mortality from cardiovascular diseases

They also found highly suggestive evidence for a link between:

- low birth weight and increased infant mortality *in developing countries*; wheezing disorders in childhood (such as asthma); coronary heart disease; lower rates of overweight and obesity in adulthood; and slightly lower IQ in adolescence

- high birth weight and all types of leukaemia; overweight or obesity in adulthood; and lower risk of coronary heart disease

However, the authors concluded that the effects of birth weight on these health outcomes are pretty small. So don't panic if your baby was born small or large – it doesn't mean that he is definitely going to have any of these health problems, it just increases his risk slightly. His early growth is also important, and in this book we have given you lots of strategies to make sure that feeding goes well once your baby arrives, to help optimise his early weight gain.

WHAT CAUSES A BABY'S BIRTH WEIGHT TO BE LOW OR HIGH?

There are some things that we know influence a baby's birth weight that can't be changed (called 'unmodifiable') and others that can ('modifiable'). Unmodifiable influences include[108]:

- a baby's own genes (although this only has a small influence on his birth weight)[109]

- sex (boys are heavier than girls)

- Mum's racial or ethnic origin (lower birth weights tend to be seen in Africa, India and the Far East, and higher weights among Europeans and white Americans)

- Mum's height and pre-pregnancy weight (taller mums have heavier babies, and those with a lower pre-pregnancy weight tend to have lighter babies), and Dad's height and weight (taller, heavier dads tend to have bigger babies)

- order of birth (first babies tend to be lighter than subsequent babies) and weights of previous babies

- general health and bouts of illness during pregnancy.

Modifiable influences include:

- gestational weight gain (mums who gain more weight have heavier babies)

- gestational diabetes (mums who develop this are more likely to have heavier babies)

- alcohol (heavy alcohol consumption leads to lower birth weight)

- smoking[110] (smoking in pregnancy is one of the most important risk factors for low birth weight in developed countries, and doubles the risk[111]).

So, we have seen that early growth is important for your baby's health and development and it's worth trying to make sure that he grows at a healthy rate during his first 1,000 days. The chapters that follow are packed full of information and advice about how to establish good feeding and eating habits as soon as your baby is born, and over the following two years. At each stage of feeding we consider all types of babies and children – from the babies with poor appetites who may be prone to weight faltering, to the eager eaters who may be prone to rapid weight gain. We have given evidence-based advice about how to interact with your baby to ensure that he gets the best possible start in life, and that your stress levels remain as low as possible.

THE BOTTOM LINE

- Growing (weight and length) at an optimal rate during the early years is important for lifelong health and development.

- It is common for babies (especially if they are breastfed) to lose up to 10 per cent of their birth weight in the days after birth, but they tend to regain this by three weeks.

- Babies tend to move around on their centile position in the early weeks, but usually settle on a more stable centile position from around six weeks onwards.

- Weight faltering is rare in the UK, while rapid growth is common, especially in babies born small who experience 'catch-up growth'.

- Growing too slowly or too quickly usually has a nutritional basis, and your baby's appetite plays an important part in his early growth.

PART 2

Milk-Feeding

Feeding a young baby can sometimes feel daunting, especially when you are doing it for the first time. A new parent has to make lots of different decisions, largely relating to:

- *what* to feed: whether to breastfeed or use formula milk, or use a mixture of both; and which type of formula milk to use

- *how* to feed: how often and how much to feed; and how to manage the actual feeding interaction (for example, feeding to a schedule or 'on demand')

There is a lot of 'received wisdom' and strong opinion when it comes to milk-feeding. A concern of ours is that the information out there isn't always evidence-based and there is an awful lot of information for parents to sift through. Scrutinising every little detail available on the Internet can seem like an insurmountable task, especially during the first few weeks after birth when sleep deprivation is at its most brutal, and you really just want practical, properly researched advice. As scientists, we have found it time-consuming and hard-going navigating the swathes of claims and exploring the scientific evidence for each one. We cannot imagine how we could have done this without the time or training we have had. This was one of the main reasons we decided to write this book – we have done the work, so you don't have to.

The topic of breast- versus formula-feeding is one that often arouses emotive discussion and many mums will have found themselves on the receiving end of those voicing strongly held – and, at times, zealous – opinions about what they should or shouldn't be doing. This can be very stressful to say the least and makes it difficult to know the facts when it comes to milk-feeding. Some mums who don't manage to breastfeed, or who choose not to, feel guilty, judged or that they have failed their baby. Other mums are put under pressure by well-meaning friends or family members to stop breastfeeding before they are ready, or are made to feel that it's inappropriate to breastfeed a baby in a public place. This can lead to mums giving up or not even starting in the first place. It is also surprisingly difficult to find good scientific information about formula milk, yet this is crucial for mums to make an informed decision about the type and amount of formula milk to feed, if this is necessary.

The decision to breast- or formula-feed is highly personal and, importantly, in some situations it isn't possible, suitable or adequate to breastfeed. We are not judging your decision; as we see it, only one thing matters when it comes to feeding your child, and that is making the choice that is right for you and your baby. We hope that by providing you with the most up-to-date evidence-based information, we can support you in making that choice. Importantly, the tips and advice that we provide in Chapter 6 on *how* to feed to support your baby's development of good appetite regulation will apply whether you decide to breast- or formula-feed.

CHAPTER 4

Breastfeeding

The World Health Organization (WHO) and the Department of Health (DoH) both recommend that babies are breastfed exclusively (i.e. they receive *only* breast milk – no other food or drink, not even water) for the first six months (26 weeks) of life.[112] The DoH recommends that breastfeeding (and/or formula, if used) should continue beyond the first six months, along with appropriate types and amounts of solid foods. The WHO advises that from six months babies should be given nutritious complementary food and continue to be breastfed up to two years or beyond. The WHO doesn't distinguish formula milk from solid food, even though formula-fed babies are still getting all of their nutrients from milk only, so it isn't clear from their advice whether formula-fed infants should also be fed milk alone for six months, although this is probably the case. It's not particularly helpful that the WHO provides guidelines on milk-feeding *only* for breastfeeding.

These are pretty uncompromising guidelines. So what is the evidence for such a strong stance? Is breast milk really best? In the next few pages we will explore the scientific facts about breastfeeding so you can make an informed decision about what is best for you and your baby.

THE CHALLENGES OF BREASTFEEDING RESEARCH

Before we summarise the scientific findings of studies that have examined the benefits of breastfeeding, it is worth reflecting briefly on the considerable challenges in this field of research. For example, trying to obtain detailed and meaningful information about the amount of breast milk versus formula milk babies receive for the duration of the milk-feeding phase is not an easy task. A lot of the time the questions need to be asked retrospectively – weeks, months or even years after milk-feeding has finished – and it is difficult for parents to remember the details of how they fed their baby when it wasn't simply one method or the other. In addition, while randomised controlled trials (see page 71 for an explanation of randomised controlled trials) would provide the most convincing evidence of the benefits of breastfeeding it isn't ethical (or feasible) to randomise babies to *not receive* breast milk, given the many proposed health advantages. However, as recently as the early 1980s far less was known about the benefits of breastfeeding and some studies were therefore able to randomly allocate premature babies on neonatal units to receive either banked breast milk or formula milk through a tube. These babies have now been followed up for many years and their health outcomes compared. Findings from these studies are important, because they are the only babies who have been truly randomised to receive breast milk.[113]

There have also been studies where mums are randomly allocated to receive either very intensive breastfeeding support or just the usual information. The assumption is that the mums randomised to receive high levels of support will be more likely to breastfeed (or to try to persist with it) than those who just get the usual information. This means that the health outcomes of the babies in the two groups can be compared to study the effects of breastfeeding. The only such study using this design randomised a whopping

17,046 mums in Belarus to receive either intensive support or the usual information (the 'Promotion of Breastfeeding Intervention Trial').[114] As expected, the proportion of mums who exclusively breastfed at three months was much higher in the intensively supported group than the usual information group (43 per cent versus 6 per cent). This study has therefore provided valuable insights about the importance of breastfeeding for long-term consequences.

Another approach is to study large numbers of babies from birth over many years and to compare the outcomes of those who were breastfed with those who were formula-fed. The main problem with this type of study is that mums who breastfeed their babies often differ from mums who formula-feed in important ways, such as income, education level, health, age and so on. This means that differences in the health outcomes of breastfed and formula-fed babies could, in fact, have been caused by any of these other factors, and not just by how they were fed.

As you can see, in reality, measurement of breastfeeding in most studies is pretty crude, by necessity, and this means that we can't always be completely sure about the role that breastfeeding plays in certain health outcomes. If researchers haven't found a clear link between breastfeeding and a particular outcome, it doesn't mean there definitely isn't one; it may just have been too difficult to find it because of the challenges of research in this area. This must be borne in mind when weighing up the evidence for the various claims that are made.

The Advantages for Your Baby

On balance, the slogan 'breast is best' is true. And there are also important practical advantages that are not to be understated: it's free, readily available and there's no need to sterilise bottles.

'When I think about the benefits of breastfeeding, it's difficult to name one particular reason – for me it's convenience
I think, then money, then health benefits.'

Marta, mum of Julia (6 weeks)

Research has established that babies who are exclusively breastfed
(usually for six months in studies) are at an advantage in terms
of a number of different health benefits, although we don't
necessarily know exactly why yet. These advantages are both
short-term (during infancy and into childhood) and long-term
(lasting into adolescence and/or adulthood). It would be fair to
say, though, that the evidence for the shorter-term benefits is
slightly clearer. There are also advantages for mum as well. Let's
take a look at the benefits of breastfeeding.

SHORTER-TERM BENEFITS

- Fewer infections (and fewer hospital visits)

- Less diarrhoea and vomiting

- Reduced risk of Sudden Infant Death Syndrome (SIDS)

There is overwhelming evidence that breastfeeding provides potent
protection against infection during infancy, and in some cases into
childhood. This is certainly true when it comes to colds, flu and
diarrhoea. This benefit comes into its own particularly in poorer
countries where universal access to clean water is not the norm,
making formula preparation and sterilisation of bottles challenging, and where infections can quickly become serious and

life-threatening because of inadequate medical care. This is the context in which the WHO developed their guidelines for breast-feeding exclusively for six months, and to continue to breastfeed after the introduction of solid foods until the age of two. But even in affluent countries, such as the UK, infection is the scourge of early life, and there is strong evidence that breastfeeding offers considerable protection against many common infections.

In 2016 the *Lancet* commissioned the most comprehensive review to date of the short- and long-term benefits of breastfeeding, using studies from all over the world.[115] They estimated that 823,000 deaths of children under five years of age could have been prevented in 2015 in low- and middle-income countries if everyone breastfed exclusively for six months. This would have prevented 13.8 per cent of all the deaths of children less than two years old, and 87 per cent of all deaths of babies less than six months old. This is a big deal in countries where infant mortality is high, and it is clear from this research why the WHO have taken such a strong stance on breastfeeding.

But it isn't just babies in low-income countries who benefit from being breastfed. The risk of SIDS is reduced by 36 per cent for babies who receive any breastfeeding at all (versus none),[116] and another review suggested that protection might be higher for babies who were exclusively versus partially breastfed.[117] Thankfully, SIDS is still extremely rare in this country – around 230 babies and toddlers die from SIDS each year in the UK[118] – but a 36 per cent reduction means breastfeeding could save approximately 83 of these lives each year.

Breastfeeding has also been shown to protect against more common afflictions – about half of all diarrhoea episodes and a third of respiratory infections in babies could be avoided by breastfeeding. When it comes to preventing hospital admissions from these infections, the protective effect is even more pronounced – it is estimated that 72 per cent of all infant hospital admissions for diarrhoea, and 57 per cent for respiratory infections, could be prevented by breastfeeding.[119] Ear infections, in particular, are reduced considerably for breastfed babies and toddlers less than two years old, and the amount of breast milk the baby gets, and for how long, both matter. Babies who are exclusively breastfed for six months are 43 per cent less likely to have an infection by two years of age than partially breastfed or formula-fed babies; and those who were 'ever' versus 'never' breastfed are 33 per cent less likely, as were those who were 'breastfed at all' for *more than* 3–4 months.[120]

It isn't always possible to know if it is breastfeeding itself that protects against SIDS and infections, or if there are other factors that cause *both* lower breastfeeding *and* worse health outcomes – such as living in poverty – but if there is any possibility that breastfeeding is able to protect against SIDS, we feel that it's worth giving it a go.

LONGER-TERM BENEFITS

- Reduced incidence of childhood leukaemia

- Reduced risk of type 2 diabetes

- Reduced risk of obesity

- Reduced risk of cardiovascular disease in adulthood

- Higher intelligence

Understanding how breastfeeding relates to longer-term health outcomes is more complicated because of the many challenges already described that make it difficult to link early-life feeding with health outcomes many years later.

Childhood leukaemia

One review concluded that babies who were breastfed at all for six months or longer had a lower risk of childhood leukaemia than those who were either not breastfed at all, or who were breastfed for less than six months.[121] It was estimated that 14–20 per cent of leukaemia cases could be prevented by breastfeeding for six months or longer, and 9 per cent of cases could be prevented by breastfeeding at all versus never. The findings were the same for high- and low-income countries. In the UK, leukaemia is the most common cancer among children, although it is still (thankfully) rare – about 470 children are diagnosed with it every year.[122] This research therefore suggests that 94 cases per year could be prevented by breastfeeding for a minimum of six months, and 42 cases per year could be prevented by breastfeeding at all versus never. The authors suggested that the biological properties of breast milk may be what offer protection. Unlike formula milk, breast milk contains a number of active components that support the development of a strong immune system, promote a healthy gut microbiome (the bacteria that lives in a gut) and reduce inflammation. However, it is also important to bear in mind that the design of these studies makes it difficult to be certain that breastfeeding itself really prevents leukaemia. These studies rely on researchers asking mums of children who have been diagnosed with leukaemia to remember how they fed them, often years afterwards. Not only does this mean that it is difficult to remember what they did with accuracy, but mums may also be influenced in their responses by their own beliefs about the role that breastfeeding may have played in their child's ill health.

Overweight and obesity

Another review estimated that any breastfeeding resulted in a 13 per cent reduction in overweight or obesity according to high quality studies.[123] So, in the UK where about 30 per cent of children have overweight or obesity at 10 years of age, this would mean that for every 100 babies who were breastfed, 26 would develop overweight or obesity, compared to 30 babies who were breastfed for a shorter duration (or not at all). However, the researchers cautioned that in studies carried out in high-income countries it is not possible to rule out the possibility that this difference results from the fact that babies who are breastfed for longer come from families with higher incomes and education levels. In fact, in countries like Brazil where income and education levels are unrelated to breastfeeding rates, there is no difference in rates of childhood overweight and obesity for babies who were breast- or formula-fed.[124]

The Promotion of Breastfeeding Intervention Trial conducted in Belarus, which followed over 13,000 babies up to 16 years of age, did not reduce rates of overweight or obesity.[125] In fact, there were slightly *more* adolescents with overweight and obesity in the group whose mums were given breastfeeding support. So, the link between breastfeeding and later overweight and obesity is not clear, and when studies have found a relationship it may just reflect other differences between the mums who do it and don't do it. There are probably other more important risk factors for overweight and obesity, such as a baby's early growth (discussed in detail in Chapter 3), which relates to *how* he is fed as well as *what* he is fed (see Chapter 6), and the parents' own weights. For example, a UK study found that 35 per cent of children with two severely obese parents had obesity, compared to only 2 per cent of children with healthy weight parents.[126]

Type 2 diabetes

There aren't many high-quality studies that have looked at the link between breastfeeding and children's later risk of type 2 diabetes. A review of these indicated that breastfeeding *may* reduce the risk of type 2 diabetes by about 24 per cent, but the small number of high-quality studies (only three) mean that this finding isn't reliable.[127] So, at present, we don't know for certain if breastfeeding really offers any protection against type 2 diabetes as good-quality research in this area is lacking.

Cardiovascular disease

Reviews have not found any conclusive protective effect of breast-feeding on symptoms of cardiovascular disease in later adulthood (high cholesterol and high blood pressure).[128] The Belarus study also found no effect of breastfeeding on later blood pressure in childhood or adolescence, but it didn't look at cholesterol. However, the UK trial of preterm babies who were randomised to receive breast milk versus formula through a tube found a very small reduction in blood pressure at six years of age, and a better cholesterol profile in terms of the ratio of 'bad' (LDL) to 'good' (HDL) cholesterol (~ 14 per cent lower), for babies who received breast milk.[129] The protective effect of breastfeeding on blood pressure and cholesterol, if there is any at all, is very small. There are probably much more important risk factors, such as family history and weight, to consider.

Intelligence

This area has long been of interest to researchers. As long ago as 1929, two researchers (Hoefer and Hardy) reported that breastfed babies had higher intelligence scores from 7 to 13 years of age.[130] There have also been various reports of superior development (for example, earlier walking) for babies who are exclusively breastfed for longer.[131] This is an outcome with strong evidence for breastfeeding playing a causal role, but the effect is pretty modest. A recent review, conducted in 2015, estimated that IQ is about three points higher among breastfed than formula-fed babies, after taking into account Mum's intelligence.[132] It is unlikely that social class is driving these findings because the randomised trials found the same, as have studies looking at the relationship in the UK versus Brazil. In the trial in Belarus, IQ was about seven points higher in the 'supported breastfeeding' group compared to the usual care,[133] and a similar effect was seen in preterm babies randomised to receive breast milk versus formula.[134] Studies have also found superior school attainment in breastfed babies from both the UK (where social class is related to breastfeeding rates)[135] and those from Brazil (where social class in unrelated to breastfeeding rates).[136] Breastfed babies had higher IQ and better school attainment in both countries, suggesting that it is breastfeeding that is responsible for higher IQ, not social class.

Of course, the question of interest is *how* breastfeeding influences intelligence. There are several plausible explanations. Breast milk itself is compositionally different to formula milk (see page 134). In particular, it contains certain long-chain polyunsaturated fatty acids – docosahexanoic acid (DHA) and arachidonic acid (AA) – that are important for brain development, and breastfed babies have higher concentrations of these than formula-fed babies. But the behaviours involved in breastfeeding versus bottle-feeding may also be important; the very act of breastfeeding is different from feeding from a bottle, and mums may talk to their baby more or interact with them slightly differently during breast- versus bottle-feeding. However, the fact that preterm babies randomised to receive breast milk through a tube had higher IQ scores suggests that breast milk itself is certainly involved, but it's a small effect – probably about three IQ points.

The Advantages for Mum

Aside from the many benefits to your baby, research has shown that breastfeeding benefits Mum as well. Benefits for Mum include:

No periods ('amenorrhoea')

Women who exclusively or predominantly breastfeed prolong the delay of their periods because it inhibits ovulation. However, this doesn't mean that you definitely can't get pregnant – you *can* still ovulate, so you do still need to use contraception to prevent pregnancy while breastfeeding.

Reduced risk of breast cancer

As long as 300 years ago, people noticed that more nuns got breast cancer than anyone else – the disease was in fact described as an 'accursed pest'. In fact, an analysis in the 1960s found that after 80 years of age, a nun's risk of breast cancer is three times higher than other women's, and this is probably because they don't have children and never breastfed. [137] A 2015 review estimated that if you ever (versus never) breastfeed, you have a 7 per cent reduced risk of breast cancer based on the highest quality studies conducted in high income countries.[138] Breast cancer is the most common cancer in the UK, affecting about 1 in 8 women in their lifetime (12.5 per cent of women).[139] At a population level the reduction in cases would be considerable, although it's only a very small reduction in risk for any individual. There were around 55,200 new breast cancer cases in 2014 in the UK, so breastfeeding may have prevented about 3846 of them. But for you, if you ever breastfeed, it means your risk goes from 1 in 8 to about 1 in 8.6.

Reduced risk of ovarian cancer

The same 2015 review estimated that there is a much larger reduction in your risk of ovarian cancer, than of breast cancer. Based on the highest-quality studies, any breastfeeding, versus none will reduce your risk of ovarian cancer by 18 per cent.[140] In comparison to breast cancer, ovarian cancer is rare; it affects only about 1 in 52 women in their lifetime. In 2014 in the UK there were around 7,400 new cases, so breastfeeding may have prevented around 1,332 of them.[141] And for you, it means your risk goes down from 1 in 52 to 1 in 61.

Reduced risk of type 2 diabetes and lower weight

A review of six large studies found that women who breastfed the longest (which varied from study to study) had a 32 per cent reduction in their risk of type 2 diabetes, and this was over and above other important risk factors such as BMI, physical activity, education, income, and even their family history of diabetes.[142] Given the effect of breastfeeding on type 2 diabetes, one would also expect to see an effect on body fat. But a review of the long-term effect of breastfeeding on later life BMI found that for every six months of breastfeeding, a woman's weight was only 1 per cent lower – so there is an effect on BMI but it is very small.[143]

A review by The *Lancet* concluded that some of the benefits of breastfeeding that you may have heard about – reduced risk of depression,[144] protection from osteoporosis[145] and higher post-partum weight loss (weight loss immediately after pregnancy)[146] – are not well supported by the evidence. In particular, a number of studies have reported that women who breastfeed have lower rates of depression, but this is probably best explained by the fact that women who develop depression are less likely to breast-feed, not because breastfeeding per se helps to protect against depression.[147]

Taking all of this into consideration, if you can breastfeed, and choose to breastfeed, you and your baby are likely to benefit, and it will probably make your life a lot easier in practical terms too. As any of you who are formula-feeding will know, preparing the feeds is a faff and there is a cost involved. There is sufficiently good evidence for breast milk offering protection against SIDS and infec-tion, even if some of the longer-term benefits for health are less clear. When it comes to outcomes such as obesity and cardiovascular disease for your baby, there are other factors that probably play a much more important role, so try not to beat yourself up about it if breastfeeding has proved too difficult or impossible for you.

HOW LONG SHOULD YOU BREASTFEED FOR?

When it comes to the short-term benefits of breast-feeding, it is generally agreed that protection is largely conferred for the period during which your baby is receiving breast milk, and any amount helps. It is harder to know about the longer-term benefits, because studies haven't always compared different durations of feeding. The review of childhood leukaemia showed much greater protection for babies who were breastfed for six months or longer, BUT there was also protection for those who were 'ever' versus 'never' breastfed. For you to reap the benefits of breastfeeding for your own health, the longer you can do it the better.

There are two implications of all this for breast-feeding your baby:

1. The longer you can breastfeed him the more he (and you) will benefit.

2. Every drop counts, so even if you can only manage it at the beginning, or for one or two feeds per day, he will still benefit from this.

Mixed Feeding

Exclusive breastfeeding will provide your baby with the best possible nutrition during his first six months. Although formula milk itself won't cause your baby any harm, it displaces breast milk, which means he gets fewer of the health benefits from it. There are indications of a *dose response effect* (more breast milk means more protection) when it comes to protection from breast-feeding – exclusively breastfed babies may have greater protection from SIDS and infections than babies who are partially breastfed. So it looks like the more breast milk, the better.

However, it's fair to say that the topic of mixed feeding (breast milk and formula milk) is an under-researched one, even though plenty of people do it – in fact, it's so common in some Hispanic communities that is has its own name: 'las dos' (meaning 'both').[148] Some mums who used this method told us that they opted for mixed feeding because it meant: feeling sure that their baby was getting enough milk (some mums were worried they weren't producing enough milk themselves) or getting enough nutrients; going back to work and being unable to express enough for all the milk feeds; getting a break from breastfeeding from time to time; having the freedom to go out and have a few alcoholic drinks. However, if you decide to supplement breast milk with formula it's important to make sure you get your milk supply up during the first month to six weeks (especially the first two weeks) before you introduce formula milk. Remember that breast milk production is all about supply and demand – if your baby takes less, you produce less. Regular expressing will help you to keep it up as well. However, no pump is as efficient as a baby at getting the milk out. So in the early weeks, until you have built up your milk supply, it is best for feeds to be directly from the breast rather than expressed milk or formula milk.

Why Women Stop Breastfeeding

A national survey of 2,683 new mums in the UK in 2010 (the Infant Feeding Survey) asked mums to report the main reasons they stopped breastfeeding in the first few weeks.[149] The following three reasons were the most important:

1. They thought they weren't making enough milk for their baby, and were therefore worried that their baby wasn't getting adequate nutrition.

2. They didn't think their baby was sucking properly or he was rejecting the breast, and therefore not feeding properly and not getting adequate nutrition.

3. It was too painful, therefore it was too difficult to feed him physically.

It's clear that most women want to try to breastfeed, but few manage to keep it up for the full six months, at least not exclusively. The Infant Feeding Survey reported that although 81 per cent of women start breastfeeding their baby from birth, by three months only 17 per cent are still *exclusively* breastfeeding, and only 1 per cent exclusively breastfeed at six months.[150]

However, one in three mums is still breastfeeding to some extent at six months, even if this is only one feed per day. When mums who had stopped breastfeeding in the first two weeks were asked what might have helped them to carry on for longer, the most common thing they reported was that they needed more support and guidance from the hospital staff, midwives and family. This underlines the importance of seeking help and advice *early*, if you are struggling. See page 129 for information about support on breastfeeding.

NOT ENOUGH MILK

This is the most common reason reported by women who choose to stop breastfeeding and substitute with/switch to formula milk, or wean onto solid food early. In the UK Infant Feeding Survey 2010, insufficient milk was the main reported reason for stopping breastfeeding and was reported by 17 per cent of mums who stopped within the first week, 28 per cent of those who stopped in the second week, and 39 per cent of those who stopped between six weeks and four months.[151]

In truth, we don't actually know how many women produce insufficient milk – or no milk at all – because data on breast-milk production haven't been collected in large population-based samples. What we do know is that there are big differences in rates of breastfeeding in different countries, indicating that cultural factors play an important part in both rates of, and perceptions about, breastfeeding. Less than 1 per cent of British mums are still breastfeeding at 12 months compared to 35 per cent of Norwegian mums; and there is virtually universal breast-feeding in low-income countries in some regions of sub-Saharan Africa, south Asia and Latin America[152]. These differences in rates of breastfeeding are cultural, not genetic.

We also know that the frequency (and duration) of feeding is probably the most important influence on milk supply. If you are keen to breastfeed, it is crucial that you try to feed whenever your baby is hungry, especially during the first couple of weeks. The volume of milk you produce six days after your baby has been born is predictive of the amount you will produce at six weeks, and a lot of stimulation of your breasts during the first few days is the key to making sure you have an ample milk supply further down the line. If you start substituting breastfeeds with formula milk too early, your milk supply will diminish. It's a deceptively simple process; when milk is removed, your body receives hormonal signals to make more – if more milk is removed, more is made, but if less is removed, the supply dries up. If you are worried about the amount of milk you are producing you can get a rough estimate by expressing it – but bear in mind that babies are often far more adept at getting the milk out than a pump, so you may in fact be producing more than you express.

I struggled to breastfeed both my children. They're now five and three, but I still find it difficult thinking back to the early days which were totally overshadowed by feeding dramas. Nothing in the world can prepare you for it but when breastfeeding doesn't work it can make you feel dreadful and like you've failed from the off. I still wince when I see one of my friends whip their boob out and effortlessly feed their baby. For me breastfeeding was a fiasco full of double pumps, multiple different types of feeding pillows, endless trips to baby cafés and clinics, and well-meaning breast-milk advocates breathing down my neck.

I ended up pumping for a year with my first baby, right up until I went back to work, so I was never able to really relax and enjoy the time that we had. You're on such a strict schedule when you pump that you can't really stray far from home. When I had my second child I was determined the feeding was going to work, and for a while it did, but my milk disappeared at six weeks and my daughter ended up in hospital, unable to drink anything at all as she'd never learned how to take a bottle. So then the pumping started again, but it was even harder this time as I had a toddler as well. I only did it for about eight months the second time round, but that was long enough.

I don't know whether the breastfeeding guilt/shame, or whatever it is, is ever really going to leave me and when I look back a large part of me wishes that I hadn't spent all that time pumping. However, when you're faced with a newborn baby and flooded with crazy hormones it's easy to feel overwhelmed by all of the pro-feeding propaganda there is out there. I found it very, very hard to step away from the pump and accept formula instead.

Katherine, mum of Isabelle (5 years)
and Beatrice (3 years)

Katherine's story highlights the challenges – emotional and physical – that some mums endure when breastfeeding their baby from their own breast hasn't been possible.

BREASTFEEDING HURTS

Breastfeeding shouldn't be painful – at least not after the first few days. Some tenderness during the very first few days is common, but it should only be mild. A state-of-the-art ultrasound study in 2014 revealed that babies 'get the milk out' by suction, rather than squeezing and kneading the nipple with their mouth (breastfeeding is not the same as milking a cow!).[153] So if your nipple is distorted when your baby comes off, then he isn't latching on correctly.

A common cause of cracked painful nipples is a shallow latch – if your nipple isn't far enough back in your baby's mouth his tongue will rub or press on your nipple, which can cause the problem. If your baby is latched well, the nipple should go right to the back of his mouth where his tongue action won't hurt it. It is worth seeking help if you have very painful nipples during the early days. Ask your midwife, a lactation consultant or someone at a breastfeeding café to help you and your baby get into a position where he is able draw in a large enough mouthful of your breast to get going. It is worth trying out a few different positions to see if you can find one that causes you less discomfort; it might be that tweaking your position just a tiny bit is all that is needed to make it less painful. If your nipples have become cracked and very painful you can apply some highly purified lanolin until they have healed again. This will keep them moist, feel soothing and will help prevent scabs from forming. There is no need to remove this before you breastfeed again and you can apply it as often as you need to. Some women also find that applying some expressed breast milk onto their nipples after a feed helps relieve soreness. You can also use a nipple shield to protect your nipples from further damage, but this can sometimes lead to other complications – the shield can open cracks (ouch!), it can be harder for your baby to get the milk out and it can be difficult to move your baby back to your bare breast once he's become used to the shield. But if you have tried everything else and not found a solution, a nipple shield is certainly worth a go.

If your nipple or breast is excruciatingly painful, red and inflamed, and you feel very unwell, you could have mastitis, which can be caused by infection or blocked ducts. The advice is to continue to breastfeed as normal and take some time to rest (as much as you can with a young baby!). If it continues to get worse, do see your GP as you may need antibiotics.

> With Grace I was able to breastfeed her with no obvious problems. With Thomas he was diagnosed with tongue tie as I was having a lot of problems with him latching on and him appearing hungry after he had fed for a long time. However, this diagnosis didn't happen until he was three days old, by which time I was extremely sore and felt unable to breastfeed him. I felt that healthcare professionals up until this point had not listened or taken my

requests for help and support seriously. I was so sore from feeding Thomas when he was three days old that, as soon as the supermarket opened, I went and bought formula. This had never been my intention as the way to feed him, but I felt that was the only option at the time. I felt so upset at buying the formula and as though I was a failure. I remember crying as I walked out of the supermarket with it.

I didn't want to formula-feed Thomas. Because of this I decided to keep trying with the breastfeeding and I struggled on for around two weeks, despite being in absolute agony and Thomas clearly not getting enough milk. I cried every day and found that I was mentally deliberating breastfeeding versus formula-feeding and what was 'right' and 'wrong'. I would make my mind up that breastfeeding just wasn't working and that if Thomas had formula he would still grow up to be a happy, healthy baby. But then I would see someone else (other than me and his dad) giving him a bottle and my heart hurt because I am his mum and I felt that I was the only one that should be feeding him and that I was failing him as a mother. I felt that I was letting him down in a huge way and that because I couldn't and he couldn't breastfeed he was not going to bond with me.

I spent a huge amount of those first few weeks completely beating myself up about the situation and feeling so low with the guilt of failure when it should have been a time of complete happiness with Thomas. All the leaflets on breastfeeding that I had from the hospital/midwife shouted out about how good breast milk is for the baby and how much better off the baby is. I remember thinking, 'Thomas will end up in hospital unwell if I don't breastfeed him.' Thinking back, that's terrible and no mother should be made to feel that way, especially when ultimately the decision is taken out of their hands for the sake of their baby's health and well-being.

Amy, mum of Grace (18 months) and Thomas (4 months)

The decision to stop breastfeeding can be devastating, as Amy's story demonstrates. If you are struggling with breastfeeding, please don't struggle alone. There is support available, so do seek it out. Our advice to you would be to do this sooner rather than later; many mums find that if they get enough support in the early days and weeks, they are able to get the hang of it in the end. The contact details of some of the organisations that can help are listed in the Useful Resources section on page 367. However, some mums still can't manage to breastfeed, after valiant efforts for many weeks and months. If you have made the decision to stop, it is not the end of the world. *How* you feed, as well as *what* you feed is important.

Breastfeeding Myths

Virtually all women are able to breastfeed. All you need is one functioning breast – women successfully exclusively breastfeed twins, with one on each breast. Your ability to breastfeed has nothing to do with any of the following: the size of your breasts before pregnancy or how much they grow during pregnancy; your age; your ethnicity; or your relatives' ability to breastfeed. You can also breastfeed if you: have had breast implants; have a nipple piercing; have flat or inverted nipples; are diabetic; or are pregnant. There are a lot of other commonly held myths about breastfeeding that are not supported by evidence. The following four myths have sometimes been powerful enough to put women off breastfeeding altogether:

1. BREASTFEEDING WILL CHANGE MY BREASTS AND MAKE THEM SAGGY

Until 2007 it was commonly believed – even by medical professionals – that breastfeeding causes breasts to sag (called 'ptosis').[154] It wasn't until Dr Brian Rinker, a plastic surgeon at the University of Kentucky, carried out the first research into this question that this myth was debunked. Anecdotally many of the women who were seeking corrective breast surgery at his clinic attributed their ptosis to breastfeeding, so he decided to find out if this was really true. He interviewed 132 women who were seeking surgery to augment or lift their breasts, and gathered detailed information about their medical history, as well as the number of pregnancies, breast size before pregnancy, BMI and whether or not they smoked. He found that the number of pregnancies was an important factor, but not breastfeeding itself.[155] During pregnancy, oestrogen and progesterone stimulate the milk-secreting glands to develop and these become engorged with milk and stretch the skin around the breast; they also stretch the ligaments that support your breast. It is these pregnancy processes that lead to breasts sagging, not breastfeeding.

2. BREASTFED BABIES DON'T SLEEP AS WELL AS FORMULA-FED BABIES

Disrupted sleep and ongoing sleep deprivation are some of the toughest challenges faced by parents with a new baby. In the UK there is strong popular opinion that formula-fed babies sleep for longer, and as such women are often advised by well-meaning friends or family either to 'top up' with a formula feed to aid sleep through the night or move to formula altogether. In fact, the jury is most definitely out when it comes to the evidence for this. It is true that some studies have found that breastfed babies sleep less during the night, wake more often and wake for longer than formula-fed babies,[156] but some researchers have found no differences at all between breast- and formula-fed babies.[157]

Importantly, over the last decade a number of studies have actually found that breastfeeding babies *and* their mums sleep for longer, that mums manage to get back to sleep more quickly after waking up in the night, and that there are hormonal mechanisms involved in breastfeeding that aid better sleep quality.[158] With sleep, we know that quality is as important as quantity, and breastfeeding may promote deep sleep, which is restorative. In particular, a large study found that those mums who were exclusively breastfeeding slept for longer, had better physical health, more energy and lower rates of depression than either mixed-feeding or formula-feeding mums.[159]

Perhaps the biggest myth that needs to be challenged is that babies *should* be sleeping through the night by the time they are 6–12 months old. In a study of 715 British babies this age, Dr Amy Brown, Associate Professor at Swansea University, found that 78 per cent will wake at least once in the night and 61 per cent will have at least one milk feed.[160] She cautioned that as a sleep-deprived mum you will be extremely vulnerable to the multi-million pound market that has a vested interest in trying to sell you a solution to a 'problem' that isn't and shouldn't be 'solved' by moving to formula.

3. BREASTFEEDING IS EASY

Just because it is the most natural thing in the world, it doesn't mean breastfeeding is easy. First Steps Nutrition, says: 'almost everyone needs support when they are starting out'.[161] It is absolutely crucial to ensure you get the positioning right in the early days. First Steps Nutrition urges new mums to make sure they seek help and guidance during the first few days or weeks. There is plenty of help in the community. NHS community drop-ins are available in most areas, where there will be volunteer mums and/or lactation consultants. Lactation consultants are professionals who have been specially trained in how to support you and your baby with breast-feeding. Private lactation consultants can also come out and see you at home. The National Breastfeeding Helpline and the NCT helpline can also provide advice over the phone. So do seek help if you are struggling; this is especially important during the early weeks when we know mums find it hardest (see the Useful Resources section on page 367). If you haven't had your baby yet, it is worth knowing where to get support from before he arrives. This could even be friends who are currently breastfeeding or have breastfed before. In fact, get friends and family to help with other things as much as you can too – doing the dishes, going to the supermarket, cooking meals, doing the laundry, changing his nappy, bathing him, to name a few! Having someone taking care of these tasks can make feeding issues much more manageable because it will allow you to focus on yourself and your baby.

Thanks to two pieces of advice I received when I was still pregnant I had very realistic expectations about breast-feeding – I knew my nipples would hurt for the first two weeks and that it was going to be hard work initially. Following Julia's delivery I had a fever so both of us had to stay in the hospital for three nights as we were given anti-biotics as a precaution. Although it didn't feel like it at the time, this was a blessing in disguise as it gave me time to get a lot of help from the midwives. When Julia would latch onto my breast I would often call for a midwife to make sure she was in the right position, which I knew was vital to avoid bleeding nipples. As a result I felt that after five days I had cracked breastfeeding, as I knew what I was doing. What also helped hugely was that Julia was a good feeder.

Despite the quick success at breastfeeding, for over one week I did dread each feed as my nipples hurt (they were still cracked and slightly bleeding!) like hell but I knew that this would eventually get better and I would have to just persevere through this early bit. The pain was so bad that I had to shake my legs (don't ask me why?!) to bear the first few sucks. I did find the help of midwives invaluable, but I also feel they never tell a mother the whole story – that at first breastfeeding is not easy; that despite a correct position of the baby on your breast your nipples will still hurt as they need to get used to it; and that latching may not come easily to all babies. This can give mothers unrealistic expectations or make them feel like a failure if they struggle with breastfeeding. Finally, I'm a confident person so I had no problem asking for help with breastfeeding, but I'm sure this may not be the case for all mothers.

Marta, mum of Julia (8 weeks)

4. YOU CAN'T BREASTFEED IN SOME PUBLIC PLACES

The Equality Act 2010 stipulates that women are allowed, by law, to breastfeed their baby wherever they need to or wish to in any public place in the UK. This means that it is unlawful for any member of staff to ask you not to breastfeed on their premises or to refuse to serve you because you are breastfeeding your baby. Although you might feel embarrassed or worried about breastfeeding in public, it is your right to do so. Some mums do feel self-conscious though; feeding scarves are a really good way to feed discretely in public if you're nervous about it – you can also use a pashmina or shawl if you have one.

Breast Milk Composition

Breast milk is a dynamic substance as it adjusts to a baby's changing developmental needs, and contains many living cells. It changes over the course of a feed, from one feed to the next, in response to environmental changes and with the age of the infant.

Important nutritional changes occur over the first few days of milk production. The very first milk to be produced is called colostrum; its main purposes are to protect the vulnerable newborn baby from infection and boost development. It is yellow in colour and is produced in very small amounts but is compositionally rich, providing a large injection of antibodies. Nutritionally, it contains about 54kcal per 100ml and is relatively high in protein (2.5g per 100ml) compared to later breast milk.

'Transitional milk' is then produced between Days 6 and 14 after birth, which differs from colostrum to support the changing needs of a rapidly growing baby. It contains around 58kcal per 100ml and has lower protein content than colostrum (1.7g per 100ml).

Mature breast milk is established by about two weeks after birth, which becomes the milk that supports the baby throughout the following few months. Mature breast milk contains around 65kcal per 100ml and 1.3g per 100ml of protein. In general it contains about 3.8g fat per 100ml (the fat provides about 50 per cent of the baby's calories), but the fat content changes substantially over the course of a single feed.[162] The initial 'fore milk' is more watery and contains less fat, but as the feed progresses the 'hind milk' becomes richer containing about double the amount of fat. But the amount of fat in 'fore' and 'hind' milk also varies in relation to the number and size of feeds that babies take. For example, the fat content changes from about 4.3 per cent to 10.7 per cent for babies taking 6–9 large feeds per day; but 'fore' milk tends to be richer for babies taking more frequent smaller feeds

(14–18 feeds per day), changing from about 4.8 per cent to 8.2 per cent fat. This probably ensures that whatever the feeding pattern, breastfeeding babies get roughly the same amount of fat.[163]

But breast milk is not just fuel. It's a complex bioactive fluid that plays a number of roles in supporting the health and development of your baby. Aside from providing optimal nutrition, it contains hundreds of bioactive molecules that contribute towards immunity and development. These are not present in formula milk because they can't be manufactured in a laboratory and/or they don't survive the production process. Although the exact composition of breast milk is still unknown, we do know a fair bit about many of its properties, which include: cells and agents that protect the baby against infection and support immune development (for example, immunoglobulins, macrophages, antiviral and antibacterial agents, living white blood cells); lactoferrin which also has antibacterial properties and helps babies absorb nutrients; fatty acids which promote development (including the brain); and growth factors. It even contains agents that appear to control wakefulness and sleepiness (nucleotides), the levels of which change at different times of the day which may help to establish and regulate a baby's body clock.

Breastfeeding mums need to take a vitamin D supplement. This is recommended for all British adults, but it is especially important if you are breastfeeding. You can buy supplements reasonably cheaply at a pharmacy or supermarket and First Steps Nutrition suggests opting for a dose between 10mcg (400 IU) and 25mcg (1,000 IU). All breastfed babies from birth to one year should also be given a daily vitamin D supplement of 8.5–10mcg. See pages 59–60 and 256–7 for more information about Vitamin D.

APPETITE REGULATION

The appetite-control centres in the brain start to develop in utero but continue to develop in the first few weeks and months after birth. The composition of breast milk may also play a role in supporting the development of optimal appetite regulation, by influencing the appetite-regulatory systems in the brain. This is less widely known, but evidence is mounting.[164] Breast milk contains many of the hormones that determine hunger and fullness in adults and children.[165] These hormones are not present in formula milk (or are present in very small amounts) due to the different composition of cows' milk and the processing of formulas to ensure that they are safe and have a long 'shelf life'.[166] For example, breast milk contains leptin, (the 'satiety hormone') which regulates feelings of hunger and fullness.[167] In children and adults leptin is a fundamental regulator of appetite and enhances satiety (fullness sensitivity). Breast milk is the main source of leptin in babies in the first six months of life and may help to regulate hunger and satiety during the early weeks and months. We know that babies consuming breast milk that contains higher levels of leptin grow less rapidly during the first few years, which we know is better for their later health (as discussed in Chapter 3).[168]

Other appetite hormones are also present in breast milk, including ghrelin (the 'hunger hormone') which stimulates hunger. These hormones are thought to play a role in the development of the appetite-control centres in a baby's developing brain, as well as the cells that line the gut. They are also thought to speed up gastric emptying (how quickly milk leaves the stomach), which happens more quickly with breast milk compared to formula milk. There are however also behavioural differences between breastfeeding and bottle-feeding which are likely to play a role in the development of appetite regulation – these are discussed in detail on page 167.

FOOD PREFERENCES

Breast milk, like amniotic fluid, reflects to some extent the flavours of the mum's diet. Your newborn baby's flavour senses are well developed, which means that breastfed babies are repeatedly exposed to a variety of ever-changing flavours for as long as they receive breast milk. This may influence their food acceptance later on, and it is probably the first way that babies learn which foods are safe to eat. One of the first studies conducted in this area randomised women to drink a glass of carrot juice four times a week during the first two months of breastfeeding or to avoid carrots altogether.[169] The babies whose mums had had carrots were more receptive to carrot-flavoured cereal later on than those whose mums had avoided them altogether. Babies whose mums eat plenty of fruit during breastfeeding are also more likely to enjoy fruit during weaning. Other studies have shown that flavours such as aniseed, garlic, ethanol, mint, vanilla and even blue cheese (!) appear in breast milk one to two hours after a mother has consumed them, and take six to eight hours to disappear.[170]

Breastfeeding may therefore provide another window of opportunity for 'programming' your baby's taste preferences in the long term and might be particularly advantageous when it comes to increasing your baby's acceptance of bitter-tasting vegetables later on. Some research has shown that children who were breastfed versus formula fed (or breastfed for longer) eat more fruit and vegetables and are more willing to try new foods during childhood and will be less picky.[171] However, this research is based on observational or small studies, rather than large randomised controlled trials. This means that we can't be completely sure if Mum's diet during breastfeeding really *causes* the baby's food preferences, or if mums who breastfeed also go on to feed their children more fruit and vegetables later, and it is this that accounts for their child's willingness to eat them rather than the flavour of the breast milk.

The early flavour experience of a formula-fed baby is pretty monotonous in comparison to a breastfed baby's. There are, however, differences in the flavours of different formulas and babies tend to learn to prefer the formula they are fed, and subsequently the foods that contain these flavours.[172] It also means that if your baby doesn't seem to like a particular brand of formula milk, they may prefer another.

VEGETARIANS AND VEGANS

Vegetarians and vegans who are breastfeeding have a fantastic opportunity to introduce their baby to all of the wonderful flavours of their own diet, if it is rich in vegetables and fruit, and varied. But if you have a vegan or vegetarian diet it's important to take vitamin B12 and vitamin D supplements alongside your diet while you are breastfeeding (you have probably already been taking these while you were pregnant). There are two supplements suitable for vegans: Veg 1 supplement (available from the Vegan Society) and Vitashine vitamin D supplement (available from most pharmacies).

There are also a couple of other dietary considerations that you will need to plan for; breastfeeding requires you to eat more protein and zinc, which you can get from pulses, tofu, cashew nuts, certain seeds (chia seeds, ground linseed, hemp seeds, pumpkin seeds) and quinoa; you will need 80 per cent more calcium than a non-breastfeeding (and non-pregnant) adult, so eating calcium-fortified foods is also important (for example, calcium-set tofu).

If you are a vegan mum who is breastfeeding, First Steps Nutrition provides fantastic information about how to ensure you get all of the nutrients you need in their booklet 'Eating Well: vegan infants and under-5s'.

THE BOTTOM LINE

- How you choose to feed your baby is *your choice*, and yours alone.

- There is convincing evidence that breastfeeding your baby will benefit both him and you, so it is worth giving it a shot if you can.

- Breastfeeding can be hard, especially in the first few days and weeks. The mums who persevere are the ones who get the help and support they need from midwives, health visitors, friends and family *early*. There is help available, so if things aren't going well and you're struggling to get the hang of it, please ask for help. Be pushy if you have to be!

CHAPTER 5

Formula-Feeding

Sometimes it isn't possible to breastfeed your baby – some mums are not able to or choose not to; some parents have adopted their baby; and some dads or grandparents are responsible for feeding their baby. Some mums have also told us that although they started off breastfeeding, after returning to work it was too difficult to provide all the required milk by expressing their breast milk. And some felt uncomfortable doing this at work or simply didn't have the time. In these instances formula offers a vital source of nutrition for your baby.

The decision to formula-feed is purely personal and depends on what is right for you and your family circumstances. Some mums are made to feel guilty about doing this, but it is your decision to make and yours alone, and all mums want the best for their baby. Life with a young baby can be very stressful and coping with the many competing demands can feel overwhelming. Sometimes the only way to keep your sanity is to take practical decisions to make your life a little bit easier and, for some, this means using formula. It is our view that parents need evidence-based information about formula-feeding, so that they can make well-informed choices about what formula milk to use. In this chapter we provide you with sound scientifically based information about formula milk.

'In the weeks and months after having your first child, you are exhausted and considerably less resilient than usual. At this vulnerable time, instead of feeling supported, I felt pressurised and judged by some family members, friends, midwives and health visitors – and even strangers – when it came to breast-feeding. This pressure even led to me sometimes hiding somewhere in order to give my baby a bottle of formula without judgement. Sadly, I look back on those first few months as an awful time. I feel women should be fully informed of the options and then supported in their choice, rather than brain-washed and forced into exclusive breastfeeding.'

Annabel, mum of Elliot (4 years) and Coram (2 years)

Reasons Why Some Parents Choose To Bottle-Feed

Some of the parents we spoke to told us about the practical advantages of bottle feeding or using formula milk. Here are some of the things they reported (some of these also apply to feeding expressed breast milk through a bottle):

- Other people can feed your baby which gives you a break.

- It gives other people the opportunity to form a close bond with your baby while feeding.

- You can be certain about how much milk your baby is taking.

- Formula has some vitamins and other nutrients that breastfed babies have to get from supplements (vitamin D).

- It avoids any embarrassment that women may feel when breastfeeding in public.

The Infant Feeding Survey reported that in the UK in 2010, 19 per cent of women are exclusively using formula milk from Day 1, 34 per cent by two weeks, 45 per cent by six weeks, 58 per cent by four months, and 66 per cent by six months.[173]

My daughter was born by emergency C-section after a long labour. In the antenatal period I had absolutely no plans to formula-feed – I'm a GP so know about the health benefits of breastfeeding. But in the first postnatal week I produced little more than about 20ml of milk per day. I invested in a well-reviewed electric breast pump, but this had little effect on my supply. I introduced formula from roughly Day 2 and by 10 days I had stopped any attempts to breastfeed. In the short term I felt deflated and inadequate, but reflecting on this experience now, my daughter is a happy, healthy and intelligent three-year-old.

The benefits of formula-feeding for my daughter, my husband and myself have been immense. I was quickly able to establish a routine, with good sleep patterns, and I do feel formula-feeding contributed to this. My husband played a large part in night feeds. I returned to work at six months and the transition to childminder, with continued formula-feeding, was easy. We travelled abroad when our daughter was 12 weeks old and, while the formula-feeding took a little more planning, it wasn't prohibitive. I believe that if I had continued to battle to breastfeed I would have been at high risk of postnatal depression. Instead I look back fondly at the first months of my daughter's life. If I do have another baby I will not plan to breastfeed even if I have a good milk supply.

Laura, mum of Elsie (3 years)

Formula-Feeding Myths

Just as there are myths about breastfeeding (see page 129), there are also a few about formula-feeding:

IT ISN'T POSSIBLE TO BOND WITH YOUR BABY IF YOU BOTTLE-FEED HIM

This is simply not true! There are plenty of ways to bond with your baby, and you can still bond with him if you are bottle-feeding. An important part of feeding your baby is *how* you feed him not just *what* you feed him. The key is to feed him responsively. You can do this whether you breast- or bottle-feed. We describe exactly how to do this in Chapter 6.

FORMULA-FEEDING IS EASIER THAN BREASTFEEDING

You may be in for a surprise if you think that formula-feeding might be easier than breastfeeding. It has its challenges as well. The biggest one is the amount of steps that you will need to go through in order to make up a feed safely. This involves sterilising the bottle as well as the formula powder (if, like most mums, you are not using ready-to-feed formula). It takes quite a while to make it up properly, so it can be a challenge when your baby is hungry and you quickly need to make up a feed. We have provided step-by-step instructions on how to do this on page 157.

'I actually assumed that I would breastfeed my first daughter and had given no consideration to bottle-feeding. However, when she arrived I found breastfeeding much more difficult than I expected. I felt so overwhelmed by the demand that I started to feel anxious when she was due a feed. I also developed mastitis so started to express, but was advised to return to breastfeeding by my health visitor to avoid 'nipple confusion'. I did this, but a combination of pain and feeling so unhappy meant that after six weeks I finally succumbed to moving her to formula. As soon as I did this I felt such a huge relief. I found I was soon able to get her into a routine to plan activities around this. My husband was able to help me and got to spend more time with her. Obviously the bottle washing and sterilising is a bit of a pain, but you soon get used to it. Formula-feeding isn't necessarily the easy option but sometimes breastfeeding just doesn't work out. I am really happy with my decision now but at the time it was very hard.'

Alison, mum of Hanna (5 years)

YOUR BABY WILL SLEEP FOR LONGER AT NIGHT IF YOU GIVE HIM FORMULA

You may be disappointed if you were counting on a full night's sleep by giving your baby formula at night, or switching over completely. Research suggests that babies wake up in the night regardless of whether they are fed formula or breast milk.[174] Your baby may not even want a feed, but he may wake up anyway (we provide information about how to check if your baby is really hungry on page 181). The myth about the different sleep patterns of breastfed and formula-fed babies is debunked in detail on page 130.

FORMULA IS VIRTUALLY THE SAME AS BREAST MILK

Although formula milk is an adequate alternative source of nutrition for your baby, it is not compositionally the same because it isn't possible to manufacture something that includes all of the properties of breast milk. There are important nutritional differences between the two. The composition of formula milk is described in detail below.

Formula Milk Composition

There have been few academic publications examining the nutritional composition of UK formula milk relative to human breast milk. However, the British charity First Steps Nutrition trust has carried out the most detailed review to date.[175] Given the dynamic and complex composition of human breast milk it isn't possible to produce an identical substance, but formula is intended to act as an effective substitute for human milk. As such, every effort has been made to mimic the nutritional profile of human breast milk.

Like breast milk, formulas contain about the same number of calories (60–70kcal per 100ml) and are largely matched in the proportions of fat, protein and carbohydrate. Most infant formulas are based on cows' milk, but the proportion of the two proteins – casein and whey – has been adjusted so it is more comparable to breast milk (animal milks have a higher casein content, while breast milk has more whey). Other ingredients, such as iron and fat blends, are also added to formula to better approximate the composition to human breast milk and increase its health benefits.

Which Formula Milk to Choose?

In the UK there are many types of formula available – powdered as well as ready-to-feed – and lots of different brands, so it can be difficult to make a decision on which to choose for your baby. Some brands make pretty bold health claims based on their ingredients, but standard formula milks in the UK must adhere to the strictest formulation regulations, which means that none of them can vary that much. In 2014 the European Food Safety Authority (EFSA) panel on Dietetic Products, Nutrition and Allergies was asked by the European Commission to review existing research on the composition of infant formulas, to provide expert opinion on which ingredients in formula milk are necessary and unnecessary, in terms of ensuring babies using these formula milks grow well and are healthy. They concluded that many ingredients that you will see advertised on standard formula milks are unnecessary because there is no evidence for a beneficial effect, including: arachidonic acid [AA], eicosapentaenoic acid [EPA], chromium, fluoride, taurine, nucleotides, non-digestible oligosaccharides ('prebiotics'), 'probiotics', or 'synbiotics' (combination of prebiotics and probiotics).[176] They even cautioned that unnecessary ingredients in formula (such as these) put a burden on a baby's metabolism because he has to excrete them.

First Steps Nutrition have published the most detailed review to date of the nutritional composition, health benefits and safety of all formula milks on the UK market.[177] They concluded that no standard 'first' milks (those marketed for babies aged 0–6 months old) are superior to any other, so when making a decision on which formula to choose, you may as well be guided by price. They also conducted a price review in 2017, and it turns out that prices really do differ.[178] Ready-to-feed milks are by far the most expensive. Though they might provide a useful option when there are no facilities to make up milk safely (and when you are new to bottle-feeding and have a crying baby they will by far feel like the quickest and easiest option), you will, however, end up spending about three times as much money compared to powdered milk. The difference in price between the most expensive ready-to-feed milk (Aptamil Profutura First Infant Milk) and the cheapest powdered milk (Mamia First Infant Milk) over one month is a staggering £110 (£138 versus £28). Formulas based on goats' milk are also an awful lot pricier than those based on cows' milk

There are also 'starter packs' of first infant formula available to buy. These are 70ml bottles with sterile teats that are ready-to-feed during the first few days after birth and all are based on cows' milk. This is an extremely expensive way to feed your baby during the first days and will provide no added benefit to your baby at all. If this makes your life easier during the first few days, it's an option; but do bear in mind that it will cost you between £61 and £102 to feed your baby just for the first week.

But are there any benefits to formulas based on cows' milk versus goats' milk, or ready-to-feed versus powdered? A common misconception is that formula based on goats' milk is less likely to cause allergies than formula based on cows' milk. However, the EFSA also reviewed the evidence for this and concluded that there is no difference at all in terms of the likelihood of an allergy, or the safety, when using one or the other.[179] Ready-to-feed formula is sterile until opened, while powered milks need to be sterilised with (nearly) boiling water in order to kill the bugs that can live in the milk powder. (Bottles always need to be sterilised whatever type of formula milk you use, because a young baby's immune system is not yet fully developed and they are at high risk of infection – sterilisation of bottles is crucial for prevention of serious infection.) This, of course, has a practical advantage – some mums prefer to use ready-to-feed formula for night feeds rather than spend time boiling and cooling water to make up formula from powder at 3am. But, other than this, there are no benefits, and the cost difference is enormous.

First Steps Nutrition concluded that more expensive milks provide no benefits at all over the cheapest ones on the market.

'All formula milks have to be of a similar composition to comply with EU compositional requirements and they are all nutritionally adequate for infants. If a substance was found that was definitely beneficial for infant health that could be added to formula milks, it would be in all formula by law.'

First Steps Nutrition Trust[180]

With this in mind, do not hesitate to pick a less expensive brand of formula for your baby if finances are a factor. You can feel confident that standard formulas are pretty much the same, and more expensive does not mean better. Pick whichever type of formula – powder or ready-to-feed – best suits your needs. It is also recommended that babies who are not being breastfed be given 'first' milks (0–6 months) throughout the *whole of the first year of life* (0–12 months), so you don't need to worry about changing to a different formula milk when your baby reaches 6 months.

'When we went to the supermarket to buy formula for Thomas we had no idea which one to get. All the ingredients on all of them were absolutely identical. We ended up going with one that was more expensive, which I suppose made us think it was better, and it advertised different things on the packaging about the benefits.'

Shane, Dad of Thomas (4 months)

In their review, First Steps Nutrition provided detailed information about all UK formula milks that are suitable for vegetarians, halal- and kosher-approved, and an evaluation of 'specialist milks'.[181] We have summarised the key bits of information from their review for you below.

FORMULA MILK FOR VEGETARIANS

Most formula milks that are based on cows' milk or goats' milk are not suitable for vegetarians because they include fish oils and/or use other animal-derived ingredients during the production process. For example, rennet is an animal-derived enzyme which is used by most manufacturers to separate curds from whey; alternatives to rennet are used for the production of the vegetarian formulas. There are no suitable ready-to-feed infant formulas for vegetarians. The following powdered milks are the only first milks that are suitable for vegetarians in the UK (we have not included soya-protein-based formula in this list because it is not recommended without medical supervision):

- Holle Organic Infant Goat Milk Formula 1

- Kendamil Mehadrin First Infant Milk

- Kendamil First Infant Milk

There are no first milks currently on the market in the UK that are suitable for vegans, because the vegetarian formulas source the vitamin D from sheep's wool. First Steps Nutrition advises parents wanting to bring up their baby as vegan to seek expert advice from their GP or midwife to ensure that their baby's nutritional needs are adequately met.

FORMULA MILK FOR A KOSHER OR HALAL-APPROVED DIET

Only one first milk has been formulated and produced in line with the requirements for the Jewish Orthodox religion, in a koshered factory: Kendamil Mehadrin First Infant Milk. The only halal-approved ready-to-feed first milk is SMA Pro First Infant Milk. All powdered first milks for the following brands are halal-approved:

- Aptamil

- Cow & Gate

- SMA

- Kendamil

SPECIALIST MILKS

Alongside the array of standard first milks available on the market, there are a host of other specialist milks that you can buy over the counter. Proceed with caution when purchasing any of these. We would not recommend using any of them unless you have been instructed to do so by a medical professional. All of the following milks, except the 'hungry-baby' milks, are classified for special medical purposes, which means that they don't need to adhere to the tight regulations that govern the formulation and preparation of standard formula milks. The following types of formula milks are available over the counter for babies aged 0–6 months:

'Hungry-baby' milks

Four brands of infant formula are marketed for 'hungry babies':

1. Aptamil Hungry Milk

2. Cow & Gate Infant Milk for Hungrier Babies

3. HiPP Organic Combiotic Hungry Infant Milk

4. SMA Extra Hungry

All four milks are very similar. The main difference between these and standard formula milks is that they are casein- rather than whey-based (the whey:casein ratio is about 20:80), which makes them more similar to animal milk. Casein is a heavier curd-like protein, which takes longer to digest. The manufacturers claim that it stays in the stomach for longer resulting in slower gastric emptying and keeps the baby fuller for longer.[182] In their review, First Steps Nutrition concluded that there is insufficient evidence that babies are less hungry after these milks and no evidence that babies sleep for longer after drinking them. These milks are also considerably higher in protein than first infant milks, which has been linked to higher weight gain in a number of studies (see page 282). Casein is also much harder for babies to digest. We therefore do not recommend any of these.

Comfort milks

Comfort milks are advertised for babies with digestive discomfort such as wind, colic or constipation. They are all based on cows' milk, but contain only whey protein (no casein). They all contain partially hydrolysed proteins and have lower lactose content than standard formulas, and some are thickened with starch. The claim is that these compositional differences make them easier to digest.

Because they are based on cows' milk they are *not suitable for babies with a cows' milk allergy*. There are four of these milks marketed in the UK:

1. Aptamil Comfort

2. Cow & Gate Comfort

3. HiPP Combiotic Comfort

4. SMA Comfort

Some parents hope that feeding a comfort milk in the evening will help to settle a fussing baby, but there are concerns over these milks and they are not recommended. Because they are for special medical purposes, they should only be used under medical supervision (even though you can buy them over the counter). First Steps Nutrition found no evidence that these milks prevent colic, wind, gastrointestinal discomfort or regurgitation. A recent large-scale and in-depth review of these milks commissioned by the Food Standards Agency (FSA) in 2016 concluded that there was no consistent evidence that they reduce the risk of any allergy (including food allergies).[183]

A 2016 paper issued by the European Society for Paediatric Gastroenterology, Hepatology and Nutrition (ESPGHAN) also supported this view and cautioned that we don't yet have health and safety information about the longer-term outcomes for babies given these formulas.[184] Wind, colic, constipation and fussing are common during the first few weeks but tend to improve as the baby matures. There are strategies you can use that don't necessarily involve changing their formula. Offering small feeds more frequently and making sure that you wind your baby during and after feeds can reduce fussing and distress. But bear in mind that babies cry for all sorts of reasons and it is not necessarily feeding-related. You can read more about how to deal with a fussing baby on page 187.

'Anti-reflux' or 'stay-down' milks

Reflux is very common in babies during the first few months and will usually have rectified itself by the time your baby turns one. The NHS describes the following common symptoms:

- Spitting up milk during or after feeds, which can happen several times a day

- Feeding difficulties, such as refusing feeds, gagging or choking

- Persistent hiccups or coughing

- Excessive crying, or crying while feeding

- Frequent ear infections

Reflux happens because the ring of muscle at the bottom of your baby's oesophagus (food pipe) that keeps food in the stomach is still developing. This means that some of the stomach contents can leak out and come back up again. But if your baby is gaining weight at a healthy rate and feeding well, there should be no cause for concern. It can still be worrying and stressful for you though (not to mention all the washing that has to be done!). But bear in mind that serious reflux that requires medical intervention is rare; and it needs to be diagnosed by a paediatrician.

There are four anti-reflux milks that are available to buy over the counter:

1. Aptamil Anti-reflux

2. Cow & Gate Anti-reflux

3. HiPP Organic Combiotic Anti-reflux

4. SMA Pro Anti-Reflux

Like other formulas that are classified as foods for special medical purposes, they should only be used under medical supervision. They are thickened using corn (maize) starch or carob-bean gum, which is not in line with the general consensus that infants less than four months old should have no food other than milk. Another concern is that these formulas are made up using cold or tepid water, which does not sterilise the powder. This introduces the risk of infection. If you are concerned about reflux, see your GP before using one of these formulas.

Lactose-free milk

Lactose intolerance is rare in babies and can only be diagnosed by a paediatrician. Symptoms begin shortly after drinking milk that contains lactose and include:

- abdominal pain

- diarrhoea

- flatulence and/or bloating

Lactose intolerance is not the same as an allergy to cows' milk protein, which is also rare but much more serious. In the UK two lactose-free formula milks are available to buy over the counter: Aptamil Lactose Free and SMA LF. Both are considered foods for special medical purposes so, again, they must only be used under medical supervision when lactose intolerance has been formally diagnosed.

The lactose has been replaced by glucose syrups, which is more likely to damage teeth, so First Steps Nutrition urges parents to make absolutely sure that they clean their baby's teeth after the last feed at night (although all babies – including those who are exclusively breastfed – need to have their teeth brushed after the last feed at night and first thing in the morning). First Steps Nutrition concluded that there is no evidence that lactose-free milks relieve symptoms of colic and they are not recommended for this use.

Soya-based milk

This milk uses protein from soya beans instead of cows' or goats' milk (no animal protein), and glucose syrup instead of lactose. There is only one soya-protein-based infant formula available to buy over the counter in the UK that is suitable from birth: SMA Wysoy (soya milk is also available on prescription). It is marketed as suitable for vegetarians, however it is *not recommended for infants under six months of age without medical supervision*. Soya is rich in phytoestrogens which are similar to the female sex hormone oestrogen, and the main concern is that these may affect babies' reproductive development. The Committee on Toxicity (COT) of Chemicals in Food, Consumer Products and the Environment has therefore cautioned that soya-based formula milks pose a potential risk to the future reproductive health of infants.[185]

Babies with cows' milk protein allergy are often allergic to soya protein as well, so this is not a good option for them. The Chief Medical Officer in the UK[186] and ESPGHAN[187] recommend that soya-based formula milks should *not* be used for babies under six months of age, including those with cows' milk protein allergy. Alternative and more appropriate options for these babies are formulas based on extensively hydrolysed proteins or other therapeutic formulations (for example, amino acid preparations). If you are worried that your baby has a cows' milk protein allergy you should see your GP. First Steps Nutrition have summarised their guidance an infant milk in a very useful table below:

TABLE 1: A SIMPLE GUIDE TO CHOOSING MILKS FOR INFANTS[188]

Type of milk	Infants 0–6 months	Infants 6 months–1 year
Breast milk	✔	✔
Whole cows' milk (or goats' milk, sheep's milk or unsweetened calcium fortified soya milk or milk alternative) as main milk drink	✗	✗
Infant formula suitable from birth (cows' or goats' milk based)	✔	✔
Infant formula marketed for hungrier babies, suitable from birth (cows' milk based)	Not recommended	Not recommended
Foods for special medical purposes available over the counter: anti-reflux, lactose-free, partially hydrolysed and comfort milks	Only use under medical supervision	Only use under medical supervision
Soya-protein-based infant formula, suitable from birth	Only use under medical supervision	Only use under medical supervision
Follow-on formula suitable from 6 months of age (cows' or goats' milk based)	✗	Not recommended
Goodnight milk	✗	Not recommended
Growing-up milks and toddler milks suitable from around 1 year of age (cows' milk, goats' milk or soya milk based)	✗	✗
PaediaSure Shake for fussy eaters	✗	✗
Rice milk – do not give to children under 5 years of age.	✗	✗

How to Make Up a Feed

After scanning the Internet and talking to lots of mums and dads it was clear to us that there is quite a lot of confusion about how to make up formula milk safely and why the recommendations are such as they are (which seem understandably draconian to most parents). We have therefore listed below the key tips and the rationale behind the steps that need to be followed. Good hygiene as well as the correct ratio of water to powder is crucial to ensure that formula milk is safe for your baby.

PREVENTION OF INFECTION

Your baby's immune system is not yet fully developed, making him more susceptible to infection. Breastfed babies receive some immunity from breast milk, but formula milk doesn't confer the same protection. This means that a number of steps need to be taken to minimise the risk of infection from formula feeds:

1. Wash your hands thoroughly. Always do this *before* you sterilise the bottle. This will mean that the germs that you have on your hands are less likely to be passed onto the sterile bottle and contaminate it.

2. All bottles and equipment need to be sterilised before each feed. Sterilisation means destroying any microorganisms that may cause harm, and boiling water suffices for this. You need to sterilise the bottle whether you use powdered milk or ready-to-feed milk.

3. Powdered milk is not sterile, and some nasty bugs can find their way in there. This means that the powder needs to be sterilised with the water used to prepare it. The advice is to use boiled water that has been cooled for no more than 30 minutes to ensure that the water temperature is above 70°C when you add the powder, but not boiling. This is the temperature above which most infection-causing pathogens are killed. Boiling water is too hot and will damage the nutrients in the powder, so water just above 70°C is the best compromise. To make sure the water is just above 70°C, *boil 1 litre of water in the kettle each time*, which is the amount required to remain above 70°C when left to cool in the kettle for 30 minutes.

4. It is recommended to make feeds up one at a time and discard any milk left at the end of the feed. The reason for this recommendation is to prevent infection by bacteria such as salmonella. Bacteria multiply rapidly at room temperature (the optimum temperature being body temperature, 37°C) and will continue, although at a slower rate, in the fridge. But making up formula properly is very time-consuming and one thing parents with a young baby don't have is spare time! So, understandably, many parents would rather not discard a lot of leftover formula that they have just prepared. If you need to store it for a while you can keep a freshly made bottle of formula in the fridge for up to 24 hours, and at room temperature for up to two hours, but never reheat it. But, always discard any formula left in the bottle at the end of a feed; once your baby has been feeding from the bottle, bacteria from his mouth will contaminate the milk and can multiply very quickly (even in the fridge)[189].

CORRECT RATIO OF WATER TO POWDER

It is crucial to make sure that the amount of water relative to powder is exactly right. Too much powder relative to water will make the formula too energy dense (too many calories per ml) and can lead to overfeeding and obesity risk, as well as constipation or dehydration. Too much water relative to powder will make the formula too diluted, which can result in underfeeding and growth faltering. Here's how to make sure you get it right:

1. **Always pour the correct amount of water into the bottle first** and check it to ensure it is the correct volume before adding the powder.

2. **Fill the scoop loosely with milk powder and level it off using** the back of a clean, dry knife or the leveller provided by the manufacturer. Always use the scoop provided by the particular formula powder you are using because scoop sizes differ between different brands (even when they are made by the same manufacturer).

3. **Add the powder to the water in the bottle.** A common mistake is to add the powder to the bottle first and then add the water to the powder. This results in the formula milk being too energy dense.

4. **The made-up formula then needs to be cooled** before giving it to your baby. This can be done by immersing the bottom of the bottle in cold water, making sure that the sterile teat doesn't have any contact with the water. Check the temperature of the formula before offering it to your baby by pouring a little bit onto the inside of your wrist, being careful not to let the teat touch your skin.

If you are using ready-to-feed formula and would like to warm it up before offering it to your baby, the safest way to do this is to stand the bottle in a bowl of warm (not boiling) water or hold it under warm water. Never heat it in a microwave. But bear in mind that formula does not need to be warmed before you offer it to your baby. So if you are using ready-to-feed formula from the beginning, perhaps refrain from warming it up because your baby will probably end up preferring it warm, which will make more work for you in the long run!

In the UK Infant Feeding Survey only 49 per cent of mothers reported that they had followed these three recommendations correctly: only making up one feed at a time, using boiled water cooled to a temperature above 70°C and adding water to the bottle before the powder.[190] If you would like further detailed step-by-step guidance on making up formula milk from powder, please go to the NHS and First Steps Nutrition websites (see pages 367–8).

There is also a machine that will prepare formula milk for you, in only a few minutes: the Tommee Tippee Perfect PrepTM Machine. You still need to sterilise all the bottles yourself, but the machine will dispense the actual formula for you. First it dispenses a 'hot shot' of water directly into the bottle. You then need to add the powder straight away (within two minutes), then shake the powder and water to mix it. You then return the bottle to the machine, which adds cold filtered tap water (using a special antibacterial filter) to make up the feed to the right volume and temperature for feeding immediately. You also need to change filters and maintain the machine according to their instructions. There are no published reports on the safety of these machines at the moment. First Steps Nutrition therefore caution against using them.[191]

THE BOTTOM LINE

- Breastfeeding isn't an option for everyone and not everyone wants to do it. Your baby will be fine if he is nurtured on formula milk – don't feel guilty about it if you can't breast-feed or decide not to.

- If you need to choose a formula milk, choose a *standard* first milk – it doesn't matter which one because none of them vary that much, so you may as well base your choice on price.

- Ready-to-feed milks are much more expensive than powdered milks, but they can be very useful for tired, stressed parents.

- Milks classified for 'special medical purposes' need not adhere to the tight regulations that govern the formulation and preparation of standard formula milks (for 0–6 months) – never use any of them without medical supervision.

- You can bond with your baby during feeding, whichever method you decide to use.

CHAPTER 6

Responsive Feeding: The *How* of Milk-Feeding

Once you have decided whether to breast- or formula-feed, you may be wondering *how* to feed your baby – for example, whether to feed him on a schedule or on demand, or whether or not to use a bottle. The 'how' of milk-feeding, is largely about understanding what type of feeder your baby is. The bottom line is that young babies are not all the same when it comes to milk. Our research with Gemini has shown that babies respond very differently to milk and the opportunity to feed, right from the beginning of life.[192] This is because appetite has a strong genetic basis, so babies are born with different predispositions towards milk and feeding right from the off.[193] Some babies inherit a set of genes that give them a very hearty appetite; these babies are more responsive to milk (they want to feed when they see, smell or taste milk), feed quickly and avidly, and need more milk in order to feel satisfied. As you might expect, these babies grow much more quickly during the early weeks and months and are at greater risk of rapid weight gain (see page 93). At the other end of the spectrum are the babies who inherit a set of genes that give them a poorer appetite; these babies have little interest in milk and the opportunity to feed, tend to feed slowly and get full up very easily. These babies grow more slowly in the early weeks and months. This research has implications for you as a parent – it means that your feeding strategies need to take into account your baby's appetite, and the challenges posed to you will be very different if your baby has an avid appetite versus a poor one. In short, babies have different needs.

While genes predispose your baby to have a larger or a smaller appetite, his early experiences with feeding are also likely to shape his appetite regulation. You could think of your baby's genes as setting his appetite potential and his early experiences as acting as the volume control. So if a baby is born with a genetic predisposition to have a large appetite, certain feeding strategies could increase his appetite even further, making him an even more avid feeder, while other feeding experiences may help to temper it. The same is true for poor feeders – within the right feeding environment a baby with a poor appetite can learn to feed well. But the crucial thing is understanding the type of feeder your baby is and responding using the most appropriate feeding strategies.

How babies are fed (via the breast versus via the bottle, for example), as well as *what* they are fed (breast milk versus formula milk, for example), seems to be an important influence on a baby's appetite.

APPETITE REGULATION

Feeding directly from the breast rather than through a bottle is thought to support the development of good appetite regulation, or rather, feeding your baby through a bottle may encourage him to overfeed. We know that babies who are formula-fed consume more milk overall during their first year of life than breastfed babies, and this process begins in the first few days. A review found that on the first day of life, breastfeeding babies consume only 21ml milk, in comparison to formula-fed babies who consume 170ml – 8 times as much. On Day 14 breastfeeding babies are still consuming a lot less – 674ml versus 762ml.[194] These small differences add up and, at eight months, a formula-fed baby has consumed about 30,000 more calories than a breastfed baby![195]

What on earth is going on? Is it that formula milk tastes better than breast milk, or is it just easier to drink milk out of a bottle? The much larger volume of milk consumed might be due partly to the fact that babies drink *three times faster* out of a bottle than out of a breast. A small study found that two-week-old breastfeeding babies were steadily drinking about 8ml per minute, while the bottle-feeding babies were wolfing down 29ml per minute.[196] Slower feeding may help babies and toddlers learn to respond to their feelings of fullness – and feeding too quickly can certainly lead to overfeeding because they have consumed too much by the time their satiety signals have had time to take effect. We are all familiar with having eaten something too quickly, only to discover a few minutes later that we have eaten too much and we feel bloated and overfull! Eating or feeding slowly is believed to help prevent this.

Breastfed babies probably consume less milk at each feed and drink more slowly, because it's just more difficult to get milk out of a breast than a bottle. Breastfeeding requires a lot more work than bottle-feeding; it's not just about sucking, a baby needs to use both their tongue and their jaw to feed from the breast, and there is no help from gravity. This early feeding experience seems to have a long-term effect on their appetite. One study found that exclusively breastfed babies fed directly from the breast had better awareness of satiety when they were three to six years old, than babies exclusively bottle-fed breast milk.[197] Another study showed that babies fed either breast milk or formula from a bottle gained weight more quickly from birth to one year than those fed directly from the breast,[198] and they also emptied bottles more often in later infancy.[199] 'Bottle-emptying' is a behaviour shown by a baby with an avid appetite. All of this research has come from observational studies rather than experimental studies (such as randomised controlled trials) which means that we cannot know for sure if *how* a baby is fed causes differences in appetite regulation later, or actually it is all down to some other factor that wasn't accounted for. Nevertheless, all of the current research points towards the bottle itself promoting overfeeding. This means that if you are expressing your breast milk and feeding it to your baby in a bottle, be mindful that this makes it easier for him to overfeed.

There are also feeding practices that can encourage overfeeding in *both* breast- and bottle-feeding babies. From as early as six weeks old babies will drink more milk if they are *offered* more. For example, one study asked mothers who were breastfeeding their babies (6–21 weeks old) to express extra breast milk to increase their milk supply, and in response their babies drank more milk and gained more weight.[200] While historically, health professionals considered more weight gain to be a good thing (in the war- and post-war days when weight faltering was a serious concern), by far the bigger concern today for obesity and other health conditions is rapid infant weight gain (which is common), not weight faltering (which is rare). In one study, two-month-old babies who were given more milk in a bottle during each feed also consumed more milk per day (114ml more per day),[201] and the babies fed a larger bottle of milk gained more weight from birth to six months.[202] In fact, exactly the same happens with children and adults when it comes to portion sizes – the more food we are offered, the more we eat.[203]

However, just as there are factors that might disrupt your baby's appetite, there are also strategies that can support good regulation. One key method is 'responsive feeding', and you can do this whether you are breast- or bottle-feeding.

What is Responsive Feeding?

Responsive feeding is a method of feeding whereby the parent feeds in response to their baby's hunger and fullness cues. It involves paying close attention to your baby's hunger and fullness signals – feeding only when your baby indicates that he is hungry and stopping as soon as he indicates he is full. This means not encouraging your baby to finish a bottle of milk or continue to feed on the breast if he indicates that he has had enough. This is supposed to teach a baby to recognise when he is hungry and full, and to respond by taking only as much milk as he needs. If your baby receives milk promptly after indicating hunger and milk stops being offered as soon as he indicates he is full, the theory is that he will learn to associate these two feelings with starting and stopping feeding and will regulate his milk intake appropriately (and later on, his food). This means that you do not feed your baby if he is not hungry and you do not offer milk for any reason other than hunger, such as feeding for comfort or because it fits in with your own plans or a routine. In particular, being fed for comfort may lay the groundwork for emotional eating (eating for comfort) later on in life, either as a child or adult.

The prevailing view is that responsive feeding is much easier for breastfeeding babies than those fed with a bottle. The reason being that the breastfed baby is more 'in charge' of feeding. A breastfeeding baby needs to make a concerted effort to get the milk out of the breast and, given the effort required, he's not going to do it unless he wants it. In contrast, drinking milk out of a bottle is much more passive – it requires virtually no effort from the baby and the milk will even drip into his mouth by itself if the bottle is in the right position. This makes it much easier to coax a baby into having a bit more, even if he's no longer hungry.

Because a mum who is breastfeeding has no idea how much milk her baby has consumed, she has to rely to some extent on her baby's behavioural cues to know when he has had enough (for example, stopping sucking). In contrast to this, parents who are feeding their baby through a bottle can see exactly how much milk the baby has taken, and often use this information to decide if their baby has finished feeding, rather than their baby's fullness signals. In fact, a small study showed that babies were more likely to be cajoled into finishing what's left in the bottle when Mum could clearly see the amount of milk left, than if she couldn't (when there was a cover on the bottle).[204] Research has also indicated that for many parents an empty bottle at the end of a feed is the desired outcome and 15–25 per cent will actively encourage it.[205]

In theory this interferes with the baby's ability to respond to his or her fullness cues, because the parent overrides them. This might mean that the baby is encouraged to continue to feed after he feels full; or doesn't have as much milk as he would like to satisfy his hunger. A chronic pattern of continuing to feed your baby after he has indicated he is full may also increase his responsiveness to food later and his risk of developing a tendency to overeat, or reinforce an already eager appetite. Though it can be quite frustrating if your baby doesn't drink all of the formula in his bottle because it takes time to prepare and costs money (especially if you are using ready-to-feed formula), as you begin to learn how much milk your baby will drink, you can avoid waste by making up less milk for each feed.

A recent review concluded that, on the whole, breastfeeding mums do tend to feed more responsively than those feeding through a bottle (whether using formula or breast milk).[206] This may partly account for the higher milk intake of formula-fed babies compared to breastfed babies from the first few days of life.

Much less is known about how responsive feeding in early infancy affects appetite regulation. A large study of over 1,000 babies showed that those who were frequently encouraged to empty the bottle during early infancy were less sensitive to satiety at six years of age, insofar as they were twice as likely to eat all the food on their plate compared to those who were rarely encouraged to do so.[207] This study suggests a relationship between responsive feeding and self-regulation. However, while researchers and health professionals pretty much universally believe that responsive feeding is crucial for the development of self-regulation skills, far more research is needed to test this theory.

A WORD OF CAUTION FOR BREASTFEEDING MUMS

Breastfeeding may promote good appetite regulation in terms of both the breast milk itself (the 'what') and the very act of feeding from the breast (the 'how'); and, as we have seen, responsive feeding is naturally supported by breastfeeding in comparison to bottle-feeding. Nevertheless, breastfed babies are not all the same; babies who are breastfed can and do differ in their appetites. Some have ravenous appetites for breast milk and will feed at any opportunity, even if they are not hungry, while others are more difficult to feed. This means it is still important to make sure that breastfed as well as formula-fed babies are fed only in response to signals of hunger and allowed to stop when they indicate that they are full.

You may have already read about responsive feeding on the websites of reputable organisations such as the NHS. When it comes to breastfeeding, the description of responsive feeding and the advice given does not completely align with that of researchers in this field. Advice focuses solely on ensuring that a baby is fed as soon as he is hungry, but there is no mention of responding to his satiety cues and making sure that you stop offering your breast when he indicates that he is full. These organisations boldly state that it is not possible to overfeed a breastfeeding baby and as such advocate, and even suggest, breastfeeding for reasons other than hunger:

'It's not possible to overfeed a breastfed baby . . .
Breastfeeding is not only about getting milk into your baby.
Your baby feeds for comfort and reassurance, too.'

'Responsive feeding is also to do with your needs. You may
want to offer a breastfeed if you need to fit in a feed
around other commitments, or if you just want to sit down
and enjoy spending time with your baby.'

NHS[208]

This advice is at odds with our research, which suggests that some breastfed babies have an avid appetite and offering them a feed when they are not hungry may encourage overfeeding. It is our view that feeding only in response to hunger and fullness is important for *both* breast- and bottle-fed babies. It is, of course, important to bond with your baby and to provide physical comfort when needed, but comfort doesn't necessarily need to come in the form of food (see page 187). ESPGHAN also cautions against feeding for comfort.[209]

WEIGHT GAIN

There have been several studies on the link between responsive feeding in early infancy and weight gain or later obesity risk. The most important of these to date was the INSIGHT study, which randomised 145 new mums to a responsive parenting group for one year, in which they were taught to recognise their baby's hunger and satiety cues, to use food *only* for hunger and never as a reward, and never to soothe a distressed but not hungry baby with food.[210] Strategies were also taught for feeding solid foods after milk-feeding. There was also a control group of 146 new mums who didn't receive any information about responsive feeding. At one year, babies in the responsive-parenting group had gained less weight than those in the control group, and this was the same regardless of whether the babies were breast- or formula-fed. Less than 6 per cent of the babies in the intervention group had overweight at one year compared to 13 per cent of the babies in the control group. This well-designed trial provides convincing preliminary evidence that responsive feeding can prevent overweight early on. It also suggests that responsive feeding can reduce excessive weight gain for formula-fed as well as breastfed babies, supporting the view that *how* as well as *what* you feed is important in this respect.

The Challenges of Responsive Feeding

One of the questions that needs to be addressed by research, and hasn't been yet, is whether responsive feeding is always the best strategy. Is it really a case of 'one-size-fits-all'? One of the main concerns is that responsive feeding could actually lead to over-feeding, if parents misinterpret their babies' fussing or crying as hunger cues when in fact the source of their distress is not hunger but some other need. This means it is crucial to understand what hunger cues really look like, as well as satiety cues (see pages 181–4).

But there are other complicated issues as well. Responsive feeding assumes that babies have a perfect appetite-control system already in place; it simply needs to be reinforced by their parents through responding appropriately to their hunger and fullness signals. But our research has shown that it isn't as simple as this. Some babies are naturally hungrier than others and therefore demand more feeds. Should parents always respond to their genuine cries for hunger? Or is it acceptable to withhold milk? On the other end of the spectrum are those babies who have a poor appetite and are undemanding about feeding. Is it right to wait until they signal hunger before offering milk? Or should you try and coax a faddy feeder to take some milk as often as possible to avoid dehydration or weight faltering? These are tricky issues for which science has not yet provided an answer.

In 2013 the National Institute of Health (NIH) in the US held a meeting to advance understanding of the causes of excessive early weight gain.[211] One of the discussions that took place was whether parents should *not* feed infants every time they signal hunger and on occasions withhold food. The conclusion was that more research needs to be undertaken to test out the pros and cons (and feasibility) of such a stance:

'We need to know how to parent infants with different appetites. It is very difficult to know whether *not* feeding a hungry baby is a practical, feasible or reasonable way of managing their risk of obesity.'

Julie Lumeng, Professor of Pediatrics and
Communicable Diseases, University of Michigan

With this in mind, we have considered the difficulties parents face with babies at each end of the spectrum and have outlined some practical, evidence-based advice on pages 173–175.

In our view, too much blame is placed on parents when it comes to feeding and early growth; especially given what we know about the strong genetic influence on early appetite. Some babies are great feeders, while others are a constant worry. Very little research has been done to examine how parents develop their feeding strategies during the early milk-feeding phase. But in Gemini we looked to see whether the extent to which parents restricted milk (the frequency of feeds or the amount during each feed) or pressured their baby to feed was related to characteristics of the baby, such as their birth weight and their appetite, or other things more related to Mum, such as her concern about her baby's under- or overweight and feeding method (breast or bottle). Our findings supported the idea that mums develop their feeding strategies in response to the type of baby they have right from the beginning.[212] Mums whose babies were born with a low birth weight, who had a poor appetite and who Mum worried were underweight were more pressuring in relation to milk-feeding; mums whose babies had a hearty appetite were more restrictive. We found no evidence that bottle-feeding mums exerted more pressure than breastfeeding mums, but they were more likely to be restrictive if they had a baby with a hearty appetite. These findings indicate that right from the beginning, mums are sensitive to their babies' needs and develop appropriate feeding strategies in response.

We followed up this research in Gemini by looking at fussy eating in toddlerhood. Along exactly the same lines we found that parents varied their feeding practices when their two twins differed in how fussy they were.[213] This indicated that faddy eaters prompt their parents to pressure them more, not that pressuring parents end up with faddy eaters. This research helps to combat the pervasive and simplistic view that the way a parent feeds their baby or child causes them to develop certain eating and feeding behaviours.

HUNGRY BABIES

Some babies are born with a larger appetite and will be much more demanding with regard to being fed; we know this is partly due to genetic endowment (see pages 32–5). These babies may cry out of hunger more often and need more milk in order to feel satisfied. In this situation, you have two choices as a parent: either feed your hungry baby or withhold milk/food. Given that we do not yet know the long-term consequences of not allowing a hungry baby to feed until they are full, or the consequences for harm in terms of the emotional bond if a parent doesn't respond sensitively to their baby's needs, this may not seem a reasonable option for parents. And many would find this unacceptable, not only because they feel uncomfortable about not responding to their baby's needs, but because it is simply not feasible to withhold a feed if a baby is hungry.

'I challenge anyone to resist giving a screaming inconsolable baby a bottle in the night.'

Amy, mum of Grace (18 months)

Another consideration is that restricting the frequency of breast-feeds increases the risk of low milk supply for breastfeeding mums. Responsive feeding may still play an important part in ensuring that a hungry baby doesn't overfeed, without having to deny a hungry baby their food. An eager feeder will happily guzzle milk if it's on offer, even if he is not hungry. For these babies it is important for you to wait until your baby signals to you that he feels hungry *before* offering milk. It is also important to be aware of what hunger cues look like and to be able to distinguish hunger cries from other sources of distress (see pages 181–83.

Feeding should not always be the first 'go-to' when your baby is fussing. There are plenty of reasons why babies fuss – it is one of the only ways they can communicate – but crying can indicate many different needs, not just hunger. And inconsolable crying is common during the early period of life (see pages 185–193). Sometimes you will have to use non-food forms of comfort and make sure that you don't routinely feed your baby to sleep or feed him just to keep him quiet. These babies will also have a tendency to feed past satiety if encouraged. For these babies you may need to pay close attention to his fullness signals and stop the feed as soon as your baby indicates fullness so as not to override his satiety and encourage overfeeding, especially if you use a bottle.

'Because my baby was hungry all the time, and I was breast-feeding on demand, I got into the habit of just offering him a feed whenever I heard the slightest whinge and he happily guzzled milk pretty much all day and all night.'

Pippa, mum of Sam (5 years)

BABIES WITH A POOR APPETITE

Some babies have a poor appetite and seem disinterested in (or even dislike) feeding. These babies are far less demanding with regard to being fed, take their time over each feed and may even fall asleep before they finish (although falling asleep on the job is something that all babies tend to do at one time or another!). These babies can be a huge source of anxiety for parents who worry that they aren't getting enough milk. In this case, is it best just to leave it up to your baby to let you know when he is hungry? Some researchers suggest that pressuring a baby or child to eat when he is not hungry or simply doesn't want to feed will lead to problems later on, such as fussiness around food or even food aversion.[214] There is still a strong sense that the way a baby feeds somehow reflects the parents' feeding strategy. However, we know little about the longer-term consequences of pressuring a poor milk feeder, because the research hasn't been done.

For young babies with a poor appetite it would seem reasonable to offer him a feed at regular intervals even if he has not indicated that he is hungry. If your baby rejects the feed, leave it for a while and try again a bit later. If you are concerned that your baby may be underfeeding and is not gaining weight (or is losing weight) then see your GP.

BARRIERS TO FEEDING RESPONSIVELY

Your baby will bring his own little quirks to the table, and you can only do your best when it comes to feeding. The first few weeks and months with a new baby can be overwhelming. Though the advice we are providing in this book is based on evidence, we appreciate that when you have a crying baby and are sleep-deprived, following any advice at all may not always seem practical.

Responsive feeding with a newborn baby can be hard; sometimes it can be difficult to judge if your baby is hungry or not, because you need to take time to get to know him. Not to mention that not all days are the same and babies can be much fussier on some days than others. There are also growth spurts, during which your baby will seem constantly and unfathomably hungry. But research has shown that it does get much easier to spot your baby's cues as he gets older – so don't worry if you can't seem to work him out all the time at the beginning.[215] This is a learning process that you will get better at over time, as you get to know your baby.

While there is widespread support for responsive feeding, some parents cannot/do not feed in this way. The Health Promotion Agency in New Zealand commissioned research in 2014 to find out why first-time mums might not do this so that they could address their concerns.[216] There were two main barriers:

1. A lack of confidence in their ability to read their baby's hunger and satiety cues:

    'I think as a first-time mum it's hard . . . You don't know. You second-guess yourself. And you think they, you know, might be hungry, but what if it's something else?'

    'It's hard to tell what the grumpiness is. It's not any different from, I'm sleepy grumpy, or I've had a hard day grumpy. It's all the same.'

2. A desire to establish a routine as soon as possible and stick to it:

    '[For some mums] it could be strictly routine as maybe like a safety net, because they feel like they're managing if they do that. So this might be quite unnerving if you don't feel supported or encouraged to do it.'

'I find my routine makes things so much easier. Because she knows when food is coming. She doesn't stress out. I don't stress out.'

Some mums in the research indicated that their baby never got to the stage of feeling hungry because they were fed so regularly. A few of the mums also did not believe their baby knew when they were full and some would even continue to eat until they were sick. Most mothers reported feeding their infants and children to a set routine, not based on the baby's or child's hunger cues.

We spoke with one mum who suggested that her baby's feeding cues seemed to diminish as she got older:

'After I gave birth to Julia in the hospital midwives told me what feeding cues look like in a newborn baby. I found it easy to spot them but now when Julia is six weeks she seems to be producing fewer clues or facial/mouth expressions than she used to, so I am feeding her if I feel at least two hours have passed since her last feed or if she is crying despite having a dry nappy and having just slept.'

Marta, mum of Julia (3 months)

Taking into account these concerns, we have put together a detailed, practical guide based on scientific research on how to feed responsively (see below). This advice is applicable for both breast- and bottle-feeding, and for every type of feeder. We know that it can be hard to think about feeding responsively, on top of everything else that is going on in the first few weeks with a newborn. But we hope that the guidance we provide here will provide you with much-needed information and clear, practical instructions that will help you to set your child on the path to a healthy future relationship with food.

How to Feed Responsively

Responsive feeding is providing a prompt and appropriate response to your baby's hunger and satiety cues.* This involves:

- your baby giving you clear, unambiguous hunger and satiety cues

- your accurate interpretation of those cues

- you responding promptly, providing adequate and appropriate nutrition (milk or withdrawal of milk)

- your baby experiencing a predictable response to his signals to you; which is his gateway to learning

Recognising your baby's hunger and fullness signals are the vital first step in feeding responsively. Parents are usually told to 'feed on demand', but if you feed whenever your baby cries this is not necessarily in response to his hunger (crying and soothing are dealt with in detail on pages 185 and 187). Parents need much more information about when and how to feed.

---

* If you are breastfeeding, it is important to feed your baby very regularly during the early weeks (especially the first two weeks) to ensure you establish a good milk supply. Once breastfeeding is established, you'll be able to focus on feeding in response to your baby's cues.

'Many parents are told to feed "on demand" but what is "on demand"? Is it when they wake up from sleep, when they fuss, when they cry, when they get squirmy, or only when they are clearly showing signs of hunger? Because a baby will usually feed in response to any of these behaviours, mothers need more precise guidance that feeding "on demand" should be reserved for hungry babies and not the default response to other normal behaviours.'

Ian Paul, Professor of Pediatrics and Public Health Sciences at Penn State College of Medicine, leader of the INSIGHT study on responsive feeding

Research has shown that parents find it much easier to spot their baby's hunger cues than their fullness cues. The typical hunger cues that parents say they recognise are: crying and fussing (most importantly), and licking their lips. And the most common fullness cues are: pulling away and stopping feeding. We also know that hunger and fullness signals are much easier to interpret as babies and children get older.[217] However, this doesn't mean that responsive feeding isn't possible during the very early weeks and months, and below we provide you with the information you need about how to spot them and how to respond to them. It takes time to learn how to interpret your baby's cues, and this will get easier as you get to know him.

Distinguishing crying for hunger from crying for other reasons is no small task, but there are two concerns about feeding a crying baby who is not hungry:

1. An avid feeder will take the milk anyway and overfeed.

2. A baby may learn to associate distress with being fed, leading to the development of emotional eating later on.

Babies cry for many different reasons. Reasons other than hunger include: fear, anger, boredom, tiredness and other discomfort, such as a wet nappy. They also cry for no apparent reason at all. If feeding is the first 'go-to' response, a parent may end up feeding a non-hungry baby, and on quite a frequent basis. The concern is that a non-hungry baby may learn to associate distress with being fed.

Using alternative soothing techniques will help a non-hungry baby to experience being soothed without being fed; in theory this should help him to learn to self-soothe and return to sleep without being comforted by food. It is important for a baby to learn to use healthy behaviours to deal with emotional distress, such as physical comfort. Responsive feeding is about finding other strategies for comfort that work and understanding how a baby's sleep patterns evolve over the first few weeks and months after birth. It is also good to understand a bit about babies' crying behaviour in the early months. We have provided information about babies' crying patterns over the first few months, and outlined some alternative soothing and calming strategies on pages 185 and 187.

In most cases, after the first few weeks you do not need to wake a sleeping baby for a feed – he will wake up of his own accord when hungry.

'Because most babies lose weight in the first days following birth, paediatricians typically recommend that babies feed 8-12 times per day (every 2–3 hours on average day and night). However, once babies regain that weight over the first week or two, paediatricians often omit telling mothers that feeding this frequently or feeding on a schedule is not necessary. I commonly see parents still waking their baby every three hours at age two months, which is completely unnecessary. In truth, once this initial weight loss is regained, the baby, not the parent, should determine when and how often feedings should occur.'

Ian Paul, Professor of Pediatics and Public Health sciences at Penn State College of Medicine, leader of the INSIGHT study on responsive feeding

There are sometimes situations when this isn't the case (for example, if your baby is unwell or taking medications that make him or her sleepy), in which case your doctor or medical professional should guide you. Otherwise you can trust your baby to let you know.

SIGNS OF HUNGER AND FULLNESS

Recognising hunger and fullness signals in very young babies can be tricky, but it is certainly possible to do this, and from a very young age.

Signs of hunger

There are some pretty universal signs that signal hunger in babies. These are easy to spot once you know what they are, and the signs become clearer as you get to know your baby better. Babies use lots of cues together, or 'clustered cues', to indicate their needs. For example, they may bring their hands to their mouth or face, clench their fingers, flex their arms and legs, root, make sucking noises and breathe quickly. All of these behaviours together indicate that a baby is hungry. A single cue does not necessarily indicate hunger. In particular, crying on its own is not a hunger cue, but rather a distress signal. Hungry babies might cry but they will *also* exhibit other hunger cues.

Early hunger signals (tend to be subtle and primarily oral):

- Stirring from side to side, opening his mouth and turning his head to the side (the 'seeking' or 'rooting reflex')

Active hunger signals (more overt and involve more full-body movements):

- Fussing

- Stretching

- Open-mouth postures and hand–mouth contacts

- Flexion of the hand

- Increased physical movements

Late hunger signals (very overt and tend to be characterised by distress):

- Distressed, intense crying

- Agitated body movements

- Turning red in the face

- Sweating

Note: once your baby is very distressed you will need to soothe him first, before feeding. A baby in a very distressed state is unlikely to feed properly, so it's best to try and calm him down before attempting a feed. Paediatricians recommend that you should hold your baby calmly and even have skin-to-skin contact once he has moved to full-blown crying.[218] (We have provided some detailed tips for how to calm a baby down on pages 187–92.)

Signs of fullness (satiety)

Research has shown that parents and caregivers find satiety signals harder to read and are more likely to miss them.[219] But it is also common practice to encourage babies to continue feeding even after their fullness cues have been noticed. It is important to respond to your baby by stopping the feeding.

Early satiety signals:

- Slows or decreases sucking

- Relaxes/extends arms, legs and fingers

Active satiety signals:

- Stops sucking

- Releases the nipple or teat

- Distracted or pays attention to surroundings more (babies over four months of age)

Late satiety signals:

- Pushes/arches away

- Turns head away from nipple or teat

- Seals lips together (4–7 months of age)

- Falls asleep (0–3 months of age)

TIPS FOR RESPONSIVE BOTTLE-FEEDING

Given that babies are more likely to overfeed when bottle-feeding, we have provided some extra tips below for bottle-feeding babies:

- Be cautious about the amount of formula or breast milk that you put into the bottle at each feed. Do not offer more than is reasonable for a single feed. If your baby indicates that he is still hungry after he has finished the bottle you can still offer more. We have provided evidence-based guidelines on page 202 about the frequency and volume of feeds for babies of different ages.
- If you have a baby who likes to guzzle milk quickly, try using a slower-flowing teat.
- Invite your baby to take the teat of the bottle, rather than force it into his mouth.
- Never add anything to the formula milk (for example, cereal or baby rice). This is not recommended; it may interfere with your baby's appetite regulation and lead to overfeeding, and can cause discomfort for babies aged 0–4 months who are not developmentally ready for non-milk foods.
- Don't prop the bottle up (for example, on a pillow or other surface) when babies are not yet able to hold it themselves.

- Do not put your baby to bed with a bottle as this might make the bottle (and feeding) an emotional comforter. Feeding to soothe may be how the groundwork is laid for emotional overeating in childhood. It may also later make it very difficult to put your baby to bed without a bottle.

- Don't pressure or force your baby to finish the bottle if he indicates he has had enough. Healthy babies know if they are hungry and when they are full. Feeding is not about you controlling your baby's milk intake; it's about trusting your baby to decide for himself. If your baby is pulling away from the teat, crying, closing his lips together and spitting out milk he is telling you he has had enough.

- Pace the feed by stopping to wind periodically.

- Avoid doing anything that might distract you or your baby while feeding (for example, browsing the Internet, texting or watching television). It is important to remain focused on your baby so that you are able to recognise his feeding cues and for your baby not to become distracted. A faddy feeder is easily distracted by things that seem more interesting than feeding (such as watching your phone or iPad), while an avid feeder may struggle to pay attention to his feelings of fullness if distracted by something else.

CRYING

The best available evidence suggests that excessive crying or fussing in the early months is, unfortunately, pretty common[220] – about a quarter of parents with perfectly healthy babies report it[221] – so if your baby never seems to stop crying, you are not alone. Dealing with crying is one of the most challenging experiences of being a new parent, and it's good to make sure you know what to expect during the first few months – not only in relation to feeding, but also for your own sanity.

The usual pattern is for your baby's crying (which will often be inconsolable) to be highest in the first 9 weeks of life and then decrease by the time he is 10–12 weeks old;[222] and it tends to be more common in the late afternoon and evening. *All babies* go through this pattern of crying, but some cry more than others and for some it can involve prolonged, unsootheable and unpredictable bouts of crying. For you as a parent, this can be frustrating and overwhelming. It has been called the 'period of PURPLE crying' by some researchers in the field, which is an acronym for the following features that are typical of this phase and completely normal:[223]

- **P**eak – the crying peaks in the first nine weeks.

- **U**nexpected – the crying bouts are unpredictable.

- **R**esists soothing – nothing you do will stop your baby crying.

- **P**ain-like face – your baby may look like he is in pain, but he's not.

- **L**ong-lasting – the crying seems to go on and on, and can last for five hours per day (and may feel like 24).

- **E**vening – your baby will tend to have these crying bouts in the late afternoon or evening.

How to manage it

It is beyond the scope of this book to go into detail about the methods and the research behind crying and soothing. However, research has suggested that there are two things you can do that might reduce your baby's crying by about 50 per cent:[224]

1. **Feed your baby promptly in response to his cues of hunger**
   This means making sure you get to know your baby's hunger signals and respond to them by offering a feed before he gets too hungry and gets himself in a tizzy, just as we have described above.

2. **Make sure you have lots of physical contact with your baby**
   Ten hours of physical contact per 24-hour period may reduce your baby's overall fussing and crying. And this can be when he is awake or asleep. Skin-to-skin contact is especially important for your baby during his first few days and weeks – this will help him to feel secure and reassured that you are there. It is also recommended that your baby be in the same room as you (not the same bed as this can increase the risk of SIDS[225]) when he sleeps for the first six months.

SOOTHING A NON-HUNGRY, FUSSING BABY

Your baby will still cry from time to time even if you do these two things. This is completely normal, but it doesn't mean that it's not stressful. As time goes on you will get to know your baby's temperament. Some babies are naturally a bit fussier or crankier than others, and there are times when a baby will be more or less fussy than usual. As you get to know your baby, you'll be able to interpret what he needs – whether this is feeding, comfort, a nappy change, entertainment or something else. Some parents claim that over time they get to know what a 'hunger cry' sounds like versus crying for some other reason. This is probably the exception rather than the rule, so don't worry if you can't. In one study the parents who reported being able to identify a hunger cry, were doing it based on the time of day, not the acoustic characteristics of the cry itself.[226] In fact, research on the acoustics of infant crying has shown that parents are no better than inexperienced adults at distinguishing the emotions behind the cries of babies less than six months old – but it gets easier as they get older.[227]

This means the best way to find out what is wrong is by a process of elimination – test one thing at a time to check for a problem – and only feed your baby if he is signalling that he is hungry.

'Although responding will often soothe a baby's crying, parents are only partly in charge of this situation. Some bouts of crying in the first few months are difficult or impossible to soothe, but most of these infants are healthy and grow and develop perfectly normally.'

Ian St James-Roberts, Emeritus Professor of Child Psychology, Institute of Education, University College London

There are a few strategies for calming a crying baby that have some evidence to support their effectiveness (some are for you as much as for him):

1. Using a dummy
Dummies have gone in and out of fashion over the years, but there is enough evidence to suggest that they are

worth using to try and calm your baby if he is fussing, and routinely when he is put down for a sleep. Paediatricians widely regard sucking as one of the best possible ways to calm a crying baby – it is also a potent pain relief for young babies – and a dummy will probably satisfy your baby's need or desire to suck without providing unnecessary milk (through what is called 'non-nutritive' sucking).

What's more, there is another big benefit too: the American Academy of Pediatrics (AAP) now recommends offering your baby a dummy during a nap and at bedtime to reduce the risk of sudden infant death syndrome (SIDS).[228] A review suggested that for every 2,733 babies who are given a dummy when put to sleep, one SIDS death could be prevented.[229] The risk of SIDS is highest during the first six months, after which dummy use doesn't really provide much benefit. However, be aware that it may also increase the risk of minor infections slightly (such as ear infections), so weaning your baby off a dummy after six months is probably wise, and is recommended. It is also recommended that a baby doesn't use a dummy past two years of age to reduce the risk of oral problems developing.

You may have heard that using a dummy too early can interfere with breastfeeding, the theory being that sucking on a dummy is different to sucking on a breast. But a review of four randomised controlled trials (the highest-quality evidence) found no evidence for this – there was no difference in the breastfeeding rates of babies who were randomised to use a dummy and those who weren't.[230] So this is probably a myth. Nevertheless, we would suggest that you only introduce a dummy once breastfeeding has been properly established. And do bear in mind that not all babies will respond well to a dummy, so don't force it if your baby rejects it, but it is worth a try. If you do use one, make sure you offer it consistently at every sleep (day and night) and sterilise it as you would a bottle.

2. Swaddling

One of the oldest tricks in the book is swaddling (wrapping your baby in a cloth or blanket to restrict their movement) – it was used almost universally before the eighteenth century, then went out of fashion, but is now coming back into vogue in the UK (and other countries). In fact, the demand for swaddling clothes increased by 61 per cent in the UK from 2010 to 2011.[231] People have very different views on swaddling, so we looked into whether it really works and is safe. A review of all studies on swaddling, including nine high-quality randomised controlled trials, concluded that swaddling is an effective strategy both for calming a baby (especially one who cries excessively) and promoting sleep, when done correctly.[232] However, another review also found that swaddling is linked to an increased risk of SIDS.[233] So, if you swaddle your baby it's important to follow the recommendations issued by the AAP to ensure that it is done properly and as safely as possible.[234]

- Place your baby on his back ('supine position'), NEVER on his front ('prone position') or side. In fact, this is standard advice whether or not you swaddle your baby – a baby who is placed on his front to sleep is at increased risk of SIDS[235]. Don't swaddle your baby if he is old enough to roll onto his front (this can start happening from around two months of age). Swaddling should only be used for very young babies.

- Make sure you only swaddle your baby's top half and allow his hips and knees to move freely – his legs should be able to bend up and out at the hips. This is because traditional swaddling (which binds the legs straight and together) can lead to problems with hip development. If you buy swaddling clothes, make sure they have a loose pouch or sack for your baby's legs and that he is able to move his hips freely.

- Never cover your baby's head if you swaddle him, because this may increase his risk of SIDS and over-heating. It is recommended that he is only swaddled in a light cotton blanket or muslin from the shoulders down.

- Don't swaddle your baby too tightly, but ensure that the blanket is securely fastened so it can't come undone. This will protect him from accidental suffocation and respiratory infections.

3. Close physical contact

There is plenty of evidence that babies like close physical contact.[236] You can either use a good old-fashioned sling or just hold your baby close to you – skin-to-skin contact is especially comforting for very young babies. You can also try picking your baby up and putting him on your shoulder which gives him a change of scene – sometimes the novelty factor will help, at least for a bit. If not, you can move gently, swaying or rocking him, which may calm him down – but bear in mind that too much rocking or singing might also stimulate him and keep him awake. While holding your baby try to keep calm yourself (easier said than done at times!) as babies pick up on others' stress, just as we do.

4. Leaving him in a safe place (his crib or cot) and taking some time out

If all else has failed and you are at the end of your tether, paediatricians recommend that you should leave your baby in a safe place (such as his crib or cot) and take a few minutes to calm down and collect yourself.[237] Then go back and check on him once you are feeler calmer. This is perfectly okay, and very much needed sometimes.

NIGHT-TIME WAKINGS

You don't necessarily have to feed your baby every time he wakes during the night. You only need to feed him if he indicates that he is hungry. This will be a lot of the time when he is really tiny, but less of the time as he gets older. Instead of feeding being your first 'go-to', try the following:

- Wait for a couple of minutes to see if he will settle on his own (lengthening the wait time as he gets a bit older).
- If not, go in and try soothing techniques besides feeding, if he is not indicating any signs of hunger.
- Feed him if he is hungry.
- Make sure that night-time visits are short and quiet so that he doesn't expect stimulation time in the middle of the night.

The researchers who coined the phrase the 'period of purple crying' say one thing is pretty certain when it comes to young babies and crying: 'some things work some of the time, but nothing works all of the time'.[238] So don't feel that you have done something wrong, or that you are failing your baby as a parent, if you cannot seem to stop him crying no matter what you do. However, if you are worried that something is very wrong then take your baby to your GP. There are a few things that can cause excessive crying that your doctor will be able to rule out, if you are worried. These can include under- and overfeeding (both of which are dealt with below), reflux, allergy and infection. The latter three are only present in about 10 per cent of babies who cry excessively[239]. If you are struggling to cope with excessive crying, there are some useful resources available online that provide more detailed information about crying and fussing, and strategies that you can use to deal with it (see Useful Resources, page 367).

Underfeeding and Overfeeding

One of the concerns with responsive feeding is how to know whether you are giving your baby enough or too much milk. Underfeeding is when a baby is not consuming sufficient calories for healthy growth, while overfeeding is consuming too many calories leading to excessive weight gain. One of the biggest concerns of new parents is whether or not their baby is getting enough milk; few are concerned about overfeeding. Overfeeding is, in fact, more common, but underfeeding is more serious in the short term. Overfeeding is probably more of a problem with bottle-fed babies, but the issue of whether or not it is possible to overfeed a breastfeeding baby is a contentious one (see pages 168–70). And breastfed babies commonly experience a form of overfeeding, called 'functional lactose overload', which we discuss in more detail on page 197.

UNDERFEEDING

Many parents become concerned if their baby does not drink as much milk as expected, or as much as they were drinking a few days before. There is some developmental variation in the amount of milk a baby needs and so a reduction in milk intake can simply be a reflection of the growth process. For example, at around four to five months of age there is a drop in the amount of energy needed (compared to three months) as a baby's rate of growth slows down. Nevertheless, there are some clear signs that point to underfeeding:

- Fewer than 5 wet nappies in 24 hours (for babies older than five days)

- The baby is restless, unsettled, irritable and wakeful

- Extremely underweight babies can become excessively sleepy and non-demanding

- Poor (or no) weight gain over a number of consecutive weeks

And here are some causes of underfeeding:

- Poor appetite (high satiety sensitivity, low food responsiveness, slow feeding, low enjoyment of feeding)

- Rigid feeding schedules, rather than feeding in response to a baby's hunger cues

- Premature and unwell babies may not have an effective sucking ability

- Congenital birth defects that affect ability to suck effectively (for example, tongue tie, cerebral palsy, cleft palate)

- Incorrect preparation of formula (too much water to powder)

- Giving a baby too much water

- A very sleep-deprived baby can be too exhausted to demand feeds, feed effectively or wake during the night for feeds

What to do:

- Make an appointment with your GP to have your baby assessed for a physical cause.

- If you have done this and there is no clear physical cause, ensure that you pay close attention to your baby's hunger cues. If he is not providing obvious hunger cues, then offer feeds at regular three to four hour intervals during the day to see if he will take one.

- Make sure you also still respond appropriately to his fullness cues and stop the feed as soon as he indicates that he wants to stop. Don't try to force your baby to finish a feed, even if you are worried about his weight gain, as this can lead to a feeding aversion.

- Make sure he is getting sufficient sleep.

OVERFEEDING

Overfeeding (or 'over-nutrition') is a common problem, especially for bottle-fed newborn babies (0–3 months old). It is a problem that is overlooked, because of the emphasis that is still placed on babies gaining sufficient weight, even if weight gain is excessive. Though it is easier for bottle-fed than breastfed babies to overfeed, it is still possible for a breastfed baby to overfeed of his own accord, if he has a voracious appetite for milk. The main symptom of appetite-based overfeeding is rapid weight gain (see page 92).

Causes of overfeeding include:

- Baby has an avid appetite and the parent offers feeds too frequently and not simply in response to hunger cues.

- Baby has an avid appetite and the parent offers too much milk in the bottle during feeds (for example, more than he needs/is recommended – see guidelines below).

- The parent doesn't recognise satiety cues.

- The parent actively encourages baby to feed past satiety.

What to do:

- Feed responsively – only feed when your baby indicates he is hungry and stop when he indicates he is full.

- Don't offer too much milk in the bottle at each feed (see Table 2 for how much milk to feed).

- Check he isn't feeding too quickly. If necessary, slow down feeds by stopping and taking regular winding breaks, or use a slower-flowing teat if bottle-feeding.

Functional lactose overload

Another form of overfeeding that is less well known and under-researched, is called 'functional lactose overload' – a common problem related to breast milk oversupply syndrome and over-feeding in formula-fed infants.[240] It is estimated that as many as two thirds of breastfed babies experience episodic symptoms associated with this form of overfeeding in the first three months, with a small percentage being affected up to six months. It can also occur in bottle-fed babies, but we don't know how common it is. Functional lactose overload (not to be confused with lactose *intolerance*, which is rare) is thought to occur when babies consume a large amount of lactose and are unable to digest it properly. In formula-fed babies, this can happen from overfeeding – simply consuming too much formula milk and becoming over-loaded with the sheer amount of lactose consumed. In breastfeeding babies researchers have proposed that it occurs when they don't get enough fat from the breast milk. The fat content of breast milk changes over the course of a feed, with the hind milk containing more fat than the fore milk (see page 134). This creamier hind milk slows down the transit speed of the milk through the intestine, allowing the lactose to be absorbed and stimulating the release of a satiety hormone called 'cholecysto-kinin', which makes the baby feel full. If a mum has an oversupply of milk or she switches her baby onto the other breast too soon, her baby won't get enough of the creamier hind milk. A recent paper on this topic suggested that some common breastfeeding practices may be contributing to functional lactose overload:[241]

- *Limiting feeds to a defined period and not allowing for cluster feeds*
  Cluster feeds are when a baby feeds every 30–60 minutes, usually during the evening. The milk your baby takes during these feeds tends to be low in volume and high in fat.

- *Always offering the fuller side first*
  This means that your baby will always get a lot of the high-volume and low-fat milk.

- *Always feeding from both sides*
  Although this is very important in the early days and weeks to get your milk supply up, it can mean that your baby doesn't get as much of the creamy high-fat hind milk, which he enjoys if he is able to finish all of the milk in one breast.

- *Expressing milk and feeding it through a bottle*
  A breast pump is not all that great at getting the hind milk out.

If the milk goes through your baby's intestine too quickly, he won't feel properly sated and the lactose won't be fully digested; instead it will ferment in his colon.[242] Babies with functional lactose overload cry and fuss a lot more, which isn't in the least bit surprising when you read the list of symptoms below! Functional lactose overload can lead to excessive weight gain, but not always; because the excess nutrients are not always digested and are sometimes excreted. This, according to these researchers, can lead to symptoms arising from fermentation of undigested lactose in the baby's large intestine (hence why overfeeding is often called 'lactose overload') and include:

- Poor satiety and wanting to feed frequently

- Crying

- Milk regurgitation

- Belching due to swallowing a lot of air while feeding too quickly

- Frequent sloppy, foul-smelling bowel motions if formula-fed; watery, explosive bowel motions if breastfed

- Extreme flatulence

- Bloating and cramps leading to fussing, crying and irritability

- Sleep disturbance

Ironically, a mum with oversupply syndrome may think she has an undersupply of milk, because her baby always wants to feed. But, according to the theory, repeated low-fat feeds will only aggravate the problem. Researchers in this field claim that functional lactose overload is entirely rectifiable through breastfeeding-management techniques – it doesn't signal an inherent problem with Mum's milk, nor does it indicate any type of lactose intolerance in the baby. Functional lactose overload is a poorly recognised problem among health professionals and one that is often missed or over-looked when there are feeding problems.[243] The Australian Breastfeeding Association have some tips on their website for feeding strategies that can be introduced to resolve it,[244] but it is best to seek advice from an international board-certified lactation consultant if you are concerned about this because there is unlikely to be a 'one-size-fits-all' solution. Tailored advice for you and your baby will be much more effective. Do bear in mind, though, that lots of these symptoms are common and will happen from time to time anyway. But lots of them together, and for several days or weeks continually, is a sign that there might be a problem. Also bear in mind that the science around this is sparse.

How Much and How Often Babies Need to Feed

Below we provide guidelines for the frequency and volume of milk that the average baby needs to consume during the first six months. These will provide you with a rough idea of whether or not your baby seems to be feeding okay. However, please bear in mind that these are just guidelines, not a hard and fast rule, as all babies are different. The key advice is still to trust your baby and feed responsively.

How much and how often your baby needs feeding during the first six months will depend on their age, sex, size (body weight) and their individual appetite. Very young babies have a tiny stomach – about the size of a cherry – and are growing very quickly, so need small feeds very frequently. As they mature they are able to take larger feeds and their growth rate slows down slightly as well; this means they don't need to feed quite as often. Boys tend to be born slightly heavier than girls and this weight difference remains, so on average boys need a little more milk than girls. Breastfed babies tend to be a little smaller than formula-fed babies and tend to grow more slowly; so *supposedly* formula-fed babies need more calories. The same is true for all babies born slightly heavier – bigger babies have higher energy requirements than smaller babies, so need more milk both to maintain their weight and to grow.

In 2011 the Scientific Advisory Committee on Nutrition (SACN) provided detailed guidance on recommended energy intakes per day for infants during the first few months of life (shown in Table 4, page 362). The recommendations vary for breast- and formula-fed infants.

In reality it is impossible to know how many calories your baby is consuming if he is breastfed, even if you are expressing, because breast milk varies in calories over the course of a feed, and from one feed to the next. Once breastfeeding is properly established, each breast contains about 180ml milk, which is far more than most babies would consume during a single feed.[245] But the storage capacity of a breast varies from woman to woman (from about 75ml to 380ml). So while it is important to keep an eye on the number of feeds your baby is taking, making sure your baby is gaining weight at an optimal rate is the best indication that feeding is going well. Weight gain is discussed in detail in Chapter 3.

For formula-fed babies, it is possible, in theory, to work out how much milk to feed your baby each day. But translating energy requirements for babies of different ages into the right number of feeds per day, the amount of milk per feed and the total amount of milk per day is a tricky business. For a start, the guidelines provided by manufacturers vary from one brand to another. On top of this, different brands don't always describe the same ages making it virtually impossible to compare.

In fact, First Steps Nutrition have highlighted that manufacturer guidelines are not completely in line with best practice guidance.[246] They suggest *too few* feeds (with a larger volume per feed) during the first few weeks and the suggested volumes at each age fit bottle size rather than the energy requirements of the baby. Offering very young babies too large a volume of milk at each feed can be problematic on two counts:

1. The baby consumes too much milk (more than is needed) at each feed, leading to overfeeding and risk of excessive weight gain (see page 196).

2. The baby can't manage the larger volume of milk offered (and shouldn't necessarily be consuming that much all in one go), and parents feel anxious.

First Steps Nutrition have used SACN's information on energy requirements to develop guidelines for *how many* feeds and *how much* milk at each feed babies should be consuming during the first six months.[247] These are shown in the table below. The guidance on how much and how often to feed takes into account the smaller amount of milk required during the first two weeks. As babies mature over the first few months they are able to take more milk at each feed and therefore require fewer feeds.

However, bear in mind that these are *just guidelines*. The appetites of different babies can vary and change over time. It is important not to become fixated on exact amounts and numbers of feeds, as long as your baby is growing and developing well. *How* you feed, and feeding responsively, is as important as *what* and *how much* you feed.

TABLE 2: MILK-FEEDING GUIDANCE FROM BIRTH TO SIX MONTHS[248]

Age	Feeding Guidance	Suggested intake per day
Birth and first few days	At least 8 feeds a day, maybe 10ml per feed	Around 80ml colostrum
3–4 days to 2 weeks	7–8 feeds per day increasing to 60–70ml per feed	420–560ml per day
2–8 weeks	6–7 feeds per day 75–105ml per feed	450–735ml per day
2–3 months (9–14 weeks)	5–6 feeds per day 105–180ml per feed	525–1,080ml per day

3–5 months (15–25 weeks)	5 feeds per day 180–210ml per feed	900–1,050ml per day
About 6 months (26 weeks)	4 feeds per day 210–240ml per feed	840–960ml per day

Keep a little diary – on your phone or on a pad of paper – of your baby's feeding patterns, sleeping patterns and behaviours such as crying. This will help you to spot patterns in his behaviour and will help you to get to know your baby. It might take some time but you will learn what his feeding and sleeping patterns are, and you can react accordingly. No one will know your baby better than you do.

THE BOTTOM LINE

- Not all babies are the same when it comes to milk – some will happily guzzle milk whenever it is offered; others don't seem to want it at all.

- *How* to feed is about understanding what type of feeder your baby is and feeding him appropriately, using responsive feeding strategies.

- This means getting to know your baby and his feeding styles right from the beginning.

- Never encourage or force your baby to carry on feeding when he has indicated that he is full – this will lead to overfeeding for an avid feeder, and can lead to food aversion for a baby with a poor appetite.

- It is easier to overfeed a baby through a bottle than from your breast, but it is still possible to overfeed a breast-feeding baby.

- Crying a lot is very common during the first three months – it can be incredibly stressful if excessive, but most of the time it doesn't mean there is anything wrong with your baby, and it doesn't necessarily mean he is hungry.

- Don't use feeding as your 'go-to' strategy to soothe your baby if he is crying – only offer him milk if you think he is hungry.

Introducing Solid Foods

Introducing solid foods (known as 'weaning' or 'complementary feeding') after you have been feeding your baby only milk can seem like a daunting task. There is a lot of information out there on weaning – when to start, which foods to start with and how to do it – and this can be confusing. We want to help you navigate what can be a tricky topic; bringing to bear the research we have done ourselves and the studies we have read. In Part 3 we will provide you with advice on solids – *when*, *what* and *how* to introduce them, based on what the science says.

Weaning can be an exciting time for a baby – his diet finally deviates from the monotony of milk and he begins to experience a whole range of new textures and flavours. But it can be stressful for some parents, especially when things don't go as planned. For example, when your baby refuses to try certain foods or doesn't seem to be eating anything at all. We will guide you through every aspect of the weaning process and will offer practical advice that we hope will reduce the chance of your baby becoming excessively fussy, maximise his preference for healthier foods, such as vegetables, and enable him to develop a varied diet that will set him up for many years to come.

Our aim is to ensure that you meet your baby's changing

nutritional needs and support him in developing his ability to self-regulate his food intake, helping him to grow up healthy, happy and with a good relationship with food.

CHAPTER 7

When to Introduce Solid Foods

The age at which to introduce solid foods is one of the most debated topics in infant nutrition. The World Health Organization (WHO) recommends exclusively breastfeeding until six months of age because breast milk protects against infection among other benefits. The UK's Department of Health also recommends waiting until your baby is six months old before weaning to ensure that his digestive system is ready. There is general agreement that babies' iron stores start to deplete at around four to six months of age, which introduces concerns about iron deficiency (anaemia), especially for exclusively breastfed infants, because breast milk is low in iron, and this is around the time that a baby needs to start sourcing his iron from food.[249] However, the exact age at which solid foods should first be introduced is hotly debated, leading to the 'Weanling's Dilemma': on the one hand, the concern that introducing solid foods before six months may displace breastfeeding and, as breast milk provides immunisation for babies, there is the possibility that early introduction of solid food could increase the risk of infection; and on the other hand, the concern that milk alone is insufficient to satisfy a baby's energy and nutrient requirements beyond four months of age. The immunisation issue is less relevant for babies who are formula-fed – formula milk does not protect against infection – and the WHO regards 'any fluid or food other than breast milk' as a 'complementary' food. Formula-fed infants technically therefore receive complementary foods at the point they start having formula milk. The recommendations are therefore difficult to apply to formula-fed infants and the majority of babies have received some formula milk before they are six months old; only 1 per cent of babies are still exclusively breastfed in the UK at six months of age.[250]

The problem with the guidelines is that they imply a one-size-fits-all approach and fail to consider the fact that all babies are different. Many parents in the UK are not still breastfeeding at six months, so if your baby is on formula do you still need to wait until six months to move him on to solid food? And what about parents who think their baby is ready for food earlier than six months? In some other countries, it is considered acceptable to introduce solid food between four and six months of age. The UK Infant Feeding Survey in 2010 found that 75 per cent of parents had offered solid foods by the time their baby was five months old.[251]

What Does the Evidence Say?

Milk can certainly provide sufficient energy for a baby who is four to six months old, even if he is big and growing quickly.[252] In fact, milk is a far better source of energy than solid food when babies are very young. This is because babies won't actually get many calories from food in the early stages; weaning is more about getting experience with tastes and textures, than wolfing down lots of food. So your baby doesn't need to be weaned, simply because he is big.

It is generally agreed that weaning before 17 weeks of age (four months) can be harmful to your baby. There has been research to suggest that introducing solid foods before 17 weeks is associated with increased risk of allergy and obesity in childhood.[253] There does not, however, appear to be any strong evidence that introducing solid food *from* 17 weeks of age is harmful.[254] A review of three randomised controlled trials (the highest quality evidence) that were carried out to explore outcomes among exclusively breastfed babies who were introduced to solid foods *earlier* than six months of age (at approximately 4 months/17 weeks) compared to those introduced to solid foods *at* six months found no difference in growth between the two groups.[255] However, babies introduced to food earlier than six months had higher iron levels. Iron is important for the development of red blood cells which deliver oxygen to organs and tissues in the body and is therefore very important as your baby develops (see page 62 for more on this). While larger trials are needed to investigate this further, the current research suggests that there is unlikely to be any harm in introducing solids earlier than six months, but not before 17 weeks, if you feel your baby is ready (see page 215 for signs your baby is ready); but we would recommend discussing this with your GP before offering your baby solid foods.

If you are exclusively breastfeeding, waiting until six months may be beneficial in terms of protecting against infection and maximising all of the other benefits that your baby receives from breast milk (such as brain development). However, because weaning allows the opportunity to introduce iron-rich foods, you should aim to start introducing solids no later than six months if your baby is healthy. The WHO recommends that you continue breastfeeding alongside the introduction of solid foods, up to two years or beyond.

Can Weaning Start Too Late?

Just as introducing solids too early can be detrimental to your baby, it is also important not to leave it too late. The European Society for Paediatric Gastroenterology, Hepatology and Nutrition (ESPGHAN) committee on nutrition recommends that complementary foods (foods and drinks other than breast or formula milk) can be introduced after four months (from 17 weeks) and *no later than six months.*[256]

Learning to chew and swallow are a crucial part of your baby's development. The way that the muscles of the mouth and tongue are used to drink milk differs greatly from the processes required to eat solid food, even when it is puréed. Introducing solid food at the right time (approximately six months) therefore helps your baby develop his mouth and tongue muscles to learn how to eat. However, the training that your baby undergoes when learning to eat solid foods also helps him to develop the necessary muscles for speech. If you leave weaning too late you may risk the chance of your child having impaired oral development. Research also suggests that babies who are introduced to solid foods after one year are less accepting of new textures.[257] This is thought to have a long-lasting impact and points towards the importance of introducing texture by 12 months at the very latest. If your baby is six months old and not yet showing signs that they are ready, seek advice from your health visitor or GP.

Some researchers have also suggested that there may be a period during which babies are more accepting of new *tastes* (between four and seven months of age). For example, one study conducted in the UK examined whether the age of weaning (either before five and a half months of age or after) influenced acceptance of vegetables in a group of 60 babies.[258] Over a period of nine days, half the babies in each age group were given either a variety of vegetables (courgette, parsnip and sweet potato) or a single vegetable (carrot) and then their acceptance of a new vegetable (pea) was assessed. The babies that were given the variety of vegetables after five and a half months ate more pea purée than those given a single vegetable but the younger infants were accepting of the new vegetables regardless of exposure to either variety or a single vegetable. This suggested two things:

1. There may be a window for the acceptance of new tastes or flavours.

2. Babies that are weaned at six months or later might benefit from being given a variety of tastes rapidly.

However, this was a very small study and far more research is needed to confirm the idea that there is a window for taste preferences.

Every baby is unique so it is difficult to recommend a definitive age to start weaning. We feel that age is not the only factor that should determine when you start introducing solids. Instead it is important to look out for signs that your baby is ready for solid food.

WHEN TO INTRODUCE LUMPS AND TEXTURES

The UK Scientific Advisory Committee on Nutrition (SACN) recommends that babies progress from smooth foods to lumpy foods and different textures over the course of weaning,[259] but does not provide any guidance on how quickly this needs to happen, due to lack of evidence. Unfortunately, there have been few studies of the age of introduction of lumps and the acceptance of food later. However, a large study of over 8,000 British babies, called the Avon Longitudinal Study of Parents and Children (ALSPAC), showed that children who were introduced to foods with lumps between 6 and 9 months had a more varied diet at 15 months and 7 years of age, and fewer feeding difficulties (not eating enough, refusing food, being choosy with food, overeating and difficult to get into a feeding routine) at 7 years, than children who were introduced to lumps after 10 months.[260]

The problem with this study is that it was observational rather than experimental (such as a randomised controlled trial). This means that it could have been some other unmeasured factor that caused the feeding difficulties in the children introduced to lumps later, rather than the timing of the introduction of lumpy food per se. For example, parents whose babies were genetically predisposed to have a poorer appetite and be faddy eaters may have delayed offering them lumpy foods until after 10 months; but these babies were more likely to grow into picky eaters with poorer appetites anyhow, by virtue of their genetic endowment. Nevertheless, given that there is no harm in introducing your baby to lumpy foods from six months of age, it is probably a good idea to move your baby onto lumps as soon as he indicates he is ready, and not to leave it too late. Parents who use 'baby-led weaning' introduce lumps and textures right from the off, and this is perfectly fine (see page 220).

KEY SIGNS YOUR BABY IS READY FOR SOLIDS

Generally there are three key signs that you can look out for to help you decide whether your baby might be ready to move on from milk to solid food:

1. He can sit upright and hold his head up. This is important to ensure he can swallow food.
2. He has good hand–eye coordination so he can look at food, pick it up and put it in his own mouth.
3. He can swallow food. If your baby is not ready he will use his tongue to push the food back out of his mouth (this is known as the 'tongue thrust reflex').

If your baby is showing all of the above signs, and is six months old, then you can feel confident that he is ready to start solids. However, if these signs are present before your baby is six months old it is probably worth speaking with your GP or health visitor before offering solid food.

Myth Busting

The three signs outlined above are the most common ways to tell that your baby is ready to start weaning. There are some things that are often mistaken as signs a baby is ready, including:

- Chewing fists. To eat food your baby needs to be able to move his tongue to the back of his mouth and swallow. If your baby is chewing on his fist, this does not tell you he is able to swallow; he might just be teething.

- Reaching for food. It is normal for babies to be interested in new things and this on its own does not tell you that your baby is ready to eat what you are eating.

- Waking in the night when he used to sleep through. Research suggests that parents will offer solid foods before six months because they believe it will help their baby sleep longer. The UK Infant Feeding Survey in 2010, for example, found that 26 per cent of parents did so for this reason, but there is no evidence that babies who start on solid foods at a younger age sleep any better than babies given solid foods later.[261] There can be lots of reasons why babies wake in the night; it does not necessarily mean that they need additional food.

- Wanting extra milk feeds. This means that your baby is hungry or thirsty but it does not have to mean that he needs more than just milk.

These are normal baby behaviours and, unless they are occurring with the three key signs listed in the box on page 215, your baby is not necessarily ready to move on from milk. What's important is whether your baby's digestive system is ready for solid foods, not how big or small he is.

PREMATURE BABIES

Premature babies often have difficulty managing lumpy foods and it is thought that introducing solid food to premature babies too early may contribute to the development of food fussiness. If your baby was premature, we would recommend waiting until six months of age and speaking with your GP or health visitor before introducing solid foods. As mentioned earlier, though, solid foods should be introduced by 12 months at the very latest.

THE BOTTOM LINE

- Weaning is a crucial period for establishing acceptance of tastes and textures and speech development.

- Introducing solids before 17 weeks could be harmful.

- Do not delay weaning beyond six months of age if your baby is healthy.

- Breastfeeding alongside solid foods will ensure that your baby continues to receive the benefits of breast milk.

- Look out for signs your baby is ready for solid food. If this is before six months speak to your GP or health visitor.

CHAPTER 8

How to Introduce Solid Foods

As well as having to think about *when* to introduce solid food, another decision is *how* you're going to do it. The two main methods used in the UK are spoon-feeding your baby (puréed or mashed) food and baby-led weaning (BLW). We have described the two methods below, including the evidence for each, so you can make an informed decision on which is best for you and your baby.

Spoon-Feeding

This traditional method of weaning involves gradually moving a baby from milk to solid food by puréeing foods and feeding them to him with a soft spoon. Babies are then moved onto thicker textures (mashed foods rather than purées) and this way they gradually learn how to move food around in their mouth and swallow it. Eventually they are able to chew food into smaller pieces and can be given soft finger foods. Advocates of this approach suggest it is a smooth transition from liquid to solid foods and the baby develops the oral skills necessary for safer eating. The Infant Feeding Survey 2010 found that 94 per cent of the infants in the study received purées as first foods.[262]

Spoon-feeding allows you to see how much your baby is eating and means that you know he is getting energy and nutrients, which can be reassuring. However, it can be time-consuming preparing purées from scratch and costly if you buy ready-made ones. In addition, it has been suggested that it is possible to overfeed your baby if you control the spoon. But just as is the case with milk-feeding, this depends on *how* you feed your baby. In Chapter 6 we covered some of the ways to tell if your baby is full or if he is hungry when he is milk-feeding. The same principles apply with weaning – it is crucial to feed *responsively*, whichever method you decide to use. Feed your baby promptly when he indicates that he is hungry and pay close attention to his satiety signals so that you stop feeding when he is full. This will help your baby to develop good appetite regulation when he moves on to solid food. We will explain how to do this in detail from page 226.

'It was difficult sticking to my own decisions and not conforming or giving in to peer pressure. I wanted to purée all the food for Grace and didn't want to do baby-led weaning. A lot of my friends would make comments about babies having "mush" as I was feeding Grace her puréed peas or Brussels sprouts! I didn't let it bother me and still stuck to what I was doing, but there was an ounce of me that felt like I wasn't conforming to the most recent weaning technique.'

Amy, mum of Grace (18 months)

Baby-Led Weaning

Baby-led weaning (BLW) has become quite popular in recent years and it does what it says on the tin – the baby takes the lead in the feeding process. The term was originally coined by Gill Rapley, a former health visitor and midwife. The basis of this method is that you decide *what* to offer, but your baby feeds himself. In theory, this means that your baby decides whether or not to eat the food at all, how much of the food to eat and how quickly to eat it. Parents often provide chunks of soft food or finger food and their baby explores the food by touching it, putting it in their mouth and feeding themselves. It is therefore recommended that you wait until six months of age if you decide to do BLW, by which age most babies are able to do this. BLW advocates suggest this approach promotes greater participation in family meals, which is a great way for babies to imitate healthy eating behaviours and learn how adults eat. It is thought to provide babies with exposure to family foods and helps a child become independent – developing skills such as hand–eye coordination – and learn by themselves when they are hungry and full. In addition, it has been suggested that babies may accept textures more readily as proper fully formed foods (with all their textures and lumps) are introduced immediately, rather than purées.

This method is less time-consuming than preparing purées from scratch but it is messier and it is not always possible to see how much your baby has actually eaten. Be prepared for a lot of the food to end up on the floor! It is also important to keep in mind that it can be unsafe to provide your baby with finger foods if he isn't yet ready. So it is important to consider his readiness cues, as opposed to his age, in order to introduce solid foods safely (see page 215). Babies who are developmentally delayed with motor skills, such as crawling or walking, might struggle with BLW as their hand–eye coordination may also be delayed. Some parents are concerned about the possibility of their baby choking with BLW, though there is currently no evidence to suggest that choking is more likely with BLW than with spoon-feeding.[263] However, as with spoon-feeding, it is important to ensure your baby is sitting upright and is supervised at all times while eating.

Whichever weaning method you choose, it is important to know the difference between choking and gagging. During weaning, babies will often gag, usually because the food is cold, they have too much of it in their mouth or they don't like what they are eating. Gagging is a very natural reflex in babies, designed to bring up whatever is in their throat, and will involve the child coughing and spluttering. It can be quite frightening for parents but it is nothing to worry about and, crucially, it is very different to choking. Choking is when something is stuck in the back of the baby's throat, blocking their airways and stopping them from breathing. If your child is choking, there will be no sound, your child may begin to turn blue, they will look frightened and may put their arms out to you looking for help. The NHS website provides guidance on how to help a choking baby and the Red Cross have a short film. We would advise all parents to look at these resources (see 367–8).

TOP TIPS TO AVOID CHOKING

1. Always supervise your child when he is feeding.
2. Ensure your child is sitting upright in a high chair when feeding.
3. Be aware of problematic foods such as cherry tomatoes and grapes – these should be cut in half lengthways, or even in quarters, to avoid the risk of choking.

4. Whole nuts, including peanuts, should not be given to children under the age of five because of the risk of choking.

5. Know the difference between choking and gagging: choking is life-threatening, while gagging is a normal part of experiencing foods for the first time.

Which Weaning Method to Choose?

There have been very few well-designed studies comparing BLW and spoon-feeding. So, in spite of its growing popularity, the benefits that advocates of the BLW approach promote are based largely on intuition not evidence. A major problem with the few (mostly small) studies that have been conducted in the past is that mums who choose BLW often differ in important ways to the general population who use traditional spoon-feeding – on average they breastfeed for longer, are wealthier, more educated, older, more likely to be married and more confident.[264] This means that we can't know what the impact of BLW really is on the baby, because all of these other factors probably influence the baby's development as well.

However, a large, well-designed randomised controlled trial was published recently that looked at whether BLW really results in a lower risk of overweight than spoon-feeding, whether it affected appetite regulation and whether or not babies are more likely to choke.[265] This two-year trial, called BLISS (Baby-Led Introduction to Solids), randomised 105 women to receive routine midwifery care and another 101 to receive additional support on BLW from pregnancy to nine months of age. Those women receiving additional support were given three contacts with a trained researcher who advised them on offering foods that are easy to pick up and eat from six months onwards, responsive feeding, paying attention to hunger and satiety cues, and providing high-iron and high-energy foods at mealtimes. They were also given very detailed resources on how to feed in a baby-led manner, food ideas and recipe books for each age, and also information about choking. The study looked at how many babies had overweight or obesity at 12 and 24 months of age to see if there were differences according to whether they were weaned using BLW or spoon-feeding. There were no meaningful differences by weaning group; at 24 months there were slightly more overweight infants in the BLW group (10.3 per cent) than in the spoon-fed group (6.4 per cent) but this was not a statistically significant difference, which means it may have been due to chance.

However, the study suggested that BLW has an impact on appetite regulation, but not in the expected way. Babies who were weaned using BLW had more avid appetites insofar as they had *lower* satiety responsiveness (they were *less* sensitive to their fullness) and *greater* enjoyment of food at 24 months. This contradicts the idea that BLW may help children learn how to self-regulate, as these aspects of appetite put children at greater risk of obesity. A thoughtful commentary about this trial by experts in child feeding suggested that giving babies complete autonomy over how much they eat at such a young age provides the opportunity for those with an already avid appetite to overeat, as there are fewer parental boundaries in place to ensure they do not overeat, if they are that way inclined.[266] In light of this, it may still be important to be mindful about the portion sizes and types of finger foods that you offer when using this approach, so as to make sure those babies with big appetites are not encouraged to overeat. While there were no big impacts on rates of overweight or obesity at 12 or 24 months, the impact on future weight is unknown and more research is needed.

On the plus side, the babies in the BLW group were less fussy about food and were no more likely to have a serious choking event, although they gagged more frequently at six months but not at eight months. This important trial indicates that weaning method does not appear to impact importantly on weight gain, but it does seem to increase appetite. The advantages of BLW are that it may help with preventing fussy eating and it appears to be safe. Much more research is needed in this area to really know if one method of weaning offers significant benefits over the other. The ESPGHAN committee on nutrition came to the same conclusion, following a recent review of the benefits of traditional spoon-feeding versus BLW.[267]

So which method to go with? Current World Health Organization guidance recommends that infants are first offered puréed foods, and that there is a progression in texture until 12 months when infants should be eating family foods.[268] Finger foods, are recommended from eight months, but alongside purées and not as the main diet. The UK Department of Health recommends that you offer finger foods from the start, even if you choose to offer purées or mashed foods on a spoon. This will help your baby to become familiar with textures as early as possible.[269] We would also advocate this approach, and in reality most parents seem to use a bit of both anyhow – it's rarely just one or the other.

We recommend that you try to combine both approaches. You can start by offering your baby spoon-fed puréed or mashed, iron-rich foods (allow him to spoon-feed himself or control the spoon if he is able to) as this will help ensure the development of the oral motor skills (tongue control, strength and stamina) necessary for chewing solid food. It will also ensure the intake of iron, important for cognitive development and the development of tissues, as puréed or mashed food is more likely to be ingested. This is especially important for breastfed babies given that breast milk is low in iron. But we would also recommend giving your baby something to hold and chew in between mouthfuls of spoon-fed food as well. This way your baby will not only obtain essential nutrients via puréed or mashed foods, but will also take some control of his eating. It will also help him to become familiar with the textures and appearances of different foods. But in the absence of any strong evidence for the superiority of one method over the other, you should feel free to choose whichever method you prefer.

Smooth foods, such as puréed broccoli, can be prepared by cooking or steaming them well and then using a blender to purée them.

Mashed foods are raw or cooked foods that are mashed, such as avocado mashed with a fork, so that they are slightly lumpy.

Finger foods are pieces of food that your baby can easily pick up, hold and feed himself. Ideally finger foods are soft and easy to bite – for example, parboiled carrot or strips of banana. Take care not to offer finger foods with the pips or stones remaining, such as cherries, as they can be a choking hazard.

'BLW suited my ethos as I think it is a respectful approach to children as you are giving them some autonomy and decision-making when it comes to their food. I think it is important to respect that children may know when they are full. I felt so secure when my son went to nursery as they were under strict instructions not to spoon-feed him and I know that my son was making his own decisions about what and how much food he eats.'

Maria, mum of Oliver (2 years and 9 months)

Responsive Feeding During Weaning

Whichever weaning method you choose, it is still important to feed your baby responsively – feed him only when he indicates to you that he is hungry and stop when he indicates to you that he is full. This is just as important when it comes to food as it was when your baby was being fed only milk (we described how to feed responsively during milk-feeding in Chapter 6). Responsive feeding is thought to be crucial for supporting babies and children in developing good appetite regulation.

Responsive feeding with solid foods has the same principles as it does with milk-feeding, except that there are a few more things to consider as your baby gets older and starts to move from a solely milk-based diet to food. In other words, things get a bit more complicated! From decades of research, we know that there are four important components of responsive feeding that are thought to support your baby in developing good appetite regulation and a healthy relationship with food:[270]

1. Let your child decide how much he wants to eat – don't pressure him

A crucial part of responsive feeding is allowing him to eat only as much as he wants to satisfy his hunger. Never pressure him to eat more than he wants to. Examples of pressuring your child to eat are: making him clear his plate even though he has had enough; refusing to let the meal finish until he has eaten certain foods, such as his vegetables; or just coercing him to eat a bit more than he wants to. Pressuring your child to eat can have detrimental consequences. For a child with a poor appetite it can lead to anxiety around food, food refusal and increasingly stressful mealtimes.[271] In fact, there is a reasonable amount of evidence to suggest that children whose parents pressure them excessively can have poorer weight gain over time and become even fussier than they were before.[272] So, although it can be frustrating when your child doesn't want to eat as much as you'd like him to, exerting large amounts of pressure on him is unlikely to help, and can even make matters worse. It's best just to leave it up to him to decide. There are plenty of positive strategies you can use with your child if he has a poor appetite and is very fussy – these are discussed in detail in Chapter 10.

On the flip side, it is also possible that pressuring a child to finish everything on the plate could potentially encourage him to ignore his hunger and satiety signals, and *overeat*. Although the evidence for this theory is lacking, probably because parents only tend to pressure their child to eat if he has a poor appetite or is a faddy eater – they don't tend to pressure the eager feeders simply because they don't need to! What we do know is that parental feeding strategies and child appetite is a two-way street: children who are gaining weight too slowly and/or have poorer appetites are pressured by their parents more, but also children who are pressured more by their parents actually become poorer eaters as time goes on, and their weight gain slows even more.[273] So this is not a good strategy to use with poor feeders. Allowing your child to decide when he has had enough is a fundamental part of the BLW approach, but it is also possible to make sure you feed your child in a responsive way if he is being spoon-fed.

2. Use covert rather than overt ways to restrict your child's intake of unhealthy food

As any parent will know, given the food environment that we live in today it is important to limit the amount of high-fat and high-sugar foods your child eats. If you don't, and your child has a hearty appetite and a penchant for these foods, he will overeat given the chance, and may develop over-weight. If your child has a poor appetite, the temptation might be to give him his favourite unhealthy foods to make sure he eats something, but this can mean that he will fill up on less healthy foods, have an even poorer appetite for healthier foods, and certainly less interest in them. Whether restricting food is a good thing, a bad thing or totally point-less in terms of a child's appetite and weight gain is something that has been hotly debated for years. One large ongoing study showed that restriction seemed to protect young children from gaining excessive amounts of weight or developing overweight, but that it didn't work for older chil-dren (over 10 years).[274] And lots of other studies haven't found any effect at all of parental restriction on children's weight gain, suggesting it doesn't work.[275] In fact, some imaginative early experimental research with a small number of children showed that restriction could even be a bad thing.[276] When young children's access to a particular fruit-bar cookie that they really liked was restricted (and placed in a transparent jar in front of them), their liking for it increased and they ate more of it when they were finally given access to it. This method of restriction is what researchers call 'overt' – the child is completely aware of the food that they are not allowed, because they can see it. This study suggested that *overtly restricting* what a child is allowed to eat could actually backfire; because the children develop an even greater desire for the restricted food and will eat more of it when it is then freely available simply because they haven't been allowed it. This has been called the 'forbidden-fruit effect' – we all want what we can't have, and children are no different in this respect.

So, what is the deal when it comes to restricting children – should you do it or not? The mixed findings in research probably reflect the fact that there are *different ways* to restrict your child's access to unhealthy food, and some ways are better than others for your child's appetite and weight in the long run. *Overt* restriction – such as having a transparent jar of biscuits on show in the kitchen that your child will ogle but isn't allowed access to – may have a detrimental effect. But *covert* restriction – restriction that your child cannot see and is unaware of (for example, not keeping chocolates bars in the house or not walking home from school via the bakery) – is probably the most effective way to restrict his access to unhealthy foods and drinks, without increasing his desire for them. But restriction should never be excessive, and it doesn't have to mean that you always decide what he eats. A good strategy is to make sure that you give your baby a range of healthy food choices – for example, offering a choice of vegetables with his meal. This will help him to feel in control and have options to choose from, but you are able to make sure that there are boundaries to his active choices.

Although restriction might not seem important when your baby is still very young, it is something to be mindful of as soon as your baby starts to eat solid food as he will become increasingly aware of the foods that are around him – in the house and out – and certainly of the foods that you are eating. An effective way of restricting unhealthy foods and increasing your child's intake of healthy foods is for you to lead by example – your child will do what you do, and we call this 'modelling'. This is described in more detail on page 267.

3. Offer him age-appropriate portion sizes

Regardless of the type of food that you offer your baby during weaning, it is important to make sure that you offer him a portion that is appropriate for his age (see page 363 for portion sizes for one-to-four-year olds) and his appetite. Babies can still overeat on healthy food. A baby with a big appetite – one who is less sensitive to his fullness and more responsive to food cues – will tend to eat more if it is there because it is harder for him to know when he is full, and because he enjoys eating. He will be guided more by the opportunity to eat than his internal feelings of hunger and fullness. Ensuring that the portion of food that you offer your baby is an appropriate size for his age (not too much) will help him to learn to eat only as much as he needs, and not more than he needs on a regular basis. If your baby indicates to you that he is still hungry after he has finished his food, you can offer him a small amount more. On the other hand, when it comes to a baby with a poor appetite, offering too much food can be over-whelming and even anxiety-provoking. For these babies, it is better to offer an amount that looks manageable. Again, once he has eaten it you can introduce a little bit more food if he indicates that he is still hungry, but leave it to him to let you know.

4. Offer food only in response to his hunger, not for any other reason

A fundamental part of responsive feeding is making sure that you only ever offer your child food because he is hungry, not for any other reason, such as comfort, enter-tainment or to control his behaviour. If your baby is upset, irritable or just bored the temptation is to offer him his favourite food to cheer him up, calm him down or keep him quiet. The problem is that we know this lays the groundwork for learning to emotionally overeat – a habit that's difficult to break, and something that many older children and adults struggle with. Gemini – which was the first twin study into the origins of emotional eating in childhood – showed that emotional eating already starts to emerge during the early toddlerhood years, and that it is entirely learned, not inherited (genes are unimportant in shaping a young toddler's tendency to do this).[277] With researchers from Norway we used a large ongoing study of 1,000 families to show that offering a young child food in order to soothe him when he is upset teaches him to turn to food to control his emotions later on.[278] Emotional feeding tends to work best with toddlers who love their food (toddlers with no interest in food find little comfort in it being offered), but they are already at higher risk of developing overweight, so it is particularly important to not use this strategy with babies who are very food responsive. Using food to deal with negative emotions isn't only a concern in relation to overweight; it also means that children won't learn positive strategies for coping with unpleasant feelings. It is important to find non-food strategies to comfort your baby if he is upset, such as giving him a cuddle or talking to him calmly.

Parents often use food for entertainment as well – we can all remember being given chocolate buttons or sweets as children to keep us quiet during a long car journey, or at a wedding or important event. But again, this can teach your baby to use food for entertainment and could lead to boredom eating. Instead try giving him a toy or game to keep him occupied.

Lastly, never use your child's favourite food as a bribe to get him to eat a healthy food that he dislikes (such as vegetables). Although this might seem like a good strategy (and it might work the first couple of times), research has shown that it will only serve to increase his dislike of the healthy food (he will conclude that vegetables are so foul that he needs to be given ice cream to compensate for eating them) and increase his desire for his favourite food, which now takes on the lofty status of a reward.[279] This is particularly problematic with very fussy children who don't need much encouragement to reject healthy foods and opt for the more palatable foods instead. The best way to get your baby to eat something that you want him to eat is to eat it yourself in front of him. This and other strategies are described in more detail on pages 265–7.

FEEDING A HUNGRY BABY

Just as some babies are eager feeders and poor feeders during milk-feeding, not all babies will respond in the same way to solid food. The four principles of responsive feeding are important to follow, whatever type of feeder you have.

If you have a baby with a big appetite, the following tips are important:

- **Don't pressure him to eat past the point at which he feels full**

    If he has low satiety he is more likely to eat more than he needs if encouraged to, because it is more difficult for him to recognise when he is full. Supporting him to learn to recognise his fullness threshold is important.

- **Try to think of covert ways to restrict his intake of high-fat and high-sugar foods**

The best way to do this is not to bring them into the house in the first place. If he sees them, he will want them, and if he knows they are there, he will want them. Offering your baby a choice of healthy food options is a useful strategy to make him feel that he has some control over what food he eats, and that you are not always just saying no, but offering him alternative options.

- **Make sure you offer him an appropriate portion size of food**

  Only offer him as much as he needs, not more, at meal-times. If he has low satiety sensitivity, then he will eat more than he needs if there is more food available. If he is food responsive, he will continue to eat the tastier foods until he has finished them simply because it is a pleasurable thing to do, not because he is hungry. You can always offer him a bit more if he indicates to you that he is still hungry.

- **Never offer him food for any reason other than hunger**

  If you have a very food-responsive baby who loves eating, he will probably respond well to bribery. For example, "if you sit quietly you can have a biscuit", and the temptation is to use this strategy to control his emotions or his behaviour. But it won't help him to develop a healthy relationship with food in the long run. He needs to learn to think of food as fuel, not as a source of comfort, entertainment or as a reward.

FEEDING A BABY WITH A POOR APPETITE

If you have a baby with a poor appetite for solid food, it can be anxiety-provoking (more so than having an enthusiastic feeder), but the same tips are just as important for different reasons:

- **Don't pressure him to eat past the point at which he feels full**

  If he is very sensitive to his internal feelings of satiety, continuing to eat past satiety is an unpleasant feeling. Pressuring him to continue to eat will make him feel stressed or even anxious. In unusual cases (with high amounts of pressure) it can even lead to food aversion. You are unlikely to get anywhere with this strategy so it's not a fruitful endeavour. Your baby will let you know when he has had enough and, once he has indicated this to you, trust him and let him finish eating at this point.

- **Try to think of covert ways to restrict his intake of high-fat and high-sugar foods**

  If you have more enticing foods in the house than the healthy ones that your baby won't eat, he will want them instead and he knows they are there. This can make it challenging to get him to even try the foods that he is automatically suspicious of. Having those healthier foods around and on show will help him to feel familiar with them, and that these are the options available. We discuss food fussiness, and strategies to deal with it in much more detail on page 330.

- **Make sure you offer him an appropriate portion size of food**

  Only provide your baby with as much as he can manage, not more. Offering a large plate of food to a child with high satiety sensitivity may overwhelm him and create anxiety.

- **Never offer him food for any reason other than hunger**

    Babies with a poor appetite are often fussy eaters, who are more likely to reject vegetables and opt for the foods they know and like already. Offering him these foods as a reward for eating the foods he doesn't like will do you no favours in the long run – it will make him even more suspicious of the foods he doesn't like and even more likely to refuse to eat them. There are far better ways to get him to eat his greens, such as 'modelling' (described on page 267).

UNDERSTANDING YOUR BABY'S HUNGER AND SATIETY CUES DURING WEANING

It is clear from research that it is important to feed your baby responsively – offer him food only when he is hungry and stop as soon as he indicates to you that he has had enough. This means that you need to be able to read his hunger and fullness cues for food, just as you did for milk. The good news is that this is a bit easier now your baby is older. An evidence-based coding tool – the Responsiveness to Child Feeding Cues Scale (RCFCS) – has recently been developed to provide a description of cues that babies provide to indicate when they are hungry and full during the weaning stage.[280]

Hunger cues
If your baby is hungry and wants food or is willing to eat he will:

- lean forward

- reach for the spoon or food

- point to food

Baby Food Matters

- get excited when you present him with food

- put the spoon or food voluntarily into his own mouth

- accept food quickly

- open his mouth when the spoon or food is a distance from his mouth

Satiety cues
Avoidance or an unwillingness to eat can be recognised if your baby:

- slows down his eating

- turns his head away

- looks away or looks down

- pulls his body away

- arches his back

- becomes fussy or cries

- pushes the spoon or the food away

- clenches his mouth shut

- becomes playful

- becomes distracted or more interested in what's going on around him

How Much Food Does My Baby Need?

Young babies are exploring food and the very beginning of the weaning process is less about calorie intake and more about engaging with and tasting a variety of foods. The idea is not for your baby to be eating three meals a day just yet and, although you do want him to be absorbing nutrients such as iron, at this stage the key is for him to get used to different flavours and textures. You should prepare for most of the food you offer your baby to end up on the floor, which can be a source of worry because many parents fear that their baby is not getting enough to eat.

The SACN suggest that at six months of age (weaning age) breastfed babies need approximately 78kcal per kg, so a baby of six months weighing 8kg (17lb 10oz) would need 624kcal per day. It is difficult to measure how much milk your baby is consuming if you are breastfeeding, unless of course you are expressing, but even if you know the volume of breast milk your baby is consuming, you still won't know the number of calories because breast milk can vary (see page 134). At six months of age the WHO recommends 500–600ml milk per day. Given that breast and formula milk both contain approximately 70kcal per 100ml, milk alone would provide your baby with 350–420 kcal, so the remaining kcals can be obtained from solid food. The guidelines change as your baby gets older as they will be consuming less milk. For example, at 12 months infants are recommended to consume approximately 350ml milk per day (providing 245kcal), so to meet their energy requirements they will require more energy from food. These numbers are here to provide you with a guide only. As we mentioned in Chapter 3, the best way of telling whether your baby is getting enough or too much food, is to monitor his growth.

MILK-FEEDING DURING WEANING

You should continue to give your baby breast or formula milk during weaning. Whole (full-fat) cows' milk can be given as the main milk source *from 12 months of age* but not before as it is difficult to digest, and early exposure to cows' milk proteins increases the risk of developing an allergy to milk proteins. In addition, several studies have shown that introducing whole cows' milk before 12 months of age is associated with an iron deficiency, as it can lead to blood loss in babies' intestines.[281] Cows' milk can, however, be used in cooking from six months of age (for example, your baby can have it in porridge).

First Steps Nutrition has provided a guide for the amount of milk required from six months to two years for babies drinking formula or cows' milk (table below).[282] First Steps Nutrition states that, 'breastfed babies will continue to take the amount of milk they need as they obtain increasing energy from food and it is not necessary to know the volume of this'.

TABLE 3: MILK-FEEDING GUIDANCE FROM SIX MONTHS TO TWO YEARS

Age	Feeding Guidance	Suggested intake per day
7–9 months	Infant formula could be offered at breakfast (150ml), lunch (150ml), tea (150ml) and before bed (150ml).	About 600ml per day
10–12 months	Infant formula could be offered at breakfast (100ml), tea (100ml) and before bed (200ml).	About 400ml per day
1–2 years	Full fat cows' milk could be offered at snack times twice a day (100ml x 2), and as a drink before bed (200ml).	About 400ml per day of whole cows' milk or another suitable milk drink

Which milk to choose?

In the UK there are many different formula and 'follow-on' milks on the market, but most formula-fed babies only need a standard 'first' milk (marketed for babies aged 0–6 months). The exception is if your baby has an allergy, in which case he may then be prescribed an alternative formula by your GP. But first milks are suitable for the majority of babies *up to one year of age.* After this your baby can move onto cows' milk, or an appropriate alternative. Any whole (full-fat) milk (cows', goats' or sheep's milk) is suitable as a main drink for babies from one year providing it is pasteurised. Unsweetened calcium-fortified soya milk, oat milk or coconut milk can also be given from one year of age. (See page 156, for guidance on choosing milks during the first year of life.)

We do not advocate using 'follow-on' formula milks which are targeted at infants beyond six months of age. The WHO states that follow-on milks are not needed[283] and, compared with standard first milks (0–12 months) or cows' milk (12 + months), they have been found to have no nutritional benefit and are far more expensive. They are fortified with nutrients such as vitamin D, iron and omega-3 fatty acids, but iron levels are higher than recommended.[284] Given that weaning should occur at around six months of age, most babies will obtain all the nutrients they need once they start on solid food. First milks are closer in composition to breast milk than follow-on milks, so these should be used for the first year of life if a baby is not being breastfed.

In Chapter 5 we also mentioned 'hungry' and 'goodnight' milks (page 151). There is no evidence that these milks offer any advantage over first milks, and there is no evidence to support the claims that these manufacturers make. What's more, using these milks at night could lead to dental caries (cavities). They are also very expensive.[285]

'Toddler' and 'growing up' milks are also marketed for babies of one year of age or older; these are high in sugar, expensive, and offer no nutritional benefit. A relatively recent product to enter the market is the PaediaSure shake. Worryingly, this is targeted at parents with fussy eaters aged 1–10 years. It claims to be 'suitable as a sole source of nutrition or as a nutritional supplement for patients who cannot or will not eat sufficient quantities of everyday food and drink to meet their nutritional requirements', as per the PaediaSure data sheet. It is available to buy in the baby and toddler snack aisle in leading pharmacies. We strongly discourage the use of such shakes – in our view they will not help your child to develop healthy eating habits and have a varied, balanced diet (see Chapter 9 for more on key nutrients and their impact on health). Children need to be encouraged to taste food and learn how to eat proper food; a shake is no substitute for a balanced diet. See page 331 for tips on how to feed a fussy eater.

THE BOTTOM LINE

- The method you choose for introducing solid food is a personal choice: there is no evidence that one is better than the other.

- Baby-led weaning is safe insofar as there is no convincing evidence that babies are more likely to choke.

- If you begin with puréed foods, gradually introduce mashed textures and finger foods as soon as your baby indicates that he is ready, and offer finger foods alongside.

- Only offer your baby food if he is hungry, and let him stop eating as soon as he is full.

- Never pressure your baby to eat if he doesn't want to.

- Provide a portion of food that is appropriate for your baby's age.

- Never use food to manage his emotions or provide entertainment.

- Never reward food with food.

- Continue with breast milk or standard formula ('first' milks) alongside solid food.

- 'Follow-on' formulas, 'toddler', 'growing-up' or 'hungry' milks, as well as food replacement shakes, are not needed or recommended.

CHAPTER 9

First Foods

Weaning is a crucial period for establishing healthy eating habits, largely because during this process your baby will develop taste preferences that may stay with him for many years. Research shows that food preferences can be 'programmed' in early life.[286] This means that tastes and foods that your baby is exposed to during weaning can shape what he likes as an older child, and even as an adult. It's therefore a great opportunity to introduce your baby to foods that you would like him to eat in order to reap the benefits for years to come.

Many new parents choose to use baby rice or rusks as the very first food, but we would strongly advise you *not* to do this. Baby rice and rusks are incredibly bland in flavour. Weaning is about developing your baby's taste preferences and openness to new textures, not simply about calories and nutrition, and it is the perfect opportunity for your baby to try new flavours. Baby rice or rusks will not achieve this.

Vegetables First

We are all born with an innate preference for sweet foods and a dislike of bitter foods. Historically, a natural liking for sweet foods meant that we were primed to eat foods higher in calories, because these foods contain more sugar. This ensured that we stored up enough energy to protect us against starvation when food became scarce. At the same time, a natural dislike for bitter tastes protected us from eating poisonous foods, which are often bitter in flavour. Today our taste biases mean we have a tendency to eat too much of the readily available and cheap, high-calorie foods (for example, chocolate) and too little of the low-calorie foods that taste bitter but are nutritionally dense (for example, vegetables such as spinach). The upshot of this is that traditional, plant-based diets rich in vegetables have been replaced with diets high in fat and sugar. Vegetables are nutrient-dense (they contain many vitamins, minerals and fibre) and have a low energy density (a low number of calories per gram) because they are low in sugar and fat. For example, there are just 23kcal in 100g spinach, but milk chocolate has 535kcal per 100g. This means we can eat large quantities of vegetables without eating too many calories and will obtain essential nutrients from them.

The benefits of eating vegetables are clear, but trying to get children to eat them can often be challenging. Vegetables are the type of food most commonly disliked by children[287] and many parents struggle to get them to eat enough, especially when it comes to the more bitter vegetables, such as broccoli or cabbage. However, even though humans have an innate tendency to dislike bitter foods and prefer sweet foods, much of what we like is learned through experience. This means that it is possible to teach a child to learn to like and eat vegetables. The very early years offer a window of opportunity for 'setting' your child's liking for vegetables, that will maximise the likelihood that he will eat and enjoy a wide variety of vegetables during childhood and later on in adulthood. Although this process may start as early as pregnancy, and continues during breastfeeding, weaning probably plays a more important role. Research suggests that starting weaning with vegetables is a good way to help your child learn to like vegetables and he will be more accepting of future vegetables and eat a wider variety of them later in life.[288] The theory is that things can only get better for them in the taste stakes. If something sweet (for example, apple) is their first taste, what is the advantage of eating broccoli when they know other foods taste much sweeter? It makes sense that they will reject the broccoli, and who can blame them?

However, it would be fair to say that there isn't a lot of high-quality research into the long-term effect of introducing vegetables first. Most studies have been observational which means we can't be sure that introducing vegetables first *really caused* babies to increase their liking for them and eat more of them later, because other factors that weren't measured could have been more important. However, researchers from our group at University College London conducted one of the few well-designed randomised controlled trials in this area; this study was able to show that weaning with a vegetable as the first food had lasting positive effects on taste preferences and this was probably due to using a vegetable as the first food.[289] In the TASTE study they randomly assigned 60 mothers of four-to six-month-olds to either an intervention group or a control group. The intervention group was visited by researchers at home and offered advice on introducing five different varieties of vegetables (on their own, not disguised with fruit) for the first 15 days of weaning; the control group was visited at home but not given advice on weaning with vegetables. After one month, the researchers assessed how much of an unfamiliar vegetable and fruit the babies ate. Babies in the intervention group ate more of an unfamiliar vegetable than infants in the control group, and the researchers and mothers also rated them as *liking* the vegetable more. What was interesting was that there was no difference between the groups in their liking or intake of the fruit. This suggests that introducing vegetables instead of fruit as first foods is a great way of improving acceptance of vegetables. On the other hand, starting with fruit might be a lost opportunity because babies tend to be accepting of fruit anyway.

'I started by giving Grace individual vegetables and then giving multiple vegetables together. I didn't give her any sweet fruit until about four to six weeks into weaning. I did that so that Grace was experiencing different tastes with the aim that she would like vegetables. It seems to have worked because she will eat anything!'

Amy, mum of Grace (18 months)

Currently in the UK few new parents offer vegetables as a first food – the Infant Feeding Survey 2010 found that the most common foods given were baby rice (57 per cent) followed by ready-made baby food (12 per cent). Eleven per cent of babies were given 'home-made foods'; 10 per cent were given rusks; 8 per cent were given fruit; and just 7 per cent were given vegetables as first foods.[290] We would recommend offering a 'rainbow' of different varieties of vegetables including lots of dark green vegetables and avoiding sticking to things like sweet potato, parsnips or carrots because they are naturally quite sweet. Start with a range of different single vegetables including the least sweet varieties (for example, broccoli and spinach). If your baby doesn't seem to like something, don't give up; offer it again another day. Exposure to a variety of flavours during complementary feeding is important for fostering healthy food preferences. A more varied diet during complementary feeding has been linked with eating a greater variety of foods later in childhood and children being more accepting of novel foods.[291] Evidence also suggests offering different vegetables each day is more successful in increasing acceptance of novel foods than giving the same vegetable for multiple consecutive days. In Chapter 10 we offer a step-by-step guide on how to introduce vegetables as first foods and we explain the science behind the benefits.

FRUIT

There is no disputing that fruit is good for us; it is full of nutrients and is unprocessed. It does, however, also contain a reasonable amount of sugar (hence the sweet taste), which is why babies tend to like it. It is highly unlikely that your baby will turn his nose up at banana, pear or apple. But if you try to give him vegetables once he has tried fruit, you may be disappointed. The key is to make sure that the first foods that are introduced to your baby are vegetables. There are some fruits, such as plums or cherries, which can be quite sour so may initially be rejected by your baby, and we recommend introducing these earlier than the sweet fruits.

Fruit juice

150ml of pure unsweetened orange juice (a standard serving) contains about 13g sugar[292] (more sugar than you would find in four digestive biscuits), and a child would need to eat several oranges to get the same amount of juice! There are currently no recommendations on sugar intake for very young children in the UK, but a child who is four–six years old is recommended to have no more than 19g sugar per day.[293] If 150ml of juice contains 13g, this is more than half their daily intake! Sweet drinks are problematic not only because they can lead children to develop a sweet tooth but they can also lead to tooth decay. Another less well-known problem is that sweet drinks are not recognised by the brain's satiety centre in the same way as solid food. This means that the calories are not compensated for (they don't make us feel any fuller) and it is easy to consume excess calories in the form of drinks (this doesn't apply to milk).

We recommend not giving your baby fruit juice; he only needs water or milk, especially during weaning. If you do choose to offer fruit juice or smoothies to your baby, always dilute them with water (1 part fruit juice to 10 parts water) and offer them with a meal, not on their own. Fizzy drinks have no nutritional value at all and should be avoided.

Juice and fizzy drinks should not be given to your baby in a bottle as this is bad for his teeth, so do not use bottles for anything other than water (boiled and cooled first for babies under six months of age), breast milk or formula milk. The NHS suggests introducing a cup rather than a bottle from six months of age, and by 12 months your baby should have stopped using bottles with teats as he may end up using these as a comforter.[294] Try using an open cup or a free-flow cup without a non-spill valve, rather than a bottle or beaker with a teat, so that your baby learns how to sip rather than suck. Sucking from a bottle or teat means the drink is in contact with your baby's teeth for longer and can lead to tooth decay.

MIXED MESSAGES

Many parents look to family, Internet forums, websites, health visitors, NHS sources, friends and parenting groups for support on infant feeding. Health visitors often suggest baby rice and porridge as first foods, followed by fruit and vegetables, so rather than the focus being on taste development and building healthy eating habits, it tends to be on the mechanics of eating.

The Internet is a minefield when it comes to weaning and if you search online for guidance, you are bound to come across advice from baby-food 'experts' that contradicts the scientific evidence. A quick glance at what's out there showed us that parents are being given advice to offer 'root vegetables and ripe fruit' as first foods because 'they are naturally sweet and can be easily puréed to a smooth texture'. Even the NHS/Start4life's 'Introducing Solid Foods' booklet suggests various fruit and vegetables as first foods, and all of them are sweet. There is very little guidance provided on how to encourage babies to accept vegetables. This is not in line with the best scientific research to date on which we are basing our guidance. Starting with fruit may make vegetable acceptance more difficult and babies can become accustomed to sweet tastes.

A similar issue is that you will find lots of recipes for weaning online, but many of them contain fruit or they mix fruit and vegetables together. We found recipes such as Celeriac, Carrot and Apple; Banana and Avocado; and Kiwi and Avocado. There are two main problems here. Firstly, mixing fruit and vegetables prevents babies from being able to identify the vegetables because the flavour is masked with the sweetness of the fruit. Secondly, in real life adults do not tend to have fruit mixed in with vegetables (although your apple sauce might get mixed in with your peas in your Sunday roast!). Children need to learn to eat how adults eat – not many of us would mix kiwi and avocado together for ourselves, so why do it for our babies?

First Steps Nutrition's website (see Useful Resources section) contains a very useful guide on introducing solids and eating well up to your baby's first birthday ('Eating well: the first year'), as well as recipes for eating well in the early years.

Baby Foods

The 2011 UK Diet and Nutrition Survey for Infants and Young Children (DNSIYC) reported that 72 per cent of babies aged four–nine months had consumed commercial baby foods.[295] Many of the ready-made baby foods on the market contain a lot of sugar, and foods with added sugar should be avoided in the first 12 months of your baby's life (see page 283). Processed baby foods, regardless of whether they are organic or not, often have fruit, such as apple or pear, as a basis, even when the product is marketed as 'savoury', for example, mixing broccoli and peas with pears. Often the first ingredient in the name of the product is a green vegetable but as much as 80 per cent of the product is actually fruit! If you try some of this food, you may be quite surprised by how sweet it tastes.

Few baby foods contain simple, individual vegetable flavours, and those that do usually have sweet vegetables, such as carrot or sweet potato, as the main ingredient which babies are more likely to accept. Less readily accepted vegetables, such as broccoli, spinach or cauliflower, are often not included, and are certainly not the dominant flavour.

In addition, jars and pouches of baby food often go through high-heat processing which may remove some of their nutritional goodness and, the quantities of iron- or vitamin D-rich foods, such as fish or meat, are likely to be much lower than a home-prepared alternative. Often these products also contain a lot more water than foods made at home, which reduces the energy density (number of calories per gram) of the food and means that a baby needs to eat greater quantities of it to obtain the same nutrients. There is the possibility this may interfere with a child's ability to respond to their feelings of fullness, if they learn to eat larger portions from a very young age. Overall the portions of jars and pouches are very big for the start of weaning, and once opened they can only be stored for limited periods of time which can lead to overfeeding or lots of waste.

Aside from the nutritional benefits of preparing food at home, there are also cost benefits. A recent review by First Steps Nutrition looked at 343 baby foods in jars, pouches and trays, and explored the cost compared to home-prepared baby food.[296] They reported that a 70g pouch of puréed organic carrots in the supermarket costs approximately 90p, whereas if you made the equivalent amount at home it would cost 14p. The cost difference is the packaging and obviously the convenience – it does take time to prepare, boil and purée your own vegetables, but it is far more cost-effective, and it can actually be very quick and easy, especially if you create a large batch and freeze portions to give to your baby at a later date (see page 263).

Commercial foods with a number of ingredients, for example, 'Parsnips, Sweet Potato and Broccoli', are labelled to imply there are just three ingredients, but water and oil are often added to bulk them out. By preparing your baby's food at home, you can be sure that you only include the main ingredients and a smaller portion would be needed to achieve the same nutrient content. Not only is home-prepared food more cost-effective, there is also a difference in appearance and texture, as the supermarket versions are highly processed.

If you do choose to purchase jars and pouches, our advice would be to start with jars or pouches that contain only individual vegetables. Unfortunately, there are not many of these available on the market so if you are able to make your own purées (from less sweet vegetables, such as broccoli and spinach) this would be ideal. Try to avoid jars and pouches that mix fruit and vegetables together, and delay giving ones that contain only fruit until later in the weaning process. Also purées in a pouch should be transferred to a spoon before being fed to your child. If you allow your child to squeeze the food straight into their mouth they may miss out on key oral development that is learned through taking food from a spoon, not to mention they may end up eating far too quickly.

Foods to Avoid

We recommend checking with your GP if your feel your baby is ready to start solids before six months, but if you choose to wean your baby *before he is six months old*, there are certain foods that should be avoided as his gut is still developing:

- breads or pastas as these contain gluten

- nuts and seeds, including nut spreads

- fish and shellfish

- eggs

- liver

- cows' milk

- soft and unpasteurised cheese

In addition, *babies under 12 months of age* should not be given the following:

- honey until one year of age as it can contain spores of a bacterium called *Clostridium botulinum*, which can cause infant botulism, a rare but potentially fatal illness of the digestive system

- raw shellfish under 36 months of age as it can lead to food poisoning

- cows' milk as a drink until 12 months of age. (From 12 months full-fat cows' milk can be given, but semi-skimmed milk should not be given until at least 24 months.) Cows' milk can be used in cooking from six months of age

- whole nuts, including peanuts – these should not be given to children under the age of five because of the risk of choking

- raw and undercooked eggs until 24 months of age because of the risk of salmonella food poisoning. Only offer hard-boiled eggs

- processed meat or fish (for example, tinned, smoked or cured meat and fish) because it can be high in salt

- ready meals and takeaways because they tend to be high in salt

- very high fibre foods (for example, bran cereals) because they can be too filling and prevent your baby from eating enough other nutritious foods

- artificially sweetened foods and drinks (for example, no-sugar fruit cordial) as these can lead to a sweet tooth

- foods and drinks with the additives E102, E110, E122, E124 and E211 as they have been linked with hyperactivity disorders

- rice milk or rice drinks until five years of age as they contain traces of arsenic (given the amount of milk babies and toddlers drink, relative to their size, this can put them at risk of consuming an unsafe amount)

- tea or coffee because they can interfere with iron absorption from food especially if consumed with a meal

ALLERGENIC FOODS

Foods that may cause allergies, such as dairy, wheat, eggs and nuts, should be introduced one at a time in small amounts. Mixed foods containing the items listed above should not be given to children unless tolerance to each item has been tested. The European Society for Paediatric Gastroenterology, Hepatology, and Nutrition (ESPGHAN) Committee on Nutrition reviewed several well-designed randomised controlled trials and found no evidence that delaying introduction to allergenic foods (foods that can cause an allergy) beyond six months of age will prevent a baby from developing an allergy, including babies with a family history of allergies. They advise that babies at high risk of peanut allergy (for example, those with severe eczema, egg allergy or both) should have peanut introduced (for example, using a spread) between 4 and 11 months, *following evaluation by an appropriately trained health professional.*[297] In a draft report published in 2017, the SACN cautioned that deliberate exclusion of hen's egg and peanut beyond 6–12 months might actually increase risk of allergy to these foods.[298] They recommend introducing them from six months and, if tolerated, including them in the baby's usual diet. They caution that if a baby doesn't continue to eat these foods after initial exposure, their risk of developing an allergy may be increased. Gluten can also be introduced at six months but large quantities should be avoided in the first weeks after introduction and during infancy.[299]

SALT

Your baby's first foods do not need salt. Babies have never experienced salt and it only masks the flavour of foods, which is not helpful when your baby is trying to develop taste preferences. Too much salt is also dangerous for babies because their kidneys are not able to deal with it and it may increase a baby's risk of developing several health problems in later life, including high blood pressure and obesity. It is very important that your baby does not have more than 1g salt per day (approximately 2 slices of unbuttered bread).[300] Stock cubes, gravy, sauces, cheese and processed foods all contain a lot of salt, so we advise you do not use these during the weaning process. Research has shown that children can develop a preference for salty foods if they are introduced to them early in life. One such study involved offering babies aged two months and six months either salty water or fruit and then assessing their preference for salty foods at three–four years of age.[301] The babies that had been exposed to the salty water preferred salty foods, to the point where they were more likely to lick salt from the surface of foods at preschool age and more likely to eat plain salt!

SUGAR

Introducing sugary foods and drinks early on is likely to enhance your child's preference for sweetness. This is not only bad news in terms of tooth decay, but also for risk of overweight and type 2 diabetes. There is no need to add sugar to your baby's food during the weaning process. Where possible offer your baby fresh fruit rather than dried. Dried fruit has had the water removed from it, which concentrates the sugars: 170g of *fresh* cranberries contains 2g sugar, while 170g of *dried* cranberries contains 37g sugar (more than a standard sized can of cola). Dried fruit also sticks to your child's teeth which increases the risk of tooth decay. If you offer your child dried fruit, include it in a meal; don't offer it on it's own. This can help prevent damage to his teeth.

Essential Nutrients

Weaning provides the perfect opportunity to expose your baby to essential nutrients, such as vitamin D and iron. However, research has shown that many young children are not consuming enough of some important nutrients and consuming too many of others. In both Gemini (21 months)[302] and the National Diet and Nutrition survey (NDNS) – an annual survey to collect dietary information from individuals 18 months or older in Britain[303] – we found that children were consuming far too little vitamin D and iron.

VITAMIN D

Vitamin D is essential for the formation of strong bones and teeth and it keeps muscles healthy. It is also important for a range of other functions, including immunity. The main source is sunlight but in the UK, sunlight doesn't contain enough UVB radiation in winter (October to early March) for our skin to be able to make vitamin D.[304] But even in sunnier months it is difficult for children to get sufficient vitamin D from exposure to sunlight, because the NHS advises that children under six months of age in the UK are kept out of direct strong sunlight from March to October.[305] Low intakes of vitamin D have been linked to health conditions such as rickets,[306] a bone condition which can result in bone pain, poor growth and deformities of bones, such as bowed legs and curved spine. This is a rare condition but there has been an increase in the number of young children in the UK with rickets over recent years. Rickets is more common among children with darker skin because they need more sunlight to get enough vitamin D. Deficiency has also been linked to a whole range of other illnesses, including some cancers, autoimmune diseases, cardiovascular disease, infectious diseases, infertility, type 1 and type 2 diabetes and neurocognitive impairments.[307]

Vitamin D is found in various foods but it is nearly impossible to get sufficient vitamin D from diet alone – sunlight is by far the best source. Also, Vitamin D tends to be found in foods that young children are not keen on eating, such as liver. It is for this reason that the UK government recommends that babies 0–1 year who are exclusively or partially breastfed are given a daily supplement of 8.5–10mcg vitamin D.[308] Babies who are having more than 500ml of formula milk don't need a supplement because formula is fortified with vitamin D. Some families are entitled to supplements free of charge and you can see if you are eligible at www.healthystart.nhs.uk. We would recommend that you give your baby vitamin D supplements but also introduce him to vitamin D-rich foods from an early age. Listed below are good animal and vegetable sources of vitamin D.

Vitamin D-rich foods

Animal Sources	Vegetable Sources
Salmon	Vegetable-fat spread
Egg yolk	Fortified breakfast cereals
Fresh tuna	
Liver*	
Mackerel	

*Liver contains a high quantity of vitamin A. This can be harmful in large amounts so ideally do not offer this to your baby more than once per week.

VITAMINS C AND A

Vitamin A is important for immunity, vision and skin health, and red blood cell circulation.[309] Severe deficiency is the leading cause of preventable childhood blindness, and increases the risk of infection and night blindness (difficulty seeing in dim light).[310] Vitamin C is needed for the growth and repair of tissues including skin, bones and cartilage. Severe deficiency can lead to scurvy, which causes fatigue, inflammation of the gums, joint pain, and poor wound healing.[311]

Deficiency in either vitamin A or C is extremely rare in the UK, even among children who are very picky eaters. Nevertheless, the UK chief medical officer recommends that all children from six months to five years of age be given a daily supplement of 233mcg vitamin A, and 20mg vitamin C to ensure they are protected from any health problems.[312] Babies who are consuming more than 500ml of formula milk per day don't need any vitamin supplements because formula contains sufficient amounts of all necessary vitamins.

Very high levels of vitamin A (intakes above 800mcg per day) can be harmful[313] so foods that are very rich in vitamin A (for example liver) should be limited to once per week. See page 61 for other food sources of vitamin A and C.

IRON

Low intakes of iron have been linked to anaemia, a condition where the body has fewer red blood cells to transport oxygen in the blood. This stops organs and tissue getting the oxygen they need and can affect your baby's development.[314] Iron found in animal foods is a key source of iron as it is absorbed at a greater rate by the body than iron found in plant foods, so animal sources are the best source of iron for your baby. Listed below are good animal and vegetable sources of iron. Introducing these foods early on in weaning could help your baby develop a taste preference for these foods and subsequently could improve his long-term health.

Iron-rich foods

Animal Sources	Vegetable Sources
Lamb	Broccoli
Salmon	Kale
Kidney	Spinach
Tuna	Broad beans
Liver*	Baked beans
Eggs	Chickpeas
	Tofu
	Lentils
	Soya beans
	Fortified breakfast cereals or breads

*Liver contains a high quantity of vitamin A. This can be harmful in large amounts so ideally do not offer this to your baby more than once per week.

THE BOTTOM LINE

- Start with vegetables, and preferably bitter-tasting ones (for example, broccoli and spinach).

- Introduce a variety of individual vegetables; don't mix vegetables together, and don't mix them with fruit.

Baby Food Matters

- Try to include iron-rich foods such as green leafy vegetables, especially if breastfeeding as breast milk is low in iron.

- Introduce fruit later in the weaning process and begin with sour fruits – for example, cherries (with stones removed) or plums.

- Avoid rusks or baby rice as first foods as they are bland in flavour: weaning is about encouraging your baby to develop taste preferences.

- Be cautious of online advice that recommends weaning with vegetable/fruit combinations.

- Avoid salt and sugar: be wary of sauces and gravies that may contain salt, and do not add salt or sugar to first foods.

- Try to offer only water and milk as drinks for your baby – fruit juices contain a lot of sugar and fizzy drinks have no nutritional value.

- Weaning is not so much about calorie intake (most of your baby's energy will still be coming from milk). It is more about experiencing food and flavours – do not worry if most of it ends up on the floor.

CHAPTER 10

Your Guide to Weaning

This chapter provides with you with some essential tips on how to introduce your baby to solids in a way that will ensure he stands the best possible chance of developing healthy eating habits that will endure for many years.

Stage 1: A Variety of Individual Vegetables (Days 1–15)

The key is to start with a *variety* of *individual* vegetables as this will introduce your baby to a wide range of flavours. We recommend introducing one vegetable at a time to begin with – this will help your baby to learn the flavour of that vegetable. That way, when you start combining foods together, he can still identify the individual vegetable and will be more likely to accept what you are offering. This applies whether you are spoon-feeding or doing BLW.

We recommend offering a new, individual vegetable every day

for five days, and then rotating this twice more so that your child gets three tastes of each vegetable over 15 days. Start with non-sweet vegetables (including some bitter-tasting ones, such as broccoli and spinach), and introduce each of these in between a milk feed so that your baby is not too hungry or too full. This can be at any time of day. An ice-cube-sized portion is enough for the first few days as most of your baby's energy will be coming from milk and this stage is really about getting him used to new flavours. Gradually you can increase the portions as your baby's milk intake decreases. The vegetables we have suggested are by no means intended to be prescriptive; they are simply an example, using non-sweet vegetables. Introduce whatever vegetables you wish to, and at a time of the day that suits you and your baby. If you are starting your baby on solids at six months and he seems enthusiastic and hungry, you can offer him two different vegetables on each day instead of one; for example, one around midday and another mid-afternoon. In general, just try to stick to three principles:

1. *Daily changes*: don't give him the same vegetable for two consecutive days; mix it up.

2. *Repetition*: make sure that you rotate the vegetables every five days so that he gets repeated exposure (three times) during the first two weeks.

3. *Variety*: during the first few weeks of weaning try to introduce him to as many different vegetables as you can.

MAKING PURÉES

Steam your chosen vegetable (or fruit) until tender (steaming will preserve more of the nutrients than boiling). Once cooked, purée in a blender or with a handheld blender, or just mash it with a fork. Adjust the texture with your baby's usual milk or with boiled water if you wish. Leave to cool before spoon-feeding to your baby.

Remember that there is no need to add salt, sauces or other flavours – the aim is for your baby to try the individual flavour of the vegetables and learn to like them so that going forward he can detect the flavours in food and enjoy them.

Freezing purées

A great way to avoid spending a huge amount of time preparing purées from scratch every day is to make a large batch and freeze them. You just need ice-cube trays, cling film and freezer bags. Make up a large batch of one or more purées and allow them to cool down. Once cooled, fill the ice-cube trays and wrap in a layer of cling film to keep them covered. Place in the freezer (-18°C) and, once frozen, pop the cubes into freezer bags. Make sure you date the bags so that you know when the purées were made, and use them within three months. Defrost each portion as you need it by placing it in the fridge for 10–12 hours. Reheat the purée if you wish in a saucepan or microwave. If using the microwave, make sure you stir thoroughly to avoid hot spots and test the temperature yourself before feeding to your baby. Do not refreeze the purée once it has been defrosted.

FIRST FOODS TIMETABLE

Day 1	Day 2	Day 3	Day 4	Day 5
Broccoli	Spinach	Courgette	Kale	Cauliflower
Day 6	**Day 7**	**Day 8**	**Day 9**	**Day 10**
Broccoli	Spinach	Courgette	Kale	Cauliflower
Day 11	**Day 12**	**Day 13**	**Day 14**	**Day 15**
Broccoli	Spinach	Courgette	Kale	Cauliflower

INTRODUCING LUMPS AND TEXTURES

It is entirely up to you to decide whether you start with puréed smooth foods, mashed foods or finger foods. We would recommend that you use a mixture. For example, if you puree or mash some foods and spoon-feed them, give your baby some finger foods to try by himself as well. This way he will get the best of both worlds. If you start off with puréed foods, it is probably a good idea to try and move him on to lumps and textures as quickly as possible, as soon as he is showing signs that he is ready. This tends to be when he uses his tongue to push the food around his mouth, almost like chewing. This helps develop muscles important for speech. Every child is different and as a parent you are likely to know if your child seems able to cope with lumps or if you need to wait a bit longer. It can sometimes be a bit disconcerting for new parents when they feed their baby lumps for the first time, as often babies will gag and parents worry they are choking. But gagging is very different to choking; it isn't anything to worry about and is common during weaning.

PERSEVERANCE IS KEY

A baby's expression of interest or surprise in response to a new food is often misinterpreted as disgust, and what tends to happen is that the parents then stop offering that food. Try to focus on your baby's willingness to continue eating rather than his facial expressions. You might indeed find that your baby does not like some of the vegetables you offer him at first, and that is fine and totally normal. It is not unusual for babies to reject vegetables when they first try them as the flavours are new to them.

It is important not to give up the first time your baby turns away or spits the food out. Experience with a taste has been shown to increase acceptance of it.[315] If you want to increase your baby's acceptance of vegetables you need to give him lots of opportunities to try them. It can be very difficult and you may lose motivation to keep offering your child a food that he seems to clearly dislike, but perseverance is the key. The scientific evidence suggests that repeatedly exposing babies to the same vegetable eventually leads to most babies accepting and liking that vegetable. In one study, 49 mothers identified a vegetable purée that their infant (aged 7 months) disliked and they offered that vegetable on alternate days for 16 days (8 exposures).[316] On the other days they offered a liked vegetable (carrot purée). They found that on first exposure, the babies ate 39g of the disliked vegetable, on average, and 164g of the liked one. Over the following days, intake of the disliked vegetable increased and by the eighth exposure they ate 174g, about the same amount as the liked vegetable (186g). Nine months later, two thirds of the infants were still eating and liking the initially disliked vegetable. This shows that if your baby initially dislikes a vegetable, the key is to persevere. It might be necessary to offer your child the vegetable as many as 15 times, which may feel like a lot and each time your child rejects it you might be very tempted to give up, but keep trying and it should pay off.

A very recent review of the scientific literature on weaning highlighted that introducing vegetables first, frequently and in variety during weaning can increase acceptance of vegetables during this period and into childhood.[317] SACN also concluded that evidence supports repeated exposure as a proven method for enhancing babies' acceptance of new foods.[318] Our suggested timetable offers a new vegetable every day for five days, and then repeats twice for another 10 days (so your baby will get three exposures to each vegetable). Be sure to offer the individual vegetable each time and repeat any that your baby seems to dislike. A 'taste' can be as small as a teaspoonful because the idea is for your baby to do just that – have a taste.

FOOD FUSSINESS

It is important to add that some children are just less likely to accept vegetables than others. Vegetable liking seems to be influenced strongly by genes, but just because some children have a genetic tendency to dislike vegetables does not mean that preferences cannot be changed. Genes alone do not tell the whole story, which means there is room for change. Following our weaning guidance will help your child to become more accepting of foods and less fussy. We cover more on fussy eating in Chapter 12 (page 331).

PRAISE, PRAISE, PRAISE

Praising your child's good behaviour helps him to learn that what he is doing pleases you and the praise acts as a reward. As psychologists, we call this 'positive reinforcement' – if something rewarding follows a behaviour, it is more likely that the behaviour will occur again in the future. This technique is deceptively simple, but is a very effective method for managing a child's behaviour, including eating. If you offer a new or disliked vegetable to your baby and praise him for trying it, he will quickly realise that eating the vegetable makes you happy, and he will be more likely to eat it again. Looking happy when you are feeding your baby achieves the same thing – lots of smiles and encouragement will help to show your child that these vegetables are to be enjoyed.

MODELLING

Babies and children learn what is safe to eat vicariously by observing other people and it's no different with food. Your baby is looking to you to let him know that a food is safe to eat – he wants you to test drive it for him. This means that if you want your child to eat something, the best way to do this is to eat it and enjoy it with him or in front of him. If there is a vegetable you don't like – a good example is probably the commonly disliked Brussels sprout – try to hide your dislike from your child. If he sees you grimacing when you feed him or when you eat them yourself, he will pick up on that. He will quickly learn that Brussels sprouts are unpleasant or unsafe and to be avoided; this will make him much more likely to reject these foods. If it is going to be too difficult to eat something you dislike and pretend to like it, don't let this stop you offering it to your child. They will never learn to like it if they never try it and you might find that they actually enjoy it.

You are a model to your child – if you don't like or eat vegetables you can expect your child to follow suit. If you want your child to eat vegetables, you must eat them too. Aim to eat *with* your child as often as you can, even if it is not every mealtime, and show him that vegetables are healthy and delicious. Your baby can be included in family meals right from the start and this can help with modelling as he will learn how to eat by watching you. It is important to always bear that in mind. We will cover more on the influence of modelling healthy eating behaviour and the importance of family mealtimes in Chapter 12 (page 315).

Stage 2: Offer Multiple Vegetables and Introduce Other Foods

When you have introduced individual vegetable tastes for the first 15 days, you can begin offering your baby two or three familiar vegetables from Stage 1 at the same time, for example courgette and cauliflower. But ensure that they are not mixed together as you want your baby to taste the individual flavours. As with Stage 1, the key is to keep trying if your baby rejects them. Start introducing new vegetables too, for example, green beans, celery, asparagus, leeks, red pepper, green pepper, pumpkin and broad beans (although the broad bean is one vegetable that Hayley has never learned to love!). At this stage you can begin introducing sweet vegetables as well, such as parsnip, carrots, sweet potato, butternut squash and swede.

Other age-appropriate foods should also be introduced at this stage. You may find that your baby will more readily accept some of these other foods than vegetables – especially fruits, because they are sweeter. Be very careful that you do not offer some fruits (such as grapes or cherries) whole to babies as they are a choking hazard. Many fruits, such as apples and pears, will need to be cooked first to soften them and we would recommend peeling them as the skin can be a bit tough. Try starting with less sweet fruits, such as cherry or kiwi, as your baby is more likely to accept these at this stage. We would not recommend combining fruit with vegetables as the sweetness will disguise the vegetable flavour (see page 337). If you are going to offer fruit, just offer it on its own. It's really important that your baby becomes familiar with the individual flavours of many different vegetables and fruit. During this stage, repeat any foods your child seems to dislike, just as you did with the vegetables during Stage 1.

It is important that other new foods such as meat, fish, beans, pasta, rice, egg and dairy foods like yoghurt, are also introduced to your baby during weaning to ensure he consumes a balanced diet and is getting all the nutrients he requires (although there are some foods that should be avoided until your baby is six months old, see page 251). It is especially important to provide foods rich in iron. While introducing solids to your baby you are preparing him for the types of foods we as adults eat so it is great for him to experience as many different food groups as possible during this stage. Your baby will be learning to chew so a range of textures is important for his oral motor development. A varied diet is also essential for providing him with a range of nutrients needed to support healthy development. It's an opportunity to introduce items that are less commonly eaten by young children, such as oily fish. Some great examples of foods you could introduce in stage 2 are:

- fish without bones (for example, salmon)

- hardboiled eggs

- meat (for example, beef or chicken)

- dairy products made from whole milk (for example, unsweetened yoghurt)

- starchy foods (for example, sweet potato or pasta)

- pulses (for example, lentils or beans).

OILY FISH

Boys should have no more than four portions of oily fish per week and girls no more than two portions a week. Oily fish contains low levels of pollutants that can build up in the body. The concern is that high levels of these pollutants could potentially affect the development of a girl's unborn baby many years in the future. To be on the safe side, girls are therefore advised to eat less oily fish than boys.[319] Avoid offering swordfish, shark or marlin to children as these fish contain high levels of mercury and this can affect a child's nervous system.

Where at all possible, offer your child foods that you are already preparing for yourself. For example, if you are making a lasagne, keep aside some of the minced meat for your baby. This will make less work for you in terms of preparation, but remember not to add salt to the dish during cooking.

FINGER-FOOD IDEAS

Offering your baby finger foods will encourage coordination and help him to develop the skills he needs to bite, chew and swallow. Finger foods can be introduced from the start if you are BLW or as your child is getting used to lumpier textures if spoon-feeding. They need to be easy to pick up and hold and free from pips, stones or bones. Below are some ideas for finger foods.

- steamed broccoli/cauliflower florets

- ripe avocado

- steamed carrot or parsnip sticks

- steamed green beans or mangetout

- cooked potato or pasta

- melon with the skin removed

- mango

- banana

- toast or bread fingers

ALLERGIES

Allergic reactions occur more commonly with dairy foods, but can occur with other types of foods as well (such as eggs, nuts, seeds, wheat, fish and shellfish). If you notice any of the following after your baby eats a new food, please consult your GP immediately:

- diarrhoea or vomiting

- a cough

- wheezing or shortness of breath

- itchy skin

- a rash

- swollen lips or throat

- runny or blocked nose

- sore, red and itchy eyes

Rarely, an allergic reaction is severe and life-threatening (in cases of severe anaphylactic reaction). If you think your baby is having a severe allergic reaction, call 999 immediately and ask for an ambulance. If your child does have an allergy, there are plenty of food options out there for him, for example, dairy-free cheese or wheat-free bread. Your health visitor or doctor will be able to assist you with this.

Stage 3: Family Food

Once you have introduced new food groups, it is time for your child to start eating a modified version of the family diet. By about seven to nine months he should be offered three meals a day in addition to breast milk or formula milk (see Table 3, page 238, for guidance on how much milk babies should be consuming from six months to two years). By the time your baby is 10–12 months he should be offered crunchier foods as well, such as raw vegetables and breadsticks. By this age food does not need to be mashed, it can be minced or chopped instead. It is important to keep offering as wide a range of flavours and textures as possible in the transition to the family diet.

There are still some things you need to be mindful of, such as not introducing cows' milk as a drink until 12 months (it is fine in cooking from six months of age) and limiting the amount of salt (avoid adding gravy and sauces to his food), but overall there is not much stopping your baby from eating the same foods as the rest of the family. Restaurants often serve 'kids' meals' and many parents will spend time preparing a different meal to the rest of the family for their young child, but this is not necessary and we wouldn't recommend it. Your baby is still learning textures at this age and he will not have a full set of teeth yet, so you may need to modify his food slightly, for example, break a slice of toast into smaller pieces or mash roast potatoes with a fork. However, most of the foods that you eat he can eat too.

An important part of learning to eat is the social context – watching others and establishing how to eat. To help with this, aim to offer your child the same meal as the rest of the family and try to sit down together as a family. As much as possible avoid eating in front of the television as this may prevent children responding to their feelings of fullness. We cover more on this in Chapter 12 (page 324).

In November 2017 Public Health England published some excellent online resources about nutrition from six months to four years that are freely available. They have been developed for child care providers, but provide detailed guidance about the types of food that infants should be offered during the weaning process, lots of recipe ideas and weekly meal plans. They're great and well worth a read for ideas when you wean your baby: www.gov.uk/government/publications/example-menus-for-early-years-settings-in-england.

THE BOTTOM LINE

- Give a different single vegetable each day for five consecutive days, and then repeat this twice. This will ensure your baby has three exposures to five different vegetables over the first two weeks of weaning.

Baby Food Matters

- Keep trying: your baby might need several tastes before accepting certain foods.

- Don't disguise or hide vegetables with other flavours, such as mixing them with fruit or covering them with a sauce.

- Try to introduce your baby to lumps and different textures as soon as he indicates he is ready; don't leave it too long.

- Make sure you offer your baby as wide a variety of foods as you can during the first few weeks and months after introducing solid foods.

- Praise your baby and give lots of smiles and enthusiasm when he tries a new food or a food he seems to dislike.

- You are a role model: if you want your child to eat vegetables, then you must as well, in front of him.

- Towards the end of the first year of life, babies can eat most of the foods adults eat – there is no need for 'kids' menus'.

PART 4

Early Childhood

From one year of age children gain more independence with eating as they become more communicative. As a parent there are lots of opportunities to make a real difference to *what* and *how* your child eats now and in the future. As your child grows, some things get easier, while some get a bit harder, especially if your child becomes excessively fussy about what he will eat. Making sure that you establish healthy eating habits in the first 1,000 days is more important than ever given the high levels of overweight and obesity among preschool children in the UK.

In 2015, the largest national survey (the Health Survey for England) estimated that 25 per cent of all preschool children aged 2–4 years of age have developed overweight or obesity.[320] And in England, one in five children have developed overweight or obesity by the time they start primary school, rising to one in three by the end of primary school.[321] In contrast to this, only about 1 per cent of children have developed underweight at either age. Although the health risks of obesity don't usually make an appearance until well into adult life, the problem is that once a child has developed overweight or obesity they are likely to stay that way as an older child, and then as an adult. Public Health England published data in 2017 showing that 31 per cent of children with overweight at age 5 still had overweight at 11, while 30 per cent had developed obesity and 13 per cent had developed severe obesity.[322] We also know from a review of over 200,000 people that most children with overweight become adolescents and then adults with overweight.[323] Maintaining a healthy weight in the first 1,000 days of your child's life is therefore crucial.

The psychological and health consequences for children with overweight can be far-reaching and enduring. Psychological consequences for children can include: depression, poorer health-related quality of life, emotional and behavioural disorders (such as depression and anxiety), and worse academic performance.[324] The longer-term consequences for children with obesity can include raised risk of type 2 diabetes, coronary heart disease and a range of cancers in adulthood.[325]

Toddlerhood provides a great opportunity to set your child on a healthy weight trajectory. Optimal nutrition (*what* your child eats) during these early years will pave the way for lifelong health, and ensure that he thrives now and well into adulthood. But it is also the time when eating habits are formed, which can set him up for life. Based on the largest study of the diets and eating habits of toddlers in the UK (Gemini), the tips and advice in the final part of this book will help you to ensure that your child is on the right track to optimal nutrition (*what* he eats – Chapter 11) and that he develops healthy eating habits for life (*how* he eats – Chapter 12).

The Importance of a Healthy Diet

A healthy, balanced diet is crucial for your toddler's health and development. But it can be difficult to know just what a healthy diet is, especially when foods can be marketed for children as healthy when in fact they are not. Part of this involves knowing the dietary requirements for your toddler, but it also means taking time to read food labels – which can be deliberately confusing. This chapter will equip you with the knowledge to understand better the UK guidelines on energy and nutrient intakes and portion sizes, and how they apply to your child. We will guide you towards choosing foods that contain essential nutrients and advise on portion sizes that are appropriate for your child.

A Typical British Toddler's Diet

So, how many toddlers actually manage to eat a healthy diet in the UK? Until recently, virtually nothing was known about the current diets and eating habits of toddlers in the UK, as there had only been a few national studies conducted, and these were either outdated or the sample of children was very small. We recognised that a larger study of the eating habits of contemporary toddlers was needed to assess whether they are meeting dietary recommendations, and if not, where the problems are.

With Gemini, we therefore conducted a large-scale dietary survey of over 2,000 children at about two years of age. Parents completed three-day diet diaries and used portion guides to record every single thing each child ate and drank, as well as the amount. The diaries were able to tell us about the average energy and nutrient intakes for the whole sample of children.[326] The important insights that this study gave us into young children's eating behaviours have fuelled our passion for this area of research and were an impetus for us writing this book. The study has paved the way for us to give parents much-needed guidance on how and what to feed their children during the toddler years.

ENERGY INTAKE

Table 5 in Appendix 2, page 362 shows the daily energy intake recommendations (kcals per day) for children one and two years of age from the Scientific Advisory Committee on Nutrition (SACN)[327]. They are just rough guides, and the exact amount will depend on other factors as well, such as how big your child is, how physically active he is, and so on. You will see that boys and girls have slightly different recommended daily energy intakes because boys tend to be a bit bigger than girls, which means they need more energy. You will also see that the values are very precise, and you will probably be thinking there is no way that you can be expected to monitor your child's intake to this extent. We would agree; it would be virtually impossible to know the energy content of every single piece of food your child eats throughout the day and we wouldn't suggest that you calorie count obsessively. Healthy eating is not just about calories, it's about making sure your child has a balanced and varied diet, and is offered age-appropriate portion sizes (see pages 363).

In Gemini we found that toddlers exceeded recommended intakes by about 70kcal per day. Though this may seem relatively small, it adds up over time, and if this is sustained day after day during childhood, it can eventually lead to overweight for some children. With an excess of 70kcal per day, within just two months children would consume about 4,000 extra calories (four whole days' worth of extra eating) and gain more than 1 excess pound in weight (~0.5kg) or 3kg extra per year. It is easy to see how a small amount of additional energy each day can lead to excess weight gain over time in young children. However, over a third of the children in the sample consumed less energy per day than recommended, so it is not the case that all children in the UK are eating too much – all children are different.

PROTEIN

The Department of Health recommends daily protein intake for toddlers of about 14g per day[328]. To put this into context, a medium sized egg contains about 6g of protein. While there is popular belief that a high-protein diet is a good way to maintain a healthy weight (or lose weight) as an adult, research actually shows that high-protein intake in infancy and early childhood is linked to obesity. For example, one study demonstrated that babies and toddlers consuming higher amounts of protein between 12 and 24 months of age had higher body mass index (BMI) and a higher percentage of body fat when they were seven years old.[329] The current consensus among researchers is that high levels of protein stimulates the production of insulin which encourages sugar in the blood to be stored as fat. It also seems to stimulate the production of insulin-like growth factor 1 which promotes faster growth (and may also 'programme' for obesity in adulthood, and related diseases such as type 2 diabetes and cardiovascular disease).[330]

In Gemini we found that toddlers were consuming, on average, nearly three times the recommended amount of protein (40g per day). What's more, the toddlers who were eating more protein also gained more weight between two and five years of age.[331] We know that protein from dairy (such as milk and cheese), rather than other animal- (such as meat or fish) or plant-based (such as pumpkin seeds and lentils) protein was driving the increases in weight gain seen in Gemini.[332] In fact, almost a quarter of the energy intake was consumed from milk and many Gemini children (13 per cent) were still consuming formula milk at two years of age.[333] This suggests they were consuming too much milk, which contributed to the excess protein and the excess daily energy intake. It is therefore a good idea to keep an eye on how much protein your toddler is getting through each day. It can easily creep up if he is drinking a lot of milk. See our guidance on page 238 on recommended quantities of milk for infants and toddlers if you feel your child is consuming too much milk.

CARBOHYDRATES AND SUGAR

Approximately 50 per cent of your child's energy intake should be coming from carbohydrates.[334] Good sources include pasta, rice, cereal and other starchy foods (see page 292 on achieving a balanced diet). There aren't specific daily intake limits for sugar for children less than two years of age, but it is recommended that they don't have any sugar-sweetened drinks or food with sugar added to it. From age two, SACN recommends that *free sugars* (added sugar and sugars naturally present in honey and unsweetened fruit juices) should contribute less than 5 per cent of a child's daily energy intake, which equates to no more than about 12g a day.[335] To give you an idea of how much this is, a small (150ml) glass of unsweetened pure orange juice contains about 13g of sugar.[336] Other drinks that contain a lot of sugar include: sugar-sweetened fizzy drinks, energy drinks, most fruit smoothies and fruit juices, milkshakes and fruit cordials. Foods that contain a lot of sugar include: biscuits, sweets, cakes, chocolate, sugared breakfast cereals and ice cream.

FAT

There are no recommended total daily fat intakes for children under five years of age in the UK. Fats are an essential part of your child's diet, but shouldn't be consumed to excess because fat is very energy dense – it contains a large number of calories even in very small amounts. To put this into context, 1g fat contains 9kcal, but 1g protein or carbohydrate contains only 4kcal (so fat has more than twice the number of calories for the equivalent quantity). Once your child is two years old you can offer him lower-fat foods over full-fat ones (for example, semi-skimmed milk instead of full-fat milk, but not skimmed milk until he is over five years old), as long as he is growing well and is healthy.[337] Fats also come in different forms; some are good for you, whereas others are less good for you so need to be limited.

Saturated fat

You may have seen conflicting advice in the media about whether or not saturated fat is unhealthy. Evidence generally points towards high intakes of saturated fat leading to higher total cholesterol and, in particular, higher levels of bad cholesterol (LDL) which blocks arteries and leads to heart disease. A large review of good-quality randomised controlled trials carried out by the World Health Organization (WHO) in 2016 concluded that replacing saturated fat with unsaturated fat (such as cooking with vegetable oil instead of butter) leads to health benefits, such as lowering bad cholesterol (LDL).[338] Although there are no guidelines for saturated fat for young children in the UK, it is a good idea to try and make sure your child doesn't eat too many non-essential foods that are high in saturated fat. These are processed food such as crisps, pastries, pies, ice cream, chocolate, biscuits and cakes.

Unsaturated fats

Unsaturated fats are the good fats, but there is no recommended amount for these. There are two main types: monounsaturated fats, which are found in olive oil, peanut oil, avocados and most nuts; and polyunsaturated fats, which are found in corn oil and safflower oil. Polyunsaturated fats are *essential* fats, which means that they are necessary for various functions in the body (for example, making new cells, blood clotting and muscle movement), and you cannot make them. Your child must therefore have these as part of his diet. There are two types of polyunsaturated fats: omega-3 fatty acids and omega-6 fatty acids. Omega-3 fatty acids may help to prevent heart disease by lowering blood pressure, raising good cholesterol (HDL) and lowering triglycerides. Foods high in polyunsaturated fats include: avocados, oily fish (such as mackerel, sardines, fresh tuna and salmon), some vegetable oils (such as flaxseed oil) and some nuts and seeds (such as walnuts and flaxseeds).

FIBRE

In the UK, children aged two to five years are recommended by SACN to have 15g per day of fibre.[339] In Gemini, fibre intake fell short of recommendations[340] (8g per day rather than 15g per day). A diet containing sufficient fibre will help to reduce constipation in young children, and later in life it is important for preventing health conditions such as colon cancer, heart disease and obesity.[341] As we mentioned on page 57, there are two types of fibre: soluble (found in bananas, baked beans or carrots) and insoluble fibre (found in high-fibre breakfast cereals, wholemeal bread or brown rice). In Gemini, toddlers were consuming only about half the amount of fibre they needed (8g per day).

VITAMIN D AND IRON

SACN recommend that children aged one to four years who are living in the UK consume 10mcg of vitamin D per day.[342] Low vitamin D intake is a widespread issue among young children within the UK and sufficient intakes of vitamin D are difficult (if not impossible) to achieve through diet alone. In Gemini, vitamin D intake was less than half that which is recommended.[343] In fact, 93 per cent of children did not meet the recommended intake, which is quite concerning. Only 7 per cent of children in

Gemini took vitamin D supplements. We would strongly recommend following the DoH's guidance to offer your child vitamin D supplements each day.

The recommended iron intake for British children aged one to three years is 6.9mcg per day.[344] Seventy per cent of Gemini children did not meet the recommended intake for iron. However, intakes were higher than they were in a much older study of the diets of toddlers conducted during the early 1990s,[345] suggesting that more parents are offering their children supplements and/or fortified milk and foods, such as cereals and breads, which have become popular over the last two decades. See pages 257–9 for good sources of vitamin D and iron.

HEALTHY START

In the UK, free vitamins are available to low-income families with young children through the Healthy Start scheme, which provides fixed-value food vouchers and vitamin coupons. However, a relatively recent study found that of the 107 families eligible for free supplementation, only 10 per cent were making use of the free vitamins as they were not even aware that they were available to them.[346] You can see if you are eligible at www.healthystart.nhs.uk.

Offering your child a varied diet with a limited amount of milk and a decent amount of oily fish and meat, as well as foods that have been fortified with vitamin D and iron, can all help to ensure that he gets enough of these important nutrients.

SALT

SACN recommend that the *maximum* daily amount of salt British children aged one to three years consume is 2g per day.[347] The British Nutrition Foundation highlights that this amount does not represent an 'ideal' or 'optimum' intake (it may still be too high), but is probably achievable for most children.[348] High salt intake increases the risk of raised blood pressure and heart disease in adulthood.[349]

Almost all children in Gemini consumed too much salt. Aside from the detrimental impact that this may have on their health, another study has shown that this may set taste preferences for the future. For example, a study showed that babies that had been exposed to starchy table foods (a source of salt) at six months preferred salty solutions, were more likely to lick salt from the surface of foods and were more likely to eat plain salt at preschool age (three to four years).[350] It is really important not to add salt to any food you prepare for your child and be mindful of processed foods (foods which have been altered in some way during preparation), such as ready meals, cheese, crisps, ham, pies, pasties, bacon and sausages as these often contain a lot of salt. The Infant & Toddler Forum (ITF) is an organisation offering evidence-based practical advice for healthy eating habits from pregnancy to preschool. They are supported by an educational grant from Danone Early Life Nutrition (who own commercial brands, including Aptamil) but the group is independent. The table contains their guidance on suggested maximum portions of salty foods with a range provided for one to four year olds:

Food	Portion size
Processed cheese	15–21g (1 slice/1 triangle or string/1 Mini Babybel™)
Ham	½–1½ small slices/1½–4 wafer–thin slices
Sausages	¼–1 medium sausage
Crisps	4–6 crisps
Samosa	½–1 samosa/1–2 small samosas
Quiche	30–90g (½–1½ small slices)

We also compared all of our findings in Gemini to dietary information from children aged 18 to 36 months in the UK-based National Diet and Nutrition Survey (NDNS).[351] While Gemini toddlers exceeded daily recommended energy intakes by 7 per cent, the children in the NDNS exceeded them by 17 per cent. Vitamin D and iron intake both fell below recommended intakes and there were high intakes of protein in both samples. The fact that both studies show similar results tells us that among the UK population, toddlers are at risk of overweight and other health problems because they are consuming too much energy and not consuming sufficient vitamin D and iron.

How to Achieve a Healthy Diet

So, how do you make sure your toddler gets optimal nutrition? It's not easy, but it's about making sure you offer him more of the nutrient-rich foods and less of the foods that are high in sugar, salt and/or unnecessary fat. Offering healthy snacks as well as healthy meals, and ensuring that portion sizes of meals and snacks are age-appropriate, is crucial too. An important part of this is familiarising yourself with food labels, so you can spot foods that are good choices and those that should be limited.

UNDERSTANDING FOOD LABELS

Food labels contain a lot of information and it can be very diffi-cult to know what you are supposed to be looking for and what it all means. Learning how to read food labels is essential in order to know what we are eating. It empowers us to make informed, healthy choices. Most pre-packed foods have a label *on the back or side of the packaging* with nutritional information.

Six key pieces of nutritional information on food labels are:

1. *Energy*
Kilocalories (kcal) and kilojoules (kJ) tell you how much energy is in a product. It's a good idea to know which foods tend to be far higher in energy than you expect, so that you can make sure your child doesn't have too many of these, if they are non-essential.

2. *Fats*

'Saturates' on the food label tells you the amount of saturated fat in the product. There is no requirement for nutrition labels to include any information about unsaturated fats.

3. *Salt*

Sometimes sodium will be listed rather than salt but you can multiply the amount in grams on the label by 2.5 and divide by 1,000 to get the salt content, for example 500mg of sodium = (500*2.5)/1,000 = 1.25g salt.

4. *Sugar*

There are two types of sugar:

- Naturally occurring sugar, such as the lactose in milk or natural sugars found in fruit and vegetables.

- Added or 'free' sugars, which include table sugar, and the sugars naturally present in honey and fresh, unsweetened fruit juices. So this will include confectionery, biscuits, fresh fruit juices and sugar-sweetened fizzy drinks.

Many of the foods and drinks containing 'free' sugars tend to have a lot of energy but few other nutrients.

5. *Reference Intake*

Reference Intake (RI) used to be called Recommended Dietary Allowance (RDA). These are guidelines on the approximate amount of energy and nutrients required for a healthy balanced diet each day. The %RI tells you how much of your daily healthy maximum is in a portion. The values listed on most foods will be for adults so they won't be relevant to your child.

6. Serving/portion size

The portion size on food packets is the manufacturer's recommendation for one portion of the product and the RI values are worked out based on this portion size. The portion size allows you to understand how much of a nutrient you are eating, to compare the nutritional content of two similar food products and to compare the serving size to the amount you eat. If you eat the serving size listed on the front of the packet, you will get the amount of energy and nutrients that are listed. But be aware that a 'portion' can be misleading and a manufacturer's idea of a portion might be very different to yours – it is often a much smaller amount than expected. As an example, one serving of Jelly Babies is four sweets (and contains 87kcal), but the packet contains far more than this. You can soon end up consuming more calories, saturated fat or salt than you realise. When comparing two products to make a healthy choice, always ensure that the serving sizes for comparison are the same. If one product gives information per 100g and another gives it per packet (200g), you would need to double the nutritional information of the first in order to compare them accurately. And some foods only include the nutritional information per 100g, but the portion included is much smaller or larger than this (for example, 28g), so you would need to calculate the values for yourself. Most of the time you would need a calculator to do this, so this type of information can be unhelpful as well as misleading.

Food manufacturers and most supermarkets now also highlight the important nutritional information (energy, fat, saturated fat, sugars and salt) using a colour-coded guide to indicate whether the product is high (red), medium (amber) or low (green) in fat, saturated fat, sugars and salt. Green labels mean the food is low in either fat, saturated fat, sugars or salt so will be the healthiest choice; amber means medium so these foods are fine in moderation, as part of a balanced diet; and red labels are high in either fat, sugars or salt and should be limited. Do bear in mind that food labels and nutritional information are based on adult serving sizes, so you would need to check the appropriate sized portion for your child (page 363). If this sounds like a lot of effort, our general advice would be to limit foods that have a red label as these will be high in fat, sugar or salt.

INGREDIENTS LIST

Food labels also have an ingredients list and this can be used to help you decide how healthy a food is. Ingredients are listed by weight starting with the ingredient that weighs the most and ending with the ingredient that weighs the least. Those that appear first in the list make up a bigger share of the food product so if these are high-fat or high-sugar, such as butter, cream or sugar, the product is usually less healthy.

ACHIEVING A BALANCED DIET

You are likely to have heard of Change4Life – the Department of Health's national campaign to prevent people from developing overweight (www.nhs.uk/change4life).[352] It provides lots of information on healthy eating. In particular, they developed the Eatwell Guide, which visually shows how much of each of the food groups everyone should be eating to achieve a healthy, balanced diet.[353] Foods are divided into five groups:

1. Bread, rice, potatoes, pasta and other starchy foods

2. Fruit and vegetables

3. Milk and dairy foods

4. Meat, fish, eggs, beans and other non-dairy sources of protein

5. Foods and drinks high in fat and/or sugar

The advice is to eat a wide variety of different foods from the *first four* groups every day. Foods in the fifth group – those high in fat and/or sugar, such as chocolate, crisps, cakes, ice cream and sweets – are not essential to a healthy diet and should only be eaten in small quantities. The guidelines are not to give these foods to children *under two years of age*. But if you choose to offer them to your child try to limit them to once or twice per week only. Breads, cereals and potatoes should make up about a third of the food that you serve each day to your child if he is one to four years old, and you should aim to give him vegetables and fruit at meals and snacks. Try to offer milk, dairy foods and dairy alternatives at two to three meals and snacks each day. If your child is one to two years old about 400ml of cows' milk a day will fit into a healthy balanced diet – this could consist of a small drink of milk in the morning with snacks, and milk before bed or a nap. Your child's main meals should always contain an item of meat, fish, eggs, pulses or meat alternatives as they are high in iron. First Steps Nutrition also has guidance on good food choices for one to four year olds.[354] They provide ideas on how to offer balanced meals to your toddler to ensure that he meets his energy and nutrient requirements.

LIMIT 'UNHEALTHY' FOODS AND SNACKS

Try to check food labels and limit the amount of unhealthy high-fat, high-sugar foods, such as pastries, sweets, chocolate and crisps, that you have in the house. This is probably the easiest way to help your child eat healthily.

To cut down on the amount of sugar you give to your child we recommend offering him water for the majority of drinks, not fruit juice. We would not recommend simply replacing sugar with artificial sweeteners because this could encourage your child to develop a preference for sweet flavours. If you have sugar in your tea, you will probably think that tea without sugar tastes terrible because you have become used to it tasting sweet. It's best not to create or encourage these preferences for sweeter flavours in the first place, to avoid encouraging a 'sweet tooth' in your child. Try to avoid purchasing too many processed foods as many of them have more sugar in than you would add if you were to make them at home.

It is also surprising how easily children can consume too much salt. For example, if your child is two years old and has a 20g bowl of corn flakes for breakfast (0.37g salt), half a cheese sandwich for lunch made up of one slice of granary bread (0.4g salt) and 30g cheese (0.5g salt), half a bag of crisps as a snack (0.17g) and an evening meal of two fish fingers (0.23g) and vegetables, they will be close to the recommended limit of 2g per day. These are common everyday foods for many children and you would probably not consider some of them to be particularly high in salt, but processed cereals, bread and cheese are foods that have a surprising amount of salt in them. Other foods that are high in salt include:

- bacon

- gravy granules and stock cubes

- soy sauce

- sausages

- yeast extract

- smoked meats and fish

- coated chicken

- ham

One good way of reducing the salt in your child's diet is to prepare food yourself rather than buying ready-made foods. You can add flavour using other ingredients, such as fresh herbs, black pepper, tomato purée, garlic, balsamic vinegar and lemon juice, and you could purchase low-salt stock cubes. Roasting vegetables is a good way to bring out their flavour rather than adding salt to the pan when boiling.

Small changes can make a big difference to your child's diet, without him feeling hard done by or hungry. Healthy swaps include:

- healthy snacks instead of unhealthy ones, such as carrot sticks and hummus instead of a packet of crisps

- a whole piece of fruit instead of dried fruit

- a frozen banana instead of ice cream

- boiled or poached eggs instead of fried eggs

- currant buns, malt loaf or fruit bread instead of cakes and biscuits

- low-sugar breakfast cereals (for example, wheat biscuits, shredded wheat or porridge) instead of those coated in honey or sugar

- low-salt stock cubes instead of standard stock cubes

HEALTHY SNACKS

Many parents are unsure what constitutes a healthy snack. A lot of the snack foods available for children are high in sugar or fat, but they are marketed in such a way as to make them appear healthy. Busy lives often mean there is limited time to prepare all of your child's food from scratch, so it's a good idea to have foods available at home that require no preparation, such as fresh fruit. There is such a wide variety of fruit to choose from, vibrant in colour so they will look appealing to young children. A wealth of research has shown that having fruit in a bowl in the house attracts children and leads to them eating more of it.[355] We would recommend that you only offer him whole fruit and give him water to drink if he is thirsty. He can be offered milk to drink as a snack.

Your child will, of course, occasionally have snack foods that are high in fat and/or sugar, such as chocolate and crisps. Simply try to be careful about how often you give these and how much you offer to your child, because they are bad for his teeth as well as his health. The images in Appendix 3 (pages 364–5) show the Infant & Toddler Forum (ITF) portion sizes for high-fat and high-sugar foods for one to four year-olds. These might seem like small portions and, indeed, they are probably far less than most children are offered. A kids' bag (20g) of soft jelly sweets, for example, contains about eight sweets – twice the recommended portion. Recommended portion sizes for several different snack foods can be found below, with a range provided for one to four year-olds:[356]

Food	Portion size
Yoghurt	1 average pot (125ml)
Apple	¼–½ medium apple
Raisins/sultanas	½–2 tablespoons
Banana	¼–1 medium banana
Celery/cucumber	2–8 small sticks/slices
Chocolate	2–4 squares
Popcorn	½–1 small cup

HEALTHY SNACK IDEAS

- Chunks of fruit: melon, strawberries, grapes (cut in half lengthways to avoid choking), apple, banana, pear, kiwi, satsuma

- Small pot of blueberries

- Plain yoghurt with sliced fruit

- Toast soldiers with hummus

- Pitta bread fingers with guacamole

- Oatcakes with peanut butter

- Sticks of carrot, cucumber or pepper with hummus or yoghurt

- Unsweetened or unsalted rice cakes with cream cheese

- Unsalted oatcakes with Brazil nut butter (or any nut butter)

- Breadsticks with tuna pâté.

Snacks that require no preparation are great if time is limited, but if you do have a bit of time it is a good idea to get your toddler involved in preparing food with you, as it will familiarise him with different foods and may make him more likely to try new ones.

CHILDCARE

It can be a bit of a sticking point for parents when they send their child to nursery or to a childminder and feel that their child is not being given 'appropriate' food.

'It's an uphill battle – when he went to a childminder she fed him fish fingers and chips and chicken nuggets and chips and pizza and chips, which is fine once in a while, but not every day. She also gave him like Ribena or sugary drinks.'

Jen, mum of Sady (20 months) and Lyla (4 years)

Public Health England have recently published meal plans and recipes for early-years settings to help them provide healthy, balanced and nutritious food and drink to under-fives.[357] The resources provided by the Children's Food Trust may also be useful to you as a parent and can be accessed via their website: www.childrensfoodtrust.org.uk.

If you have concerns that your child is not being fed in line with how you would like him to be, you need to talk with the nursery staff or your childminder. It is okay to tell them what you do and do not want your child to have; he is your child and some of you are paying a lot of money for them to look after him, so you have a say in what happens when he is in their care. For example, feel free to say: 'I don't want my child to be given any fruit juice or fruit cordial; he is only to have water.' The same applies with grandparents; it is quite often the case that grandparents like to spoil their grandchildren with 'treats' and this can undermine the efforts you go to to ensure your child eats healthily. It can be a tricky issue because you are grateful to the grandparents for looking after your child but equally you want them to follow the rules you have set out at home. Talking to them is the best way of dealing with this; explain how you do things at home and why you would like to keep it that way.

Portion Size

It is sometimes difficult to know whether your child is eating enough or eating too much, but parents tend to worry much more about their child undereating than overeating. Children all differ in their appetites and how often and how much food your child eats will vary depending on his appetite (as well as other things, such as how fast he is growing at that particular time).

Many parents struggle to know what an appropriate portion size is for babies and toddlers. This isn't surprising because it is really difficult to find evidence-based guidance on age-appropriate portion sizes for young children. Parents often worry that their child is not eating enough, but some recent research conducted by the ITF suggests that many parents in the UK are actually serving their young children *too much* food in one go – the portion sizes they are offering are too large for a child of that age.[358] A survey was conducted with 1,000 parents of infants in the UK and many were serving their child *adult-sized* portions.

Large portions are problematic because research has shown very consistently that children (and adults) will eat more food if they are served more.[359] We all have a tendency to eat a bit more, *if it is there*, simply because we can. One study involved 35 children aged 3–5 years old being served snacks differing in portion size.[360] The amounts eaten during the snack and a subsequent lunch were measured and, regardless of age, the children that had been served larger snacks ate more. Another study that looked at the daily food intake of 16 children aged four to six years old found that the most powerful influence on the amount children ate was the amount served to them.[361] These studies were small, but this effect has been observed over and over again in all sorts of other studies, and with older children and adults as well. This tendency to eat more when served more was probably helpful many thousands of years ago, when food was less plentiful and it was wise to eat every last scrap when you came across it. But in the current food environment, where there is virtually no limit to food for most people in the Western world, this tendency can quickly lead to excessive weight gain. And children who are less sensitive to their fullness and more responsive to food cues are more susceptible to overeating.

Now this might sound obvious, but there are two ways to eat more calories during a meal: a large volume of food is eaten (more grams), or a small volume of food is eaten (fewer grams) but it is higher in energy density (more calories per gram). Therefore, another important consideration when thinking about the portion size of foods you serve your child is the energy density of that particular food.

ENERGY DENSITY

Energy density is the amount of energy (calories) per gram of food. Lower energy-density foods, such as soups, stews, fruit and vegetables, tend to have a higher water content, so they provide fewer calories per gram of food. High energy-density foods, such as biscuits, cakes, crisps, peanuts and cheese, tend to be high in fat and have a low water content.

In theory, if a food is high in energy density, your child should naturally eat *less* of it through the process of self-regulation, but this doesn't seem to happen (at least not for every child). In the study of four- to six-year-olds mentioned above, the children did not adjust the amount they ate based on the energy density of the food. If the children were served more, they ate more. There is also a perception among researchers that children should eat less following a snack before a meal; so if you go for a meal and your child has a starter, he should eat less of his main course to compensate. But again, research has shown that not all children do this.

Studies such as these provide evidence that some children, like adults, can be influenced by certain aspects of their eating environment (for example, portion sizes and energy density), rather than their internal feelings of fullness. Even babies as young as six weeks old have shown this tendency – mothers of 18 breastfed infants aged 6–21 weeks old expressed extra breast milk as a means of increasing milk production and, as a result of the increased supply of milk, their babies drank more, and had a greater energy intake.[362] This suggests that serving large portions interferes with our ability to regulate our intake, even for very young babies. A summary of evidence for the impact of portion sizes on the consumption of food and drinks was conducted in 2015.[363] Fifty-eight studies involving a total of 6,603 participants were assessed and it was concluded that exposure to larger portion sizes increased quantities of food consumed among children and adults. The authors suggested that if portion sizes were reduced across the whole diet, average daily energy intake could be reduced by 144 –228kcal. This is actually quite a lot, and could make the difference between maintaining a healthy weight, and developing overweight for some children.

WEIGHT GAIN

In a large national sample of British babies and toddlers we looked at whether those who consumed larger portions were more likely to have overweight.[364] We found that all children ate, on average, five times per day (three meals and two snacks) but the children with overweight ate larger portions at each meal or snack. In Gemini we looked at how portion size affected the children's rate of weight gain between two and five years of age.[365] We found that children who consumed larger average portions gained more weight than those who consumed a smaller portion each time. Our research suggests that, in toddlerhood, overweight is strongly linked to eating larger portions during each meal/snack, highlighting the need to be vigilant about the portion sizes that you offer to your child.

PORTION SIZE GUIDANCE

The ITF has been running a portion-size campaign – #RethinkToddlerPortionSizes – which focuses on ensuring young children are served age-appropriate portions. They used the research we published from Gemini as evidence that large portion sizes put children at higher risk of overweight and launched their campaign to help take the guesswork out of how much food is enough. They have developed a 'Tot It Up' calculator – a food tracker that enables you to add up everything you have served your toddler over the course of a day, as well as input his physical activity. It will give you a summary of your toddler's daily and weekly food intake, and also provides you with tips on how to make small changes to ensure he has a healthy balance. You can find the 'Tot It Up' calculator on the ITF website: www.infantandtoddlerforum.org.

'I don't have enough information on portion size. Just the other day I read something about toddlers only needing a spoonful of baked beans as a portion and I realised there must be all sorts of foods that I don't know the recommended portion for.'

Peter, dad of Daniel (18 months) and Isabelle (4 months)

Many parents of young children are not sure where to go for portion-size guidance. The ITF provides a range of evidence-based portion sizes suitable for children aged one to four years in the UK.[366] In Appendix 3 (page 364) there are a few example food items and images of appropriate portion sizes for children of this age. You can access the complete set of portion sizes on the ITF website: www.infantandtoddlerforum.org. A range is given for each food and this is because of the wide age bracket (one to four years). A four year old child is likely to require more energy than a one year old. The ITF recommends that: 'portion sizes for very young toddlers aged 12–24 months are those at the lower end of the portion size ranges in the tables. The energy requirements of these young toddlers are considerably lower than those for children two years and over.'

First Steps Nutrition also has guidance on portion sizes for one- to four-year-olds.[367] They have photos of appropriate portion sizes that were developed based on balanced food plans that meet the average energy and nutrient needs of children aged one to four years.

In general, younger children should be eating slightly less than older children for each type of food. We suggest that the best way of judging how much food your child needs is to know what type of 'eater' he is and respond accordingly. (See the next chapter for more on this.) As was the case with milk-feeding your baby and weaning him, the principle that we would suggest you follow is *responsive feeding*.

THE BOTTOM LINE

- Familiarise yourself with your child's dietary requirements.

- Use The Eatwell Guide to provide a balanced diet for your child.

- Read food labels to inform your food choices and compare food products.

- A few healthy swaps can make a big difference to your child's diet.

- Be mindful of portion sizes. Large portions have been shown to influence weight gain in young children.

- Children will eat more when served more so they need child-sized portions.

- Portion sizes are not an exact science – the amount your child needs will depend on his weight (and his appetite – discussed in the next chapter).

- Use the 'Tot It Up' calculator to monitor your child's food intake (see page 303).

- If you are concerned about the quality of the food your child is being offered in childcare, then speak to them and make your wishes clear. It is okay to tell them what you do and do not want your child to have; he is your child.

CHAPTER 12

Responsive Feeding in the Toddler Years

The first 1,000 days provides a unique window of opportunity for you to lay down the foundations for your toddler's eating habits that will endure for many years. *What* he eats during this period is important, but *how* he eats matters too. During toddlerhood, the way you feed your child and the routines you establish can help to optimise his appetite regulation, ensure he likes healthy foods, doesn't hanker after unhealthy foods and is open to trying new ones. You can help him to foster a good relationship with food so that he views it as fuel rather than comfort, entertainment or a reward.

You will now be well versed in the principles of responsive feeding – recognising what type of eater your child is, and using appropriate feeding strategies that support his particular eating styles. You should continue to use this approach now that he is becoming a more integrated member of family meals. But ensuring that he develops good eating habits goes further than responsive feeding now that he is older. It will also involve establishing structured mealtime routines and including him in the preparation of meals and shopping for food. All of this will pave the way for him to make good choices when the time comes for him to start making decisions about food on his own. Responsive feeding is thought to lay the foundations for good appetite regulation and a healthy relationship with food, and will allow you to feed your child in way that suits his particular eating style.

WHAT THE EVIDENCE SAYS

Systematic reviews of responsive feeding, weight gain and appetite regulation in toddlerhood and childhood have highlighted that responsive feeding is linked to better appetite regulation and healthier weight gain.[368] But, the vast majority of studies haven't been designed in such a way that it is possible to know if unresponsive feeding is really the cause of poor appetite regulation and risk of overweight, or whether parents tend to use less responsive feeding methods when their children have avid or poor appetites and are already either gaining weight too rapidly or too slowly – the chicken-or-the-egg issue. The only way to really find this out is through a randomised controlled trial. A recent review of all randomised controlled trials to prevent overweight and obesity in infancy and childhood concluded that the most promising trials were those that focused on responsive feeding, as well as diet.[369]

The most important trial to date on responsive feeding during weaning and appetite regulation is NOURISH, which randomised 352 Australian women to receive 12 group sessions on how to feed responsively, and what foods their babies should be given when they were between 4 and 7 months old (6 sessions) and again when they were 13–16 months old (6 sessions).[370] Another 346 mums were randomised to be in the control group – they had access to all the usual health services, but no extra information on feeding. At two years of age the toddlers whose mums were in the intervention group had better appetite control – they were less food responsive (less likely to want to eat, or eat more, when they see, smell or taste palatable food), had better satiety sensitivity (more sensitive to their feelings of fullness) and were less likely to emotionally overeat (wanting to eat when feeling upset, anxious or annoyed).[371] They were also less fussy with regard to food. Many of these effects were still there when the children were three to four years old – they were still less food responsive and more satiety sensitive.[372] The intervention did not have a big effect on children's weights, however.[373] At five years of age there were fewer children with overweight in the intervention group, but this difference was not considered 'statistically significant' (meaning it could have been due to chance). Nevertheless, it showed that responsive feeding has important and long-lasting effects on appetite.

How to Feed Your Toddler Responsively

As mentioned in Chapter 6, responsive feeding involves feeding your child only when he is hungry, and stopping as soon as he indicates to you that he is full. The good news is that, now that your child is older, it is much easier to read his hunger and satiety signals – these gestures tend to be far easier to read in a toddler than a baby, probably because he will sometimes just tell you, so you don't have to rely solely on his body language.

Hunger cues from around 12 months of age include:

- leaning towards food

- visually tracking food

- excited arm and leg movements

- opening his mouth as the spoon approaches

- asking for or pointing towards food

Satiety cues from around 12 months of age include:

- shaking head to say 'no more'

- using words like 'all done' and 'get down'

- playing with food or throws food

- pushing food or plate away

However, for toddlers and young children, responsive feeding gets a little bit more complicated than simply looking out for his hunger and fullness signals. It involves much more than that. Broadly speaking, it means you taking care not to be too controlling or dominating in feeding interactions with your child and of his 'food world'. This certainly doesn't mean giving him free rein and letting him rule mealtimes – overindulgence and lack of control can lead to nothing short of chaos with a two-year-old! At the same time, a laissez-faire approach to feeding, or being uninvolved or disinterested, means he won't get the support that he needs to nurture good eating habits. In order for your child to develop effective appetite regulation, healthy food preferences and a good relationship with food, he needs to learn which foods are good and safe to eat, what hunger and fullness feel like, and that he should only eat when he is hungry and stop when he feels full – you are an important part of this learning process.

The trick is to find the right balance – not being too controlling, but not leaving everything up to him. In practice, this will mean making sure that you respond appropriately to your child's needs when he signals them to you – not ignoring them, then overruling him – and giving him a sense that he has *some* control over how he eats (how much and how often) and what food he chooses to eat, while also setting some boundaries (like anything with young children). Children differ in their natural dispositions towards food – some have hearty appetites and want to eat all the time, while others are harder to feed – and different types of eaters pose very different challenges for you as a parent. We will discuss specific tips for different types of eaters in detail on page 319 and offer tailored strategies that you can use to manage eager eaters and very picky ones.

However, there are a few principles of responsive feeding that are important to follow, whatever your child's appetite and eating style, and we have outlined these below.

1. Let your child decide how much to eat – don't pressure him

Although it can be tempting to pressure your child to finish the meal that you have spent ages preparing, don't make him finish everything on the plate or encourage him to eat more if he has indicated that he is full. This will help him to learn what fullness feels like and to stop eating in response to his satiety. Encourage him to have autonomy over his intake, by self-feeding – this may mean accepting there will be some mess!

2. **Avoid excessive restriction of unhealthy food and use covert rather than overt ways to restrict your child's intake**

   As he gets older your child will begin to have more autonomy around his eating. This, of course, means that it can be difficult to monitor your child's eating when they go to parties and there are cakes, crisps and other unhealthy foods freely available. At times you may have to simply accept that your child will indulge, but the key is not to make these foods out of bounds. Birthday parties don't happen every day (although they can be every weekend when they are little!), and it is fine for your child to enjoy these foods from time to time. As we mentioned in Chapter 8, being overly restrictive with certain foods can backfire and your child may be more likely to want the foods he is never allowed. If you allow 'unhealthy' foods but limit them, hopefully when he attends parties he won't go over the top. Try to restrict foods in a covert way, for example, by not keeping chocolate in the house, rather than in an overt way, for example, by eating chocolate in front of him but not allowing him any. This will make your life easier insofar as it will minimise pestering, but it will also guard against the 'forbidden-fruit effect' – your child wanting more than ever the food that he isn't allowed.

3. **Offer him a range of healthy foods to choose from**

   Offering your child a choice of healthy options will help him to feel like he has some control over *what* he eats and will teach him to make decisions about food for himself. If you offer your child two or three alternatives, it will also soften the blow of saying 'no' to something that he wants. You can read more on this below.

4. Offer him age-appropriate portion sizes

Make sure you pay attention to the portions of food that you serve your child at meals and for snacks (see page 303). Some toddlers will eat more if served larger portions, simply because the food is there and they can. In addition, it is good to teach your child what a healthy portion of food looks like; this will lay the groundwork for when he gets older and makes decisions about portion sizes for himself.

5. Offer food only in response to hunger, not for any other reason

This means making sure you only feed your child because he needs the fuel, not because you want to soothe him if he is upset, control his behaviour or distract him. If your child is only ever given food in response to hunger, it will support him not only in developing good appetite regulation, but it will also help to ensure that he develops a healthy relationship with food, and doesn't come to rely on it as a source of comfort or entertainment.

6. Give him lots of praise when he eats healthy foods that he is reluctant to eat or even try

To your toddler, your praise is a reward worth working for. If he sees that you are pleased with him when he tries certain foods, he will be more likely to do it again next time. This is a fundamental part of becoming familiar with a food and learning to like it – repeated tastes of a food result in increased exposure, and ultimately liking. Expect that he will refuse some foods; this is normal in toddlerhood. If he refuses to eat something don't make a fuss or try and coax him. Just offer it again tomorrow.

7. Use non-food rewards to reward him for trying a new healthy food or for eating a food he doesn't like

Non-food rewards are a great way to motivate your child to try a food they are suspicious about or refuse to eat. Stickers or a star chart work well for some children, but you know your child best and will have a good idea about what motivates him. But be sure never to use his favourite unhealthy food as a bribe to get him to eat healthy foods he doesn't like – it will only result in him disliking the healthy food even more and increasing his desire for his favourite unhealthy food, which has now become a reward as well as something that tastes good.

8. Make sure there are no distractions

Distractions, such as the television or other screens, should be avoided during mealtimes so that your child is able to focus on eating; the taste of the food and the feeling of fullness as he eats.

9. Be a good model for him yourself

It is so important when it comes to healthy eating that you act as a role model by eating healthy foods yourself, in front of your toddler. This is the most important way that he will learn about which foods are safe and good to eat. As your child gets older, an important part of this is allowing him to participate in family mealtimes (see below). You can also include him in food shopping and preparing meals and snacks. All of these activities are opportunities to teach him about eating healthily. But being a good role model is not just about your behaviour, it also involves you having a healthy attitude towards food and eating, and using positive language to describe foods.

10. Establish structured mealtime and snack routines

Try to get into a routine whereby your toddler has three meals each day that are always served at the same time, and two snacks (one mid-morning and one mid-afternoon). This will mean that your child learns what to expect in terms of food and is less likely to pester you for food when it's not a set time to eat. It's really important not to skip meals – a child with an avid appetite will be extremely hungry and may then overcompensate at the next meal, while a child who has a poor appetite may not sufficiently compensate at the next meal. In particular, eating a healthy breakfast is an important habit for your toddler to develop (see page 316). We would also advise limiting mealtimes to 30 minutes. This is plenty of time for children to get all the nutrition they need; dragging out a mealtime for a picky eater will only lead to a battle of wills. There are many more effective strategies for encouraging healthy eating for faddy eaters on page 330.

'My son will not eat certain things like tomatoes and carrots, despite them being a regular feature of his baby-led weaning diet. I just continue with my ethos of not force-feeding and accept that at the moment he does not like these food items. I can already see that with age he is more willing to try new things. We do not cook separate meals for him and it is nice to see what he is willing to eat, even if you think it is something he will dislike.'

Maria, mum of Oliver (2 years and 9 months)

Feeding your child responsively may seem quite a difficult task and sometimes you will just want an easy life and will give in to what your child will or will not eat, but following the tips above will be worth it in the long run. Your child will be more in tune with his feelings of hunger and fullness, and less fussy, and you will feel more confident about how often and how much he should be eating.

FAMILY MEALTIMES

Eating together as a family appears to benefit children's health and well-being in numerous ways. Children who participate in shared family mealtimes have better language development and academic achievement, better-quality diets and reduced risk of childhood obesity.[374] A recent analysis of 17 different studies explored the nutritional health of almost 200,000 children who participated in family mealtimes with varying frequency.[375] The analysis found that children who ate with their family three or more times per week were more likely to have healthier eating patterns and be a healthy weight than children who ate fewer than three family meals together. Another study of two- to five-year-old children found that children's vegetable consumption and liking reflected the extent to which they ate the same food as their parents at mealtimes.[376] This highlights the importance of eating together, giving your child the same food that you eat and modelling healthy eating behaviours in front of your child by eating the same food as them.

However, we do appreciate that it is not always possible to sit down together and eat as a family when work schedules, childcare and other commitments don't allow it. But, if possible, try to get into a routine where you have a meal together once or a few times a week; for example, dinner together at home every

Wednesday or breakfast together every Saturday morning. A family meal doesn't have to include anyone other than you and your toddler, but if there are other family members, try to encourage them to join in as often as they can. The most important thing is that you or someone else sits down with your toddler and eats with him, as often as possible, so that he can watch you eat and learn about foods and behaviours during mealtimes. Family meals also provide time to engage in conversation and spend quality time together. Even if you are not eating with your child, it is still an opportunity to talk and you can engage with him about what he is eating. The same applies with grandparents and childminders; it does not necessarily have to be immediate family. When you have your meal, aim to sit down together without the television on so that there are no distractions.

'We try to sit down and eat as a family as much as possible but the thing that stops us is Grace tends to need dinner before Shane has got in from work. Last night we had dinner at the table and it was absolutely lovely. Thomas sat in his high chair with us next to Grace and it was just perfect.'

Amy, mum of Grace (18 months)
and Thomas (4 months)

BREAKFAST – AN IMPORTANT MEAL

Try to always make time for your child to eat breakfast. Concentration and performance at nursery or school can suffer if a child is hungry and lacking energy. One review of 45 studies evaluated the effects of breakfast on children's cognitive performance and the evidence indicated that breakfast consumption is more beneficial than skipping breakfast, particularly among children that are less well-nourished (such as picky eaters).[377] There is also research to suggest that children who skip breakfast tend to be at greater risk of overweight. A review of 16 studies involving almost 60,000 children and adolescents from Europe looked at the evidence on the effects of breakfast consumption on weight.[378] Thirteen of the studies consistently showed that breakfast had a protective effect against developing overweight or obesity. It could, of course, be the case that children and adolescents with overweight skip breakfast in an attempt to control their weight; or it could be the case that by skipping breakfast they subsequently gain weight, perhaps because they feel hungry and overcompensate by eating too much later in the day. Either way, it seems important to ensure that children do not skip breakfast.

Breakfast cereals can be a good source of energy and are usually fortified with vitamins and minerals including iron. However, there are many that contain a lot of sugar and salt so be aware of these. Good options are cereals such as bran flakes, puffed rice or shredded wheat as these are lower in sugar and contain fibre. Porridge with fruit is an excellent option for breakfast.

TAKE YOUR CHILD FOOD SHOPPING

A great way of helping your child learn which foods are good for him and which are not so good is to involve him when you buy and prepare food.

'I am getting her to look at the food, find the food, help me buy the food and unpack the food so she understands where food comes from, how it's prepared and that there are some healthy foods and some unhealthy foods.'

Gemma, mum of Lilly (2 years)

Some parents avoid taking their children with them to do the family food shop because of 'pester power' – children pressure parents to buy certain foods, often those that they have seen advertised on the television. However, if you can fend off this pressure then taking your child with you to do the family food shop can be very beneficial. It gives you an opportunity to show him that you read food labels and to teach him about the different food groups and making healthy choices. He can contribute towards choosing foods for the family meals and will feel like his input is valued.

Involving your child in the preparation of meals, for example, by washing fresh vegetables and measuring and counting ingredients, also gives him an understanding of how meals are prepared, and he may be more inclined to try the food if he has seen how it has been made. It will also provide a 'norm' of eating food that has been prepared from scratch.

OFFER HEALTHY CHOICES

From about the age of two your child will be able to verbalise which foods he likes and dislikes, and which foods he does and doesn't want to eat. But remember that the choices you offer him will influence what he likes and what he will eat as well. If you give your child total control over what to choose for his meal, there is a strong chance that he will opt for something that doesn't include vegetables. Fish fingers and chips is much more appealing for many young children than, for example, fresh fish with vegetables and boiled new potatoes. Similarly, if you offer them a choice between a bag of crisps and an apple, most children would choose the crisps (adults struggle with these choices too, even though we know there are health benefits to choosing the apple over the crisps). Therefore, it is important to think about the choices you offer. At a mealtime, for example, offering a choice of broccoli or carrots, rather than broccoli or chips, means that your child will probably end up eating some fresh vegetables. But remember as well to make sure that you always include some food that he likes.

'If I put broccoli in front of him and then I put chips in front of him, I know which one he's going to go for.'

Chris, dad of Ollie (2 years old)

How to Feed Different Types of Eaters

Responsive feeding, and good mealtime habits are important for all children, regardless of what type of eater they are – those with an eager appetite who like big portions and want to eat constantly, those who have a poorer appetite, low interest in food and who are fussy, and those who are in between. However, different types of eaters also present unique challenges to parents. There is currently no science to guide us – studies linking responsive feeding with appetite and weight never look at whether different strategies work better for different types of eaters. But ensuring that you feed responsively can be challenging if you have a child with a voracious appetite or one that seems to not want anything at all. The strategies you use will need to be tailored for your child. It is our view that it's important to learn what type of eater you have, so that you can then feed your child using responsive strategies that will be effective and relevant for him. We have provided a whole range of guidance below, based on responsive feeding principles, for each type of feeder.

What Gemini has shown us is that some toddlers are much better at regulating their food intake than others. This is based on their appetite or the type of eater they are. Below we have provided you with our tips on how to feed 'eager eaters' (those with an avid appetite who have a tendency to eat too much) and 'faddy eaters' (those with a poor appetite who have a tendency to eat too little). There are distinct eating behaviours that each type of child engages in that can be difficult to manage and we have developed guidance for how to deal with the key challenges of each.

EAGER EATERS

Children with a hearty appetite tend to be less sensitive to their internal feelings of fullness (low on satiety sensitivity), are very food responsive (want to eat when they see, smell or taste palatable food, and derive a lot of pleasure from eating), eat quickly and are more likely to develop a tendency to use food for comfort (emotional overeating). We know from our research and others that babies and children with these characteristics gain more weight over time, because these behaviours can quickly lead to overeating, so management early in life is vital.[379] In particular, in Gemini we found that toddlers with lower satiety sensitivity consumed larger portions every time they ate, but did not compensate for the larger portions by eating less often throughout the day.[380] The Infant & Toddler Forum (ITF) suggests using your child's appetite to gauge how much food he needs, but this is not straightforward because a child who is food responsive and less sensitive to his satiety will eat beyond fullness, if given the opportunity. As a parent in this situation, with a seemingly ravenous child, how do you know if you have given him enough or too much? Your child might be indicating that he is still hungry, when in fact he may have had enough food but carries on eating because the food tastes good and because it is there. And what do you do if your child eats everything that you provide for him, and then always says he is still hungry for more? We call this 'plate-clearing'.

How to manage plate-clearing

If your child will eat everything he is served, this can be very fulfilling for you as a parent and often allays any concerns that he is not eating enough. However, it is important to be mindful of serving large portions. We recommend using the ITF portion sizes to guide you (see page 363), and advise you against getting into the habit of providing large portions of food for your child. Start with a reasonable portion (based on the guidelines for his age); if he finishes it and then asks for seconds, ask him if he is still hungry and suggest he waits a few minutes to let his food go down. This will give his satiety time to kick in (we know from research that the hormones that control satiety take about 10–15 minutes to be released in response to food intake and take effect[381]). If he is still hungry after waiting 10 minutes, you could offer him a small portion more or a low-energy-density snack, such as vegetables or fruit. These foods take a while to eat because they require a lot of chewing and will give his satiety more time to come into effect. They tend also to be high in fibre so are filling.

Children with an avid appetite tend to eat very quickly and this impacts their ability to feel full. Eating quickly also reflects a person's enthusiasm to eat that particular food – we all eat super-delicious food faster than we eat blander food – so food-responsive children tend to eat faster, especially when the food tastes really good. But the problem with eating too quickly is that we outpace the biological mechanisms that control satiety, and it is easy to eat too much before we realise we have had enough because our feelings of fullness come into effect too late. We have all been in the situation where we have eaten a large amount of tasty food quickly, only to feel horribly full afterwards! A recent review of 22 studies concluded that we eat more food when we eat it quickly rather than slowly, and that slowing down eating rate is an important approach to help people control how much they eat.[382] So, if your child has a tendency to eat quickly, it is a good idea to try and encourage him to slow down the pace. This is no easy task, but some of the following strategies might work (you'll soon figure out what works best for your particular child):

- teach him to put his spoon or fork down between bites, as this will allow more time for him to feel full after each mouthful

- encourage him to have a sip of water throughout the meal to introduce pauses

- cut his food up into smaller pieces that he can eat one at a time so it takes him longer to eat the whole meal

- remind him to chew his food properly before he swallows it

- give him low-energy-density foods that require a lot of chewing and that he can eat larger portions of, such as lean meat or fish and vegetables. Try to limit processed energy-dense foods, such as macaroni cheese. It is easy to eat large quantities of these quickly before feeling full.

In general, different types of foods vary in how filling they are and how long they will keep us full for. The glycaemic index of food (GI; discussed on page 56) determines how much insulin we produce in response to eating it, and there is a considerable body of research showing that low-GI meals and snacks keep us fuller for longer.[383] Offering your child low-GI foods might therefore be a good strategy to help him to feel fuller for longer, so it's worth giving them a go. However, bear in mind that not all foods with a low-GI are healthy, for example, chocolate is low-GI because the high fat content slows down the absorption of the carbohydrate. So make sure that any low-GI foods you offer are also healthy. Examples of healthy low-GI foods include:

- most fruit and vegetables

- wholegrain cereals, such as porridge

- wholegrain, granary and rye bread

- pulses, such as beans, lentils and peas

- milk

- basmati or easy-cook rice

- pasta and noodles

- sweet potatoes

We would caution against routinely serving your child second portions – always wait for him to indicate he is hungry before offering him more. If he is participating in family meals with you, remember that he will be watching you and the rest of the family as part of the process through which he learns about how to eat. If you tend to serve yourselves large portions, and routinely have seconds or thirds, your child will also want them, and will come to regard this as normal and develop this habit too. A good tip to guard against this is putting leftovers away as soon as you have served everyone, to avoid temptation (out of sight out of mind), and use them for another meal. It is also probably a good idea not to get into the habit of always offering dessert, and only offer it if your child is hungry. If you offer it at every meal, he may start to expect sweet foods after each meal and take this habit with him throughout life. However, if you think he is still hungry, a piece of fruit and some yoghurt is a good, healthy option.

It is especially important for a child with an avid appetite that you never encourage him to clear his plate or to eat past the point at which he indicates to you that he is full. He needs to be supported in learning what fullness feels like and to stop eating when he has those sensations. In the modern environment where we are served large portions, if a young child learns always to clear his plate, he may learn to overeat as he grows up into adulthood. He should be guided by his internal feelings of satiety, not the amount of food left on the plate or on the table.

We recommend limiting the amount of time your child eats in front of the television or while playing on an iPad or mobile phone. There has been research to suggest that this may be linked to overeating.[384] One possible reason is because children focus on the external stimulus rather than on their internal feelings of fullness, and are then unaware how much they are eating. How often have you been to the cinema and got through an entire tub of popcorn without even realising? Or demolished half a packet of biscuits in front of the television and have no memory of eating them? Another possible reason why media use has been linked to overeating is exposure to food adverts, which can make food responsive children hungry. Imaginative experimental studies have shown that children eat more after they have watched food adverts than non-food adverts, and that the effect is much greater for more food-responsive children and those with overweight.[385] Having the television on while your child is eating could prime him to want to eat more. He may also start to associate watching television with eating. Food adverts aren't only on television – they also dominate the Internet, so be aware that your child will be exposed to these regardless of the type of media he interacts with.

We would also encourage you to start talking openly with your child about satiety as early as possible. Explain to him what a full tummy feels like and that it is something to pay attention to while he is eating, and to stop when his tummy feels full. A fantastic experimental study by an American researcher showed that it is possible to train preschool children (three- to four-year-olds) to improve their ability to self-regulate their food intake by teaching them how to recognise their feelings of hunger and satiety, and pay close attention to them when starting and stopping eating.[386] The children were taught what the signs of hunger are (a rumbling and empty-feeling stomach), what eating to fullness feels like (stomach extension and satisfaction) and what the consequences of overeating feel like once satiety has been passed (stomach discomfort). They were taught basic things about eating – biting, chewing, swallowing and where the food then goes. Researchers used a doll with a transparent stomach to teach them about how the doll might be feeling with different amounts of food in her stomach. The six-week programme led to improved appetite regulation for all of the children – both those who were initially prone to overeating as well as those who were initially prone to undereating.

TOP TIPS FOR PLATE-CLEARING

- Serve age-appropriate portions to your toddler – these will be a lot smaller than an adult portion.

- Use the ITF portion sizes to guide you (see page 363).

- Do not encourage plate-clearing.

- Do not routinely offer second helpings; only offer them if your child indicates he is still hungry.

- Encourage your child to wait 10–15 minutes after eating to check he is still hungry before offering him more food.

- Put leftovers away (out of sight out of mind).

- Only offer a dessert if your child is still hungry.

- Try to avoid technology during meal times to focus attention on hunger and fullness.

- Offer foods with a low-GI that will help your child feel fuller for longer, such as porridge, beans or wholemeal bread (see page 56 for more on GI).

- Encourage slower eating to allow time for your child to feel full.

- Encourage your child to take sips of water throughout the meal.

- Talk to your child about hunger and fullness – explain what it feels like and that it is important to stop eating when his tummy feels full.

How to manage snacking

From Gemini we know that more food-responsive toddlers eat more often,[387] and one of the challenges that parents face with a food-responsive child is that they are constantly asking for snacks. They may also ask for more palatable foods (those high in fat and sugar that taste really good), usually in response to seeing or smelling something appetising and wanting it. As a parent of a toddler who loves his food, you might be struggling with what sort of snacks to offer, and how much and how often to give them. Most parents tend to offer their toddler three meals (breakfast, lunch and dinner) and two snacks per day, and this is what the ITF recommends. In both Gemini and a large national survey of infants and toddlers, we found that toddlers were eating on average five times per day, so this would seem about right. So how do you deal with your child if he wants snacks constantly throughout the day?

If your child is very food responsive, seeing, smelling or tasting delicious food will make him want to eat it. We all do this to some extent (have you ever ordered your favourite dessert in a restaurant, even if you're full after the main course?), but some of us find temptation much harder to resist than others, and act on our urges. Some toddlers will therefore want to eat something nice when they see it and can get very upset or annoyed if they can't have it. The problem is that in the current food environment we are bombarded with food cues – it is virtually impossible to walk down a high street without a waft of something nice finding its way up your nose . . . and your toddler's. While you can't necessarily protect your child from food cues in the wider environment, you can certainly control your food environment at home and what he sees you eating.

If your toddler has a tendency to want to eat all the time, some level of restriction over what and how much he eats is necessary. Unfortunately, the world we live in today has meant that you will come up against this challenge more and more as he gets older and gains increasing independence to interact with the outside world. So it's wise to try and get some strategies in place early. There hasn't been a huge amount of research on this, but there is some evidence that *covert* restriction is a better way to go than *overt* restriction (see page 227)[388], and that any form of restriction should never be too extreme.[389] Covert restriction is making sure that your child is *unaware* of the fact that you are limiting his access to unhealthy food (as opposed to *overt* restriction, when your child is fully aware of the fact that you are denying him access). The most effective way to do this is not to have foods in the house that you don't want him to eat. But this is not realistic for everyone and may feel a bit draconian. If this is the case for you, do try to control the sheer volume of these foods that you have in the home and keep them out of sight (for example, in a cupboard) so your child doesn't have to sit and ogle them! We would suggest having a bowl of fruit and ready-to-eat vegetables available as your child will then learn that those are the foods he is able to have, and it will help to encourage healthy eating. If a bag of crisps is on the side next to a fruit bowl, which one are most children likely to choose? Do also bear in mind that you are your child's model. If there are foods you don't want him to eat, then don't eat them yourself in front of him. Wait until you are on your own (after he has gone to bed or is having a nap). If not, you will end up having to say no to him and dealing with the consequences! But in general, some access to his favourite food is fine; it's about setting limits and boundaries – some foods should only be eaten in moderation.

Controlling your home food environment is one thing, but what do you do if you are out and about and your child is asking for food? We would still suggest that you try and limit the number of snacks your child regularly eats, regardless of whether they are 'healthy snacks' or not. We know from Gemini that children who snack more often do not compensate enough for these additional snacks by reducing the amount they eat at mealtimes, and this can lead to them eating too much on a daily basis. And small amounts add up over time if this happens regularly. But we appreciate that it isn't always possible or easy to say no, and if your child is genuinely hungry then you need to provide something for him to snack on. In this situation we would suggest that you offer a nutritious snack that is low in energy density and has a low-GI (such as fruit) – we have provided healthy-snack ideas on page 298. If your child has a tendency to ask for foods when you are out (such as at the supermarket), then you could pre-empt this by taking a healthy snack with you.

When you are on the go and you haven't brought your own snack for your child, try to purchase food items that are in small snack packs as this puts a limit on the portion size. It can be difficult to determine what an appropriate portion looks like if you have a large bag of rice cakes for example, and as we mentioned earlier, children are likely to eat more when there is more available. Consider how much your child has already eaten when you offer him snacks, for example, offer smaller snacks if he has had a large lunch. It can be difficult not to give in to requests for food because you worry that your child is hungry, but try not to offer food if the request is being made in response to a food cue, such as walking past a bakery or the sweet aisle in the supermarket. Only offer snacks if your child is genuinely hungry, for example, if it has been a few hours since he last ate. A good way to test this is to offer him a drink of water (it might simply be that he is thirsty, not hungry) and if he is still hungry, then offer him a healthy snack.

TOP TIPS FOR SNACKING

- Put palatable snacks away (out of sight, out of mind).

- Have fruit and vegetables available and on display: keep the fruit bowl stocked.

- Try to limit the number of snacks to two per day: one in the morning and one in the afternoon.

- Offer low-GI snacks that are also lower in energy density.

- Buy snack packs rather than large packs – the more there is available the more children will eat.

- Decide on snack sizes according to how much your child has eaten already that day: use the ITF portion sizes for guidance (see page 363).

- Try to avoid offering snacks when your child responds to food cues; make sure he is genuinely hungry.

FADDY EATERS

While some children show a great interest in food and are prone to overeating, there are others who are far less interested in food, and some who are also very picky about what they will eat. These children are known as 'fussy eaters' (the term 'food neophobia' is also sometimes used, but this is more of a reluctance to try new foods). Fussy eating can be a great worry for some parents and often leads to concerns that their child is not getting the right nutrition. Fussy eating becomes a lot more common as children approach two years of age and is seen in as many as 50 per cent of toddlers.[390] If you have a child who seems incredibly fussy about what he eats at this age, even though he seemed to eat perfectly well when he was younger, you are not alone! A large US study of children found that fussy eating increased as children reached two years of age.[391] Children this age were less likely to eat vegetables and more likely to eat energy-dense foods, such as sugary cereals and chips. This resulted in a lack of variety in their diet. As omnivores, humans are capable of consuming a wide variety of different foods. This makes us extremely adaptable but also means we must quickly learn to distinguish between safe and poisonous foods. In this context, fussiness makes sense – fear or refusal of unknown foods protects against harm. Because it emerges shortly after babies start to walk (usually in the second year of life) it is thought to prevent newly mobile toddlers from eating harmful substances. But what do you do if your child is suspicious of most new foods and won't even eat the foods that he seemed to like before? Fussiness can be one of the most challenging aspects of parenting a toddler, but scientists have tried and tested a few strategies that seem to work pretty well with most children.

How to manage fussiness

Research from our group has shown that fussy toddlers are pressured to eat more by their parents.[392] We also found that fussy toddlers in Gemini were having more formula milk and, more often than not, 'follow-on' formulas (instead of or as well as cows' milk) at two years than non-fussy toddlers. These children also ate less solid food. Their mothers perceived this to be because their child was not interested in food and reported using the formula to provide their child with nutrients and to make sure they were getting enough calories.[393] However, there is the real possibility that the toddlers were full up on milk so they were not hungry for solid food, and were not being given the opportunity to develop healthy eating behaviours and become less fussy through exposure. We would therefore not recommend using milk to compensate for low food intake and instead focus on the strategies below to help your child develop healthy eating habits. If you introduce your child to a wide variety of foods there is no need for, nor any evidence of benefits to using fortified milks, such as 'follow-on' formulas, 'toddler' or 'growing-up' milks (see Chapter 5).

A good strategy is to try and ensure your child is hungry at mealtimes. A child with a poor appetite will feel too full to eat a proper meal if he has had a snack too close to it being offered. This can even include a glass of milk. So make sure meals and snacks are spaced out during the day. Parents of fussy eaters often report struggling at mealtimes and, as a result, they limit their child's exposure to new or disliked foods. However, as we explained in Chapter 9, food preferences develop through exposure; children become familiar with foods the more often they taste them and in turn this leads to greater liking. Toddlers may need to be exposed to a disliked food up to 15 times before they accept it. This is because children go through neophobia during toddlerhood so it becomes harder to accept new food (much harder than when they were babies). Don't be tempted to replace the disliked food with something your child does like, for example, don't remove the broccoli and give chips instead – this is what we call 'negative reinforcement'. Your child's dislike of broccoli will be reinforced because it is taken away and replaced with something he sees as better. Of course, it can be very demoralising when you have cooked or prepared food for your child and they will not eat it, but if each time they reject a food it is replaced with something nicer that they do like, then it stands to reason that they will keep rejecting foods they are not that keen on. It's best not to get into the habit of giving in to what your child does and does not like. You are the parent, and sometimes being tough is in your child's best interests.

It is also important not to reward the consumption of the disliked food with your child's favourite food, for example, if he loves ice cream do not tell him that if he eats all of his broccoli he can have some ice cream. This reinforces the fact that the broccoli is not something to be enjoyed – it only gets eaten because he wants the ice cream. This will not improve your child's liking of the broccoli; in fact, it will just enhance his liking of the ice cream because it has now acquired the lofty status of a reward, as well as tasting good. Instead, try rewarding with something other than food if your child eats, or at least tries, the broccoli, such as a sticker or a new toy.

One of the first studies to explore the combination of rewards with exposure was conducted by our department at UCL in 2010.[394] Four- to six-year-olds were given a taste of a vegetable they disliked, every day for 12 days and they either received a physical reward (sticker), social reward (praise) or no reward. There was also a control group in which children were not given a disliked vegetable over the 12 days. The children who were given a reward ate more of the disliked vegetable than those who were simply given the vegetable with no reward, or not given the vegetable at all. Within Gemini we ran something similar called 'Tiny Tastes'.[395] When they were three years old a sample of children were randomised either to be given daily tastes of a disliked vegetable over 14 days in their home with a sticker reward if they tasted it or not to be given daily tastings at all (the control group). The children who were given daily tastings of the vegetable and a reward ate far more of it and liked it far more, compared to those in the control group. Asking your toddler to try a disliked vegetable, or a vegetable they have not had before, and offering a non-food reward is an excellent way of improving his acceptance of vegetables and other problem foods.*

Below is a simple and effective technique for fussy eaters that you can try at home. Play this game at snack time when your child is hungry.

- Choose a vegetable that you would like your child to eat or that your child does not like.

- Show your child the whole vegetable, name it and say that you are both going to have a small taste of it.

- Cut two small pieces – one for you and one for your child.

- Try your piece and say how delicious it is.

- Ask your child to taste their piece – and if he doesn't want to, tell him he can spit it out if he really doesn't like it.

- Give lots of praise if he tastes it and give him a sticker or an alternative non-food reward.

- Repeat with the same vegetable every day for up to 15 days depending on how long it takes for your child to accept it.

- Choose another vegetable and start again.

We must stress that it is important to use non-food related rewards, such as stickers or praise, rather than offering your child a food

---

* If you have a fussy eater, you can purchase Tiny Taste packs containing full instructions, stickers and reward charts online at: www.weightconcern.org.uk/tinytastes.

you know he likes as a reward. Try not to use food for any reason other than to satisfy his hunger (see page 312). It is important not to use food to soothe, for example, offering your child his favourite food if he is upset, or to use food to control behaviour, for example offering his favourite food if he sits quietly. This is likely to enhance the liking of that food and potentially make it more difficult to get your child to eat the foods he does not like.

'Miles was very reluctant to try anything new, which was particularly frustrating when we'd spent ages preparing something for him. Sometimes he wouldn't eat very much at all, then wake up in the middle of the night to demand a banana – which we'd give him, despite our better judgement, simply because it was 3am and we wanted to go back to sleep. We found ourselves increasingly relying on a small number of dishes that he would (normally) eat. They were all beige for some reason: bananas, omelettes, toast, fish fingers, pasta, beans and Weetabix. Occasionally we'd try to sneak something green past him, usually while he was busy watching television, but he wasn't often very enthusiastic.'

Jack, dad of Miles (2½ years)

How to keep mealtimes stress-free

Mealtimes can be stressful if your child will not eat a certain food or does not try everything he is served. One way to overcome this is to provide a healthy balanced meal and allow your child to serve himself, or at least play a part in what he is served and how much. There is then less pressure on him and you can relax a bit knowing that he may not be eating everything on offer, but what he does have is healthy.

Feel free to put a new or disliked vegetable on your child's plate every day even if he doesn't eat it for several days in a row. This process will help to familiarise him with it – what it looks and feels like – and eventually he is likely to try it. Modelling is also a very useful strategy to improve your child's acceptance of healthy foods. This is particularly important when it comes to new foods. If he sees that you dislike a certain food, he will regard it with suspicion as well, and is likely to reject it too. Try to show him that healthy foods are enjoyable and are a routine part of everyday life. You can't expect your child to do something you are not prepared to do yourself.

It's so important not to pressure your child to eat or to clear his plate. Some children can become very anxious when they are forced to eat certain foods and those foods then become associated with anxiety. The effect you intend to have (your child eating the food) will in fact do the opposite (your child will not want to eat it now, and possibly not in the future either). Try to have a relaxed attitude towards feeding (as hard as that might be sometimes!). If your child does not want to eat something, that is fine – you can try again another day and repeat the exposure.

As difficult as it can be not to lose your temper when you have tried everything to get your child to eat, children start to associate ill feeling and conflict with certain foods. They are then likely to avoid those foods even more, so do try not to get cross with your child or punish him by removing his favourite foods (for example, saying, 'If you don't eat your vegetables you won't get dessert'). This could only serve to reinforce your child's desire not to eat the disliked foods. In fact, pressuring him to eat is not a good idea with any food – even one that he likes. If he has had enough, let him finish eating. Eating past satiety for a child with a small appetite can feel very unpleasant, and it will make him feel stressed.

There is a growing trend for parents with fussy eaters to disguise the flavour of vegetables among other foods. Though it's very tempting to 'hide' vegetables among other flavours, for example, in a sauce or by adding a flavour that's more appealing, such as the sweetness of fruit, this means that your child will not actually taste the flavour of the vegetables. Your child needs to identify the flavours to get used to them and like them. It is also not uncommon for parents to try and make food look more appealing to children for example, by making smiley faces on the plate with the vegetables. This is fine – we as adults tend to enjoy food more if it is well presented, hence why many chefs add fancy garnishes to their dishes. If your child is more likely to eat a carrot if it is a 'nose' on the plate then go ahead and do this. And while it is good to keep introducing your child to new foods and flavours and including foods you know he doesn't like, always provide some foods that you know he likes as well. This will ensure he eats something and it will make him feel as though he has some control over his eating, and will help to keep your anxieties at bay as well.

Whatever food you end up offering your child for a meal, bear in mind that children with a poor appetite can easily feel overwhelmed by food. Make sure that you provide small portions that look manageable to him, and cut the food up into little pieces so he can eat a small amount at a time. You can always offer him some more if he indicates to you that he is still hungry.

It may seem counter-intuitive to limit the length of a meal when your child eats slowly and doesn't eat much at all. But limiting the total mealtime to 30 minutes will help to reduce your child's anxiety levels because he knows that the ordeal is time-limited. Dragging out the meal past this length of time is unlikely to result in him eating any more.

And, finally, don't give up! As we mentioned on page 336, repeatedly exposing your child to a disliked food can result in liking, so be assured that your efforts will pay off in the end.

TOP TIPS FOR FADDY EATERS

- Praise your child when he tries a new food or eats something he says he dislikes. Reward him with praise – let him know you are happy that he has eaten something he doesn't like (for some children this can be quite an achievement).

- Reward with stickers or a reward chart (or another non-food reward that you know your child likes) if your child tries a new healthy food or eats a disliked food. Children learn to associate eating the disliked foods with something positive and rewarding, and that positive reinforcement can lead to liking. Never reward food with food.

- Try offering your child a little piece of the new/disliked food everyday alongside other foods that he will eat.

- Offer small portions so that your child does not get overwhelmed by a large amount of food.

- Eat the new/disliked foods with your child and model healthy eating behaviour. Remember, you are your child's best teacher.

- Ensure the family all eat the same foods but try to allow your child to serve himself.

- Limit the meal to 30 minutes. A long, drawn-out meal will stress everyone out and is unlikely to result in your child eating more.

Having read about these different eating styles can you identify these behaviours in your child – plate-clearing, constant snacking or fussiness? Parents tend to be able to identify with one or other of these, but there are children who simply do not fit into a category. You may have no concerns at all about your child's eating habits and simply want some general advice on how to help your toddler develop healthy eating habits and a good relationship with food. If that's the case, you can still make use of the tips we have provided here as they apply to all children. For example, generally it is a good idea not to routinely offer second helpings, not to have energy-dense foods on display at home and to praise your child for trying healthy new foods.

If you can identify with one of these eating styles and you implement some of the tips we have provided, it's worth bearing in mind that it's not always going to be easy. You may start out with the best of intentions, but children can be rather wilful; if your child is pestering you for food, you may find yourself becoming impatient and just giving in to his requests, or if your child will not eat what you have served, you may become worried that he is not eating enough and give him his favourite food. This is normal, but tomorrow is another day and you can try again. All is not lost if you give up sometimes.

THE BOTTOM LINE

- Establish a mealtime and snack routine, feeding at the same time each day.

- Don't let your toddler skip meals; always offer him breakfast.

- Include your child in food shopping, preparation and family meals.

Baby Food Matters

- Feed your child responsively.

- Understanding your child's appetite is key; use feeding strategies that are tailored to his eating styles. There will be an element of trial and error, but the more you experiment the more you will grow in confidence.

- If you have a 'plate-clearer', be mindful of portion sizes, second helpings and do not encourage plate-clearing.

- If you have a 'snacker', put palatable snacks out of sight.

- If you have a 'fussy eater', do not pressure him to eat or use food to control his behaviour, such as offering him his favourite food if he eats a disliked food.

Final Thoughts

Our mission with this book was to provide you with everything you need to know about food and feeding for the first 1,000 days from a *scientific perspective*, to help you support your child in developing healthy eating habits for life. As such, we have tried to give you the facts, not the fads, about feeding, dispel some of the commonly believed myths and correct misinformation that we know is out there.

We now know quite a lot from science about where appetite and food preferences come from, how they develop and why they're important. One thing is for sure – healthy eating is about both *what* and *how* your child eats. And we hope we have armed you with lots of useful strategies and tips that you can use to help your baby develop a good relationship with food as you navigate your way through the first 1,000 days. Here are our final tips on *what* and *how* to feed.

THE BOTTOM LINE ON *WHAT* TO FEED

The first 1,000 days offer a window of opportunity for 'setting' your baby's food preferences – making sure he likes healthy foods, such as vegetables and fruit, and eats them willingly without making a fuss. The keys to liking are familiarity and feeling sure that foods are safe. This process probably starts in pregnancy, continues during breastfeeding, and is more firmly established when your baby is weaned onto solid foods.

Do...

1. *Eat the foods you want your baby to eat when you are pregnant*

    Your baby may start to get a taste for vegetables and fruit (and other foods) through your own diet when you are pregnant, and then from your breast milk if he receives this.

2. *Try and breastfeed him if you can*

    Both of you will reap the benefits, but don't feel like it's the end of the world if this hasn't worked out for you. Seek help and support early on if you are struggling in the first few days or weeks. This can make the difference between giving up and carrying on. Every breastfeed counts, so celebrate each one.

3. *Don't wait until later than six months to wean*

    If your baby is healthy, then start weaning around six months of age in order to make sure you make the most of his openness to new flavours and textures, and that he gets the nutrients he needs and has timely oral development for speech.

4. *Use a bitter vegetable as his first food*

    During weaning, start with lots of different vegetables and try to choose bitter-tasting ones (such as spinach) over sweet ones (such as carrot) initially. Once your baby has had a taste for sweet foods it might be harder to convince him that the bitter-tasting foods will be just as nice. Don't disguise vegetables in sauces and don't mix them with fruit. Babies and toddlers need to get to know what each separate vegetable tastes like and become familiar with its texture.

5. *Persevere with new foods*

You may have to offer a new food up to 15 times to get your toddler to like it, but repeated tasting is the most effective way for you to increase his liking for foods, especially those he doesn't seem keen on.

6. *Praise him for eating a healthy food*

Give him lots of praise and encouragement. This will act as a reward for the behaviour and will make him more likely to want to do it again.

7. *Reward him with a non-food for trying a healthy food*

Stickers and other age appropriate non-foods work well for most young children when it comes to motivating them to try new foods. You could even try a star chart so your child can see his progress.

8. *Lead by example and eat what you want him to eat*

Once your baby starts solid foods he will be looking to you as his main source of information about what foods are safe to eat. You need to show him by happily eating and enjoying healthy foods in front of him. If you give your baby the impression that you don't like what you are eating, you can be sure he will trust you on this! He will copy your behaviour. That's how he learns.

9. *Have fruit and vegetables available as snacks and always on show*

Your baby is more likely to eat them if they are readily available, such as in a fruit bowl, and if he can see them.

10. *Provide lots of variety*

Make sure you give your baby the opportunity to try as many different flavours and textures as you can – this is the best way to ensure he will eat a varied diet now and later.

Don't...

1. *Reward non-liked food with his favourite food in order to get him to try something*

This is not a good way to get him to eat healthy foods – it only serves to make him think the healthy food is so dreadful that it requires a reward to be given, and increases his desire for the unhealthy food which becomes both a reward as well as a nice-tasting food.

2. *Replace food with milk*

If you have a picky eater who has a poor appetite, the temptation is to keep giving him milk to ensure he's getting enough calories. But this usually means he fills up on milk and has even less of an appetite for proper food. Persevere with the food using the techniques we have provided in this book and try to limit the milk to sensible amounts.

3. *Replace food with any food substitute*

Never use a food substitute (such as a milkshake or similar) – these are packed with sugar and will only hinder your baby's ability to develop healthy eating habits. He needs to learn how to eat proper food, not avoid it by having a substitute. This will only make it harder to get him to eat a varied and healthy diet.

4. *Make a separate meal for your toddler*
The best way to model healthy eating behaviour is to eat the same food with your child at the table. There is no need to buy special snacks for toddlers or make them separate meals – they can eat whatever you eat, just in smaller portions and with no sugar or salt added.

5. *Order something off the children's menu*
Your child doesn't need special 'babified' meals in any context. He can have a smaller portion of most adult meals, as long as they don't have added salt or sugar. He can have a small portion of the meal you order yourself, and this will mean he gets used to eating the types of foods and meals that adults eat.

THE BOTTOM LINE ON *HOW* TO FEED

Babies and toddlers are all different when it comes to milk and food – some have hearty appetites, while others are faddy eaters, and this is partly down to their genes. These eating styles bring with them unique feeding challenges for you as a parent. *How* to feed your baby or toddler means making sure you know what type of feeder your baby is and responding to him appropriately through *responsive feeding*. Babies and toddlers who have a hearty appetite will have a tendency to overeat, especially in response to larger portions and food cues, such as sight, smell or taste. They need to be supported in learning to pay attention to their feelings of hunger and fullness, stopping eating as soon as they are full, being offered smaller portions and making sure they are offered healthy snacks if regularly hungry. Children with a poor appetite will struggle to eat a proper meal if they have filled up on other snacks beforehand (this includes milk), and tend to be more reluctant to eat vegetables, fruit and protein foods (meat and fish). They need to be supported by not being pressured to eat certain foods, by being praised if they try a healthy new food and being offered smaller portions so that they are not over-whelmed by a large amount of food. It goes without saying that parents need to use different strategies with the two types of children, but there are some general tips that will apply to all children.

Do...

1. *Learn to read your baby's or toddler's hunger and fullness signals*

Crying on its own doesn't signal hunger – hunger cues cluster together, and crying is only one indication. Hunger and fullness cues are easier to read in toddlers than young babies, but try to get to know your baby's cues from Day 1.

2. *Only ever feed in response to hunger*

Don't feed your baby or toddler for any reason other than hunger, for example, for comfort or to keep them quiet. This may be very difficult to do when you know feeding will soothe him, but there are other ways to comfort your baby or toddler without offering food. Always try these first.

3. *Stop feeding your baby or toddler as soon as he signals he is full*

Trust your baby on this – he will let you know. A baby or toddler with a hearty appetite doesn't need much encouragement to feed beyond fullness, and will do so given the chance. This will lead to overeating. Pressuring a baby with a poor appetite to keep on feeding or eating after he is full will make him feel stressed, and can even lead to food aversions.

4. *Provide baby- or toddler-sized portions*

Make sure that you provide appropriate portion sizes for your child – this includes the amount of milk offered in a bottle (if you bottle-feed him), as well as meals and snacks. If he has a hearty appetite, he will have a tendency to eat whatever is there. This means you need to provide the right amount so you don't encourage him to overeat. Faddy eaters can feel overwhelmed by too much food on their plates, so offer meals and snacks that look manageable.

Don't

1. *Use food to control your child's emotions or behaviour*

Don't use your child's favourite foods as a bribe to make him behave, keep him quiet or soothe him if he is upset or cranky. This will teach him to use food in order to regulate his emotions rather than learning positive strategies for coping.

2. *Have too many sugary and fatty foods in the house*

If you have them on show, he will want them. If you lock them in a cupboard, he will want them even more because they are then seen as 'forbidden'. The best way to get around this problem is not to have them in the house in the first place, at least not all the time, and in limited quantities.

3. *Make a fuss about all the fuss*

Try not to lose control. This is easier said than done – babies and toddlers' eating can be maddening at times, especially when they won't eat what you have prepared for them. But if you get stressed, your baby will too and this can intensify the stress around mealtimes, leading to food refusal.

4. *Eat with the television or computer on*

Faddy feeders are easily distracted and they may have far more interest in watching television or playing on the iPad than eating their meat and two veg. And children who are less sensitive to satiety are more likely to eat too much if they are distracted by the television. This is because they are preoccupied with the screen and it prevents them from paying attention to their food and the feeling of fullness while eating. Food advertising can also act as a food cue for food-responsive children and can make them want to eat more.

SOME FINAL REFLECTIONS

In writing this book, we have had a chance to reflect at length on what science has shown us about how your baby's eating behaviour develops in his first 1,000 days. In writing every chapter, we have been struck by how extraordinary the human body is. Your amniotic fluid is already a bath of flavours to prepare your baby for the outside world, helping him to learn what foods are safe to eat when the time comes. Breast milk does this too, but so much more than that as well – it provides sustenance, immunity, fuels your baby's brain development, and may even help him get his sleep–wake cycle sorted. And your body will adapt your breast milk to meet your baby's nutritional needs at every stage – not just from one month to the next, or in the morning versus at night, but from one feed to another, and even during the course of a single feed.

The 'terrible twos' are so-called for a reason – toddlers are renowned for being fusspots and, for some parents, mealtimes can become a bit of a misery. But even this frustrating developmental phase serves an important function – being naturally suspicious of potentially harmful substances is probably nature's way of protecting an extremely vulnerable newly mobile person from eating things he shouldn't. We hope we have given you some tips that will help you work with your baby, at each stage of his development, to support him on his journey into the grown-up world of eating.

We've also felt incredibly privileged that so many parents have shared their experiences of feeding their little ones with us. A couple of the stories we listened to moved us to tears. There is little in life that brings more intensity of emotion than a tiny baby or toddler who won't feed. This was one of our motivations behind writing this book – to try and give you some tips that will help things go as smoothly as possible. But importantly as well, we have provided you with sources of information about where to seek help if you are finding things very tough. Things don't always go to plan and there is help available – don't struggle alone; do seek advice and support if you need it. If you have tried everything and you are at a loss, take your baby or toddler to your GP.

A final message we want to leave you with is that it's never too late to intervene. Clare is a prime example – a random social intervention as an adult meant she finally started eating properly after 19 years! So never lose hope. Even if things have gone well so far, you may face new challenges as your baby or toddler grows into an older child. With increasing age comes independence, and sometimes defiance! And you will be less able to control what and how your child eats at school. But laying the groundwork now will help him to establish healthy eating habits that set him up for life.

The Eating Behaviour Questionnaires

The Baby Eating Behaviour Questionnaire (BEBQ) (0–6 months)

This questionnaire will give you an idea about the type of milk-feeder your baby is – whether he has a big or a small appetite. Answering these questions will help you to understand him and the feeding strategies that might suit him best. The questions are about all the different aspects of his appetite during his first few months of life, when he is still being fed milk only. How would you describe his feeding style at a *typical daytime feed*? Answer each statement using any of the following response options: 'never', 'rarely', 'sometimes', 'often' or 'always'. Instructions about how to interpret your answers are on page 354.

MILK RESPONSIVENESS

- *My baby frequently wants more milk than I provide.*

- *If allowed to, my baby would take too much milk.*

- *Even when my baby has just eaten well he is happy to feed again if offered.*

- *My baby is always demanding a feed.*

- *If given the chance, my baby would always be feeding.*

- *My baby can easily take a feed within 30 minutes of the last one.*

ENJOYMENT OF FEEDING

- *My baby seems contented while feeding.*

- *My baby loves milk.*

- *My baby becomes distressed while feeding.**

- *My baby enjoys feeding time.*

SATIETY RESPONSIVENESS

- *My baby gets full up easily.*

- *My baby gets full before taking all the milk I think he should have.*

- *My baby finds it difficult to manage a complete feed.*

- *My baby has a big appetite.**

SLOWNESS IN FEEDING

- *My baby finishes feeding quickly.**

- *My baby takes more than 30 minutes to finish feeding.*

- *My baby feeds slowly.*

- *My baby sucks more and more slowly during the course of a feed.*

SCORING INSTRUCTIONS FOR THE BEBQ

Look at your general responses for each aspect of appetite – for example, did you tend to answer 'always' for most of the statements for 'milk responsiveness'?

Your baby has a *big appetite* if:

- You answered mainly 'often' or 'always' for statements relating to 'milk responsiveness' and 'enjoyment of feeding', except for the statement with an asterisk to which you answered either 'rarely' or 'never'. This pattern of responses means your baby is very milk responsive and derives a lot of pleasure from feeding.

- You answered mainly 'rarely' or 'never' for 'satiety responsiveness' and 'slowness in feeding', except for the statements with an asterisk to which you answered either 'often' or 'always'. This pattern of responses means your baby is not very sensitive to his internal satiety and feeds quickly.

Your baby has a *small appetite* if:

- You answered mainly 'rarely' or 'never' for 'milk responsiveness' and 'enjoyment of feeding' except for the statement with an asterisk to which you answered either 'often' or 'always'. This means your baby is not very milk responsive and has low interest in feeding.

- You answered mainly 'often' or 'always' for 'satiety responsiveness' and 'slowness in feeding', except for the statements with an asterisk to which you answered either 'rarely' or 'never'. This means your baby is very sensitive to his internal satiety and feeds slowly.

The Child Eating Behaviour Questionnaire (CEBQ) (12 months+)

This questionnaire will give you an idea about the type of eater your toddler is – whether he has a big or a small appetite. Answering these questions will help you to understand him and the feeding strategies that might suit him best. The questions are about all the different aspects of his appetite for solid food. How would you describe his eating styles on a *typical day*? Answer each statement using any of the following response options: 'never', 'rarely', 'sometimes', 'often' or 'always'. Instructions about how to interpret your answers are on page 358.

FOOD RESPONSIVENESS

• *My child is always asking for food.*

• *Given the choice, my child would eat most of the time.*

• *Even when my child has just eaten well, he is happy to eat again if offered.*

• *If allowed to, my child would eat too much.*

ENJOYMENT OF FOOD

- *My child looks forward to mealtimes.*

- *My child loves food.*

- *My child is interested in food.*

- *My child enjoys eating.*

SATIETY RESPONSIVENESS

- *My child leaves food on his plate or in the jar at the end of a meal.*

- *My child gets full before his meal is finished.*

- *My child cannot eat a meal if he has had a snack just before.*

- *My child gets full up easily.*

- *My child has a big appetite.**

SLOWNESS IN EATING

- *My child finishes his meal quickly.**

- *My child eats slowly.*

- *My child takes more than 30 minutes to finish a meal.*

- *My child eats more and more slowly during the course of a meal.*

EMOTIONAL OVEREATING

- *My child eats more when irritable.*

- *My child eats more when grumpy.*

- *My child eats more when upset.*

EMOTIONAL UNDEREATING

- *My child eats less when angry.*

- *My child eats more when he is happy.**

- *My child eats less when upset.*

FOOD FUSSINESS

- *My child refuses new foods at first.*

- *My child enjoys a wide variety of foods.**

- *My child enjoys tasting new foods.**

- *My child is difficult to please with meals.*

- *My child decides that he does not like a food, even without tasting it.*

- *My child is interested in tasting food he has not tasted before.**

SCORING INSTRUCTIONS FOR THE CEBQ

Look at your general responses for each aspect of appetite – for example, did you tend to answer 'always' for most of the statements for 'food responsiveness'.

Your baby has a *big appetite* if:

- You answered mainly 'often' or 'always' for statements relating to 'food responsiveness', 'enjoyment of feeding' and 'emotional overeating'. This pattern of responses means your toddler is very food responsive, derives a lot of pleasure from eating and has a tendency to want to eat more when he is upset or annoyed.

- You answered mainly 'rarely' or 'never' for 'satiety responsiveness', 'slowness in feeding', 'emotional undereating' and 'food fussiness', except for the statements with an asterisk to which you answered either 'often' or 'always'. This pattern of responses means your toddler is not very sensitive to his internal satiety, eats quickly, doesn't lose his appetite even when he's upset or annoyed and will eat most foods without a fuss.

Your baby has a *small appetite* if:

- You answered mainly 'rarely' or 'never' for 'food responsiveness', 'enjoyment of feeding' and 'emotional overeating'. This means your toddler is not very food responsive, has low interest in food and doesn't take much comfort from food when he is upset or annoyed.

- You answered mainly 'often' or 'always' for 'satiety responsiveness', 'slowness in feeding', 'emotional undereating' and 'food fussiness', except for the statements with an asterisk to which you answered either 'rarely' or 'never'. This means your toddler is very sensitive to his internal satiety, feeds slowly, tends to lose his appetite when he has been very upset or annoyed, and is picky about what foods he is willing to eat or even try.

Average Energy Requirements in the First Two Years of Life

TABLE 4: AVERAGE DAILY ENERGY REQUIREMENTS FOR BOYS AND GIRLS IN THE FIRST YEAR OF LIFE[396]

Age (months)	Breastfed (kcals per day)	Formula-fed (kcals per day)
Boys		
1–2	532	604
3–4	577	632
5–6	607	652
7–8	649	687
9–10	704	736
11–12	754	781
Girls		
1–2	476	552
3–4	525	586
5–6	560	612
7–8	590	634
9–10	640	679
11–12	685	720

TABLE 5: AVERAGE DAILY ENERGY REQUIREMENTS FOR BOYS AND GIRLS AGED 1 AND 2 YEARS[397]

Age (years)	Calories Per Day	
	Boys	Girls
1	765	717
2	1,004	932

Portion Sizes for One- to Four-Year-Olds[398]

**Bread slices (fresh or
toasted) – granary**
½–1 medium slice

**Dry flaked cereal
(e.g. corn flakes)**
3–6 heaped tablespoons

**Celery/cucumber/
radishes**
2–8 small sticks/slices

Peas
½–2 tablespoons

White/oily fresh fish
¼–1 small fillet or
1–3 tablespoons

Sausages
¼–1 medium sausage

Poached/boiled/fried
½–1 egg

Digestive (plain)
½–1 biscuit

Bar of chocolate/
chocolate biscuit
2–4 squares of chocolate

Soft sweets (e.g. jelly tots/
jelly beans)
2–4 sweets

Crisps (e.g. Wotsits™/Hula
Hoops™
4–6 crisps

Useful Resources

Association of Breastfeeding
Mothers
0300 330 5453
www.abm.me.uk

Australian Breastfeeding
Association
www.breastfeeding.asn.au

British Nutrition Foundation
www.nutrition.org.uk

The Breastfeeding Network
0300 100 0210
www.breastfeedingnetwork.org.uk

The Caroline Walker Trust
www.cwt.org.uk

Change4Life
www.nhs.uk/change4life

Child Feeding Guide
www.childfeedingguide.co.uk

Children's Food Trust
www.childrensfoodtrust.org.uk

Cry-sis
0845 122 8669
www.cry-sis.org.uk

Drinkline
0300 123 1110

First Steps Nutrition Trust
www.firststepsnutrition.org

Healthy Start
www.healthystart.nhs.uk

Baby Food Matters

The Independent School Food
Plan
www.schoolfoodplan.com

Infant & Toddler Forum
www.infantandtoddlerforum.org

International Federation of
Gynecology and Obstetrics
www.figo.org

La Leche League GB
0845 120 2918
www.laleche.org.uk

Mothers Matter
www.mothersmatter.co.nz

National Breastfeeding Helpline
0300 100 0212
www.nationalbreastfeeding
helpline.org.uk

National Childbirth Trust (NCT)
0300 330 0771
www.nct.org.uk

NHS Choices
www.nhs.uk

NHS Smokefree
0300 123 1044

Public Health England
www.gov.uk/government/
publications/example-menus-for-
early-years-settings-in-england

The Period of PURPLE Crying
www.purplecrying.info

Red Cross
www.redcross.org.uk

Royal College of Obstetricians
and Gynaecologists
www.rcog.org.uk

Royal College of Paediatrics and
Child Health
www.rcpch.ac.uk

School Food Plan
www.schoolfoodplan.com

Unicef UK Baby Friendly
Initiative
www.unicef.org.uk/babyfriendly

Weight Concern
www.weightconcern.org.uk

Zero to Three
www.zerotothree.org

References

1. Development of the children's eating behaviour questionnaire. *J Child Psychol Psychiatry* 2001; 42: 963–970.
2. Development and factor structure of the Baby Eating Behaviour Questionnaire in the Gemini birth cohort. *Appetite* 2011; 57: 388–396.
3. Continuity and stability of eating behaviour traits in children. *Eur J Clin Nutr* 2008; 62: 985–990.
4. The NOURISH randomised control trial: positive feeding practices and food preferences in early childhood-a primary prevention program for childhood obesity. *BMC Public Health* 2009; 9: 387.

    Child eating behavior outcomes of an early feeding intervention to reduce risk indicators for child obesity: the NOURISH RCT. *Pediatr Obes* 2014; 22: e104–e111.

    Child dietary and eating behavior outcomes up to 3.5 years after an early feeding intervention: The NOURISH RCT. *Pediatr Obes* 2016; 24: 1537–1545.
5. Picky/fussy eating in children: review of definitions, assessment, prevalence and dietary intakes. *Appetite* 2015; 95: 349-359.
6. Appetite and growth: a longitudinal sibling analysis. *JAMA Pediatr* 2014; 168: 345–350.
7. Prospective associations of appetitive traits at 3 and 12 months of age with body mass index and weight gain in the first 2 years of life. *BMC Pediatrics* 2015; 15: 153.
8. Appetite and adiposity in children: evidence for a behavioral susceptibility theory of obesity. *Am J Clin Nutr* 2008; 88: 22–29.

    Appetitive behaviours of children attending obesity treatment. *Appetite* 2011; 57: 525–529.

Do maternal ratings of appetite in infants predict later Child Eating Behaviour Questionnaire scores and body mass index?. *Appetite* 2010; 54: 186–190.

The Children's Eating Behaviour Questionnaire: factorial validity and association with Body Mass Index in Dutch children aged 6–7. *Int J Behav Nutr Phys. Act* 2008; 5: 49.

Examining behavioural susceptibility to obesity among Canadian pre school children: The role of eating behaviours. *Int J Pediatr Obes* 2010; 6: e501–e507.

Children's Eating Behaviour Questionnaire: associations with BMI in Portuguese children. *Br J Nutr* 2008; 100: 445–450.

Eating behaviour and weight in children. *Int J Obes* 2009; 33: 21–28.

9. The extent of food advertising to children on UK television in 2008. *Int J Pediatr Obes* 2011; 6: 455–461.

10. Advertising as a cue to consume: a systematic review and meta-analysis of the effects of acute exposure to unhealthy food and nonalcoholic beverage advertising on intake in children and adults. *Am J Clin Nutr* 2016; 103: 519–533.

11. Appetitive traits and food intake patterns in early life. *Am J Clin Nutr* 2016; 103: 231–235.

12. Ibid.

13. Nature and nurture in infant appetite: analysis of the Gemini twin birth cohort. *Am J Clin Nutr* 2010; 91: 1172–1179.

14. Central nervous system control of food intake. *Nature* 2000; 404: 661–671.

15. Defining the neural basis of appetite and obesity: from genes to behaviour. *Clin Med (Lond)* 2014; 14: 286-289;

Unravelling the brain regulation of appetite: lessons from genetics. *Nat Neurosci* 2012; 15: 1343-1349

16. The home environment shapes emotional eating in childhood. *Child Dev* 2017; In Press.

Emotional over- and under-eating in early childhood are learned not inherited. *Sci Rep* 2017; 7: 9092.

17. Emotional feeding and emotional eating – reciprocal processes and the influence of negative affectivity. *Child Dev* 2017; In Press.

18. Global and regional mortality from 235 causes of death for 20 age groups in 1990 and 2010: a systematic analysis for the Global Burden of Disease Study 2010. *The Lancet* 2012; 380: 2095–2128.

19. The role of nutrition in brain development: The golden opportunity of the first 1000 days. *J Pediatr* 2016; 175: 16–21.

Early nutrition and long-term health: a practical approach: Symposium on 'Early nutrition and later disease: current concepts, research and implications'. *Proc Nutr Soc* 2009; 68: 422–429.

20. The role of nutrition in brain development: The golden opportunity of the first 1000 days. *J Pediatr* 2016; 175: 16–21.

21. Early nutrition and long-term health: a practical approach: Symposium on 'Early nutrition and later disease: current concepts, research and implications'. *Proc Nutr Soc* 2009; 68: 422–429.

22. The sweetness and bitterness of childhood: Insights from basic research on taste preferences. *Physiol. Behav.* 2015; 152, 502–507.

23. Are there sensitive periods for food acceptance in infancy? *Curr Nutr Rep.* 2017; 6: 190–196.

24. Nature and nurture in children's food preferences. *Am J Clin Nutr* 2014; 99: 911–917.

25. The importance of exposure for healthy eating in childhood: A review. *J Hum Nutr Diet* 2007; 20: 294–301.

26. Understanding the basic biology underlying the flavor world of children. *Curr Zool* 2010; 56: 834–841.

27. Garlic ingestion by pregnant women alters the odor of amniotic fluid. *Chem Senses* 1995; 20: 207–209.

28. Infant salt preference and mother's morning sickness. *Appetite* 1998; 30: 297–307.

29. Understanding the basic biology underlying the flavor world of children. *Curr Zool* 2010; 56: 834–841.

30. Effect of women's nutrition before and during early pregnancy on maternal and infant outcomes: a systematic review. *Paediatr Perinat Epidemiol* 2012; 26: 285–301.

31. Ibid.

32. A review of the impact of dietary intakes in human pregnancy on infant birth-weight. *Nutrients* 2014; 7: 153–178.

33. Developmental programming of appetite/satiety. *Ann Nutr Metab* 2014; 64(Suppl. 1): 36–44.

34. Developmental and epigenetic pathways to obesity: an evolutionary-developmental perspective. *Int J Obes* 2008; 32: S62–S71.
    Fetal programming from maternal obesity: eating too much for two? *Endocrinology* 2008; 149: 5345–5347.

35. Garlic ingestion by pregnant women alters the odor of amniotic fluid. *Chem. Senses* 1995; 20: 207–209.

36. Prenatal and postnatal flavor learning by human infants. *Pediatrics* 2001; 107: e88–e93.

37. Nutritional Support in Obstetrics and Gynecology. *Clin Obstet Gynecol* 1976; 19: 489–513.

38. Gestational weight gain. *Am J Obstet Gynecol* 2017; 217: 642–651.

39. Ibid.

40. The International Federation of Gynecology and Obstetrics (FIGO) recommendations on adolescent, preconception, and maternal nutrition: "Think Nutrition First". *Int J Gynecol Obstet* 2015; 131: S213–S253.

41. Weight management before, during and after pregnancy. Public health guideline [PH27]. *National Institute of Health and Care Excellence* 2010. [Online resource accessed February 2018].

42. Effects of low-glycemic-index diets in pregnancy on maternal and newborn outcomes in pregnant women: a meta-analysis of randomized controlled trials. *Eur J Nutr* 2018; 57: 167–177

43. Dietary fiber intake, dietary glycemic load, and the risk for gestational diabetes mellitus. *Diabetes Care* 2006; 29: 2223–2230.

    Dietary fiber intake in early pregnancy and risk of subsequent preeclampsia. *Am J Hypertens* 2008; 21: 903–909.

44. SACN report on carbohydrates and health report. *The Stationery Office* 2015. [Online resource accessed February 2018.]

45. Maternal and Child Nutrition. NICE guideline [PH11] *National Institute of Health and Care Excellence.* [Online resource accessed February 2018].

46. The International Federation of Gynecology and Obstetrics (FIGO) recommendations on adolescent, preconception, and maternal nutrition: "Think Nutrition First". *Int J Gynecol Obstet* 2015; 131:S213–S253.

47. Vitamin D status during pregnancy: maternal, fetal and post-natal outcomes. *Curr Opin Obstet Gynecol* 2011; 23: 422-426

48. The International Federation of Gynecology and Obstetrics (FIGO) recommendations on adolescent, preconception, and maternal nutrition: "Think Nutrition First". *Int J Gynecol Obstet* 2015: 131: S213-S253

    Vitamin D: Supplement use in specific population groups. NICE Guideline (PH56). *National Institute of Health and Care Excellence* 2017. [Online research accessed February 2018].

    SACN Vitamin D end health report. *The Stationery Office* 2015. [Online resource accessed February 2018].

49. Vitamin A. Present knowledge in nutrition (9th Edition) *International Life Science Institute* 2006; pages 157-183.

50. Maternal iron status: relation to fetal growth, length of gestation and the neonate's iron endowment. Nutr Rev 2011; 69(Suppl. 1): 523-529

51. Eating well for a healthy pregnancy: a practical guide. *First Steps Nutrition Trust* 2017. [Online resource accessed February 2018.]

52. Effect of inadequate iodine status in UK pregnant women on cognitive outcomes

in their children: results from the Avon Longitudinal Study of Parents and Children (ALSPAC).*Lancet* 2013; 382: 331-337

53. The International Federation of Gynecology and Obstetrics (FIGO) recommendations on adolescent, preconception, and maternal nutrition: "Think Nutrition First". *Int J Gynecol Obstet* 2015; 131:S213–S253.

54. Ibid.

55. Ibid.

56. The Eatwell Guide. *Public Health England* 2016. [Online resource accessed February 2018.]

57. SACN report on carbohydrates and health report. *The Stationery Office* 2015. [Online resource accessed February 2018.]

58. SACN Salt and health. *The Stationery Office* 2003. [Online resource accessed February 2018.]

59. Toxoplasmosis in pregnancy: prevention, screening and treatment. *J Obstet Gynaecol Can* 2013; 35: 78-79

60. Listeriosis in England and Wales in 2014: summary report. *Public Health England* 2015; Infection reports, vol. 9 (6). [Online resource accessed February 2018.]

61. Ibid.

62. Why should I avoid some foods during pregnancy? *NHS Choices* 2015. [Online resource accessed February 2018.]

63. Environmental exposures and adverse pregnancy outcomes: a review of the science. *Reprod Sci* 2008; 15: 631-650.

64. Caffeine intake during pregnancy and adverse birth outcomes: a systematic review and dose–response meta-analysis. *Eur J Epidemiol* 2014; 29: 725–734

65. Foetal alcohol syndrome. *NHS Choices* 2017. [Online resource accessed February 2018.]

66. Guidelines for pregnancy: what's an acceptable risk, and how is the evidence (finally) shaping up? *Drug Alcohol Rev* 2012; 31: 170-183.

67. Information for you: Alcohol and Pregnancy. *RCOG Patient Information Committee* 2015. [Online resource accessed February 2018.]

68. What is an alcohol unit? *Drinkaware* 2016. [Online resource accessed February 2018.]

69. Effective techniques in healthy eating and physical activity interventions: a meta-regression. *Health Psych.* 2009, 28(6), 690–701.

    State of the evidence regarding behavior change theories and strategies in nutrition counseling to facilitate health and food behavior change. *J Am Diet Assoc* 2010, 110(6), 879–891.

    A systematic review investigating healthy lifestyle interventions incorporating goal setting strategies for preventing excess gestational weight gain. *PloS one* 2012, 7(7), e39503.

70. The effect of electronic self monitoring on weight loss and dietary intake: a randomized behavioral weight loss trial. *Obesity* 2011; 19: 338–344.

71. Morning sickness: a mechanism for protecting mother and embryo. *Q Rev Biol* 2000; 75: 113–148.

Nausea and vomiting of pregnancy: an evidence based review. *J Perinat Neonatal Nurs* 2004; 18: 312–328.

72. Ibid.

73. Interventions for nausea and vomiting in early pregnancy. *Cochrane Database Syst Rev* 2015; Issue 9 Art no: CD0075.

74. Dietary cravings and aversions during pregnancy. *Am J Clin Nutr* 1978; 31: 1355–1362.

Influence of cravings and aversions on diet in pregnancy. *Ecol Food Nutr* 1985; 17: 117-129

Cravings and aversions of pregnant adolescents. *J Am Diet Assoc* 1992; 92: 1479–1482.

Food cravings and aversions during pregnancy: relationships with nausea and vomiting. *Appetite* 2002; 38: 45–51.

Food cravings and aversions during pregnancy: a current snapshot. *J Ped Mother Care* 2017; 2: 110.

75. Ibid.

76. Psychosocial characteristics and gestational weight change among overweight, African-American pregnant women. *Obstet Gynecol Int.* 2012; 878607.

77. Effect of diet and physical activity based interventions in pregnancy on gestational weight gain and pregnancy outcomes: meta-analysis of individual participant data from randomised trials. *BMJ* 2017; 358: j3119.

78. Weight management before, during and after pregnancy. Public health guideline [PH27]. *National Institute of Health and Care Excellence* 2010. [Online resources accessed February 2018].

79. Physical activity for pregnant women: infographic. *Department of Health* 2016. [Online resource accessed February 2018.];

Physical activity for pregnant women: infographic guidance. *Department of Health* 2016. [Online resource accessed February 2018.]

80. Your pregnancy and baby guide: exercise in pregnancy. *NHS Choices* 2017. [Online resource accessed February 2018.]

81. Energy requirements of infants. *Public Health Nutr* 2005; 8: 953–967.

82. BMI healthy weight calculator. *NHS Choices* 2015. [Online resource accessed February 2018.]

83. Your pregnancy and baby guide: Your baby's health and development reviews. *NHS Choices* 2017. [Online resource accessed February 2018.]

84. Postnatal weight loss in term infants: what is "normal" and do growth charts allow for it? *Arch Dis Child Fetal Neonatal Ed.* 2004; 89: F254–F257.

85. Using the new UK-World Health Organization 0-4 years growth charts: information for healthcare professionals about the use and interpretation of growth charts. *Department of Health and Social Care* 2009. [Online resource accessed February 2018.]

86. The risk of obesity by assessing infant growth against the new UK-WHO charts compared to the UK90 reference: findings from the Born in Bradford birth cohort study. *BMC Pediatr* 2012; 12: 104.

87. Prediction of childhood obesity by infancy weight gain: an individual level meta analysis. *Paediatr Perinat Epidemiol* 2012; 26: 19–26.

88. Catch-up growth in small for gestational age babies: good or bad? *Curr Opin Endocrinol Diabetes Obes.* 2007; 14: 30–34.

    Timing and tempo of first-year rapid growth in relation to cardiovascular and metabolic risk profile in early adulthood. *JAMA* 2009; 301: 2234–2242.

89. Age at menarche and risks of all-cause and cardiovascular death: a systematic review and meta-analysis. *Am J Epidemiol* 2014; 180: 29–40.

    Puberty timing associated with diabetes, cardiovascular disease and also diverse health outcomes in men and women: the UK Biobank study. *Sci Rep* 2015; 5: 11208.

    Infancy weight gain predicts childhood body fat and age at menarche in girls. *J Clin Endocrinol Metab* 2009; 94: 1527–1532.

90. Genetic and environmental influences on infant growth: prospective analysis of the Gemini twin birth cohort. *PLoS one* 2011; 6: e19918.

    Inherited behavioral susceptibility to adiposity in infancy: a multivariate genetic analysis of appetite and weight in the Gemini birth cohort. *Am J Clin Nutr* 2012, 95(3), 633–639.

91. Catch-up growth in small for gestational age babies: good or bad? *Curr Opin Endocrinol Diabetes Obes* 2007; 14: 30-34

92. Weight faltering and failure to thrive in infancy and early childhood. *BMJ* 2012; 345: e5931.

93. Ibid.

94. Faltering growth: recognition and management of faltering growth in children. NICE guideline [NG75]. *National Institute of Health and Care Excellence* 2017. [Online resource accessed February 2018.]

95. Using the new UK-World Health Organization 0-4 years growth charts: information for healthcare professionals about the use and interpretation of growth

charts. *Department of Health and Social Care* 2009. [Online resource accessed February 2018.]

96. Weight faltering and failure to thrive infancy and early childhood. *BMJ* 2012; 345: e5931.

97. What is the long term outcome for children who fail to thrive? A systematic review. *Arch Dis Child* 2005; 90: 925–931.

   To what extent is failure to thrive in infancy associated with poorer cognitive development? A review and meta analysis. *J Child Psychol Psychiatry* 2004; 45: 641–654.

   Criteria for determining disability in infants and children: failure to thrive. Evidence reports/technology assessments, no 72. *Agency for Healthcare Research and Quality* 2003. [Online resource accessed February 2018.]

   To what extent is failure to thrive in infancy associated with poorer cognitive development? A review and meta analysis. *J Child Psychol Psychiatry* 2004; 45: 641–654.

   Weight faltering in infancy and IQ levels at 8 years in the Avon Longitudinal Study of Parents and Children. *Pediatrics* 2007; 120: e1051–e1058.

98. Weight faltering and failure to thrive infancy and early childhood. *BMJ* 2012; 345: e5931.

99. Failure to thrive. Role of the mother. *Pediatrics* 1960; 25: 717–725.

100. Weight faltering and failure to thrive infancy and early childhood. *BMJ* 2012; 345: e5931.

101. Ibid.

102. Ibid.

103. Failure to thrive in a population context: two contrasting studies of feeding and nutritional status. *Proc Nutr Soc* 2000; 59: 37–45.

   Mealtime energy intake and feeding behaviour in children who fail to thrive: a population-based case-control study. *J Child Psychol Psychiatry* 2004; 45: 1030–1035.

   Feeding behaviour in young children who fail to thrive. *Appetite* 2003; 40: 55–60.

   Postnatal factors associated with failure to thrive in term infants in the Avon Longitudinal Study of Parents and Children. *Arch Dis Child* 2007; 92: 115–119.

   How does maternal and child feeding behavior relate to weight gain and failure to thrive? Data from a prospective birth cohort. *Pediatrics* 2006; 117: 1262–1269.

   The detection of early weight faltering at the 6–8-week check and its association with family factors, feeding and behavioural development. *Arch Dis Child* 2009; 94: 549–552.

104. Birth characteristics in England and Wales: 2015. *Office for National Statistics* 2016. [Online resource accessed February 2018.]

   Mean, median and quantiles for live births born to mothers aged between 20 and 41 and birthweight between 300g and 5,000g, 1990 to 2014. *Office for National Statistics* 2016. [Online resource accessed February 2018.]

105. Birth of the big one. *The Times*; 13 July 2011. [Online resource accessed February 2018.]

   Why are today's babies being born so big? *Daily Mail*; 4 August 2011. [Online resource accessed February 2018.]

106. Secular trends in birthweight. In *Recent Advances in Growth Research: Nutritional, Molecular and Endocrine Perspectives*, 2013 71: 103–114. Karger Publishers.

107. Birth weight in relation to health and disease in later life: an umbrella review of systematic reviews and meta-analyses. *BMC Medicine* 2016; 14: 147.

108. Determinants of low birth weight: methodological assessment and meta-analysis. *Bulletin of WHO* 1987; 65: 663–737.

109. Genetic and environmental influences on infant growth: prospective analysis of the Gemini twin birth cohort. *PloS One* 2011; 6: e19918.

   A comparison of twin birthweight data from Australia, the Netherlands, the United States, Japan, and South Korea: are genetic and environmental variations in birthweight similar in Caucasians and East Asians?. *Twin Res Hum Genet* 2005; 8: 638–648.

110. Maternal active smoking during pregnancy and low birth weight in the Americas: a systematic review and meta-analysis. *Nicotine Tob Res* 2017; 19: 497–505.

111. Determinants of low birth weight: methodological assessment and meta-analysis. *Bulletin of WHO* 1987; 65: 663–737.

112. Infant feeding recommendation. *Department of Health* 2003 [Online resource accessed February 2018.]

   Infant and young child nutrition: Global strategy on infant and young child feeding. *World Health Organisation* 2002. [Online resource accessed February 2018.]

113. Early nutrition in preterm infants and later blood pressure: two cohorts after randomised trials. *The Lancet* 2001; 357: 413–419.

114. Promotion of Breastfeeding Intervention Trial (PROBIT): a randomized trial in the Republic of Belarus. *JAMA* 2001; 285: 413–420.

115. Breastfeeding in the 21st century: epidemiology, mechanisms, and lifelong effect. *The Lancet* 2016; 387: 475–490.

116. Breastfeeding and maternal and infant health outcomes in developed countries: Evidence Reports/Technology Assessments, No. 153. *Agency for Healthcare*

Research and Quality 2007; 07-E007. [Online resource accessed February 2018.]

117. The role of breastfeeding in sudden infant death syndrome. *J Hum Lact* 2000; 16: 13–20.

118. Statistics on SIDS. *The Lullaby Trust* 2018. [Online resource accessed February 2018.]

119. Short-term effects of breastfeeding: a systematic review on the benefits of breast-feeding on diarrhoea and pneumonia mortality. *World Health Organisation* 2013.

120. Breastfeeding and childhood acute otitis media: a systematic review and meta analysis. *Acta Paediatr* 2015; 104: 85–95.

121. Breastfeeding and childhood leukemia incidence: a meta-analysis and systematic review. *JAMA Pediatr* 2015; 169: e151025.

122. Childhood cancer info. *Children With Cancer UK* 2017. [Online resource accessed February 2018.]

123. Long term consequences of breastfeeding on cholesterol, obesity, systolic blood pressure and type 2 diabetes: a systematic review and meta analysis. *Acta Paediatr* 2015; 104: 30–37.

124. What are the causal effects of breastfeeding on IQ, obesity and blood pressure? Evidence from comparing high-income with middle-income cohorts. *Int J Epidemiol* 2011; 40: 670-80.

125. Effects of promoting long-term, exclusive breastfeeding on adolescent adiposity, blood pressure, and growth trajectories: a secondary analysis of a randomized clinical trial. *JAMA Pediatr* 2017; 171: e170698.

126. Comparing maternal and paternal intergenerational transmission of obesity risk in a large population-based sample. *Am J Clin Nutr* 2010; 91: 1560–1567.

127. Long term consequences of breastfeeding on cholesterol, obesity, systolic blood pressure and type 2 diabetes: a systematic review and meta analysis. *Acta Paediatr* 2015; 104: 30–37.

128. Ibid.

129. Effects of prolonged and exclusive breastfeeding on child height, weight, adiposity, and blood pressure at age 6.5 y: evidence from a large randomized trial. *Am J Clin Nutr* 2007; 86: 1717–1721.

130. Later development of breast fed and artificially fed infants: comparison of physical and mental growth. *JAMA* 1929; 92: 615–619.

131. Effects of exclusive breastfeeding for four versus six months on maternal nutritional status and infant motor development: results of two randomized trials in Honduras. *J Nutr* 2001; 131: 262–267.

Duration of breastfeeding and developmental milestones during the latter half of infancy. *Acta Paediatr* 1999; 88: 1327–1332.

132. Breastfeeding and intelligence: a systematic review and meta analysis. *Acta Paediatr* 2015; 104: 14–19.

133. Breastfeeding and child cognitive development: new evidence from a large randomized trial. *Arch Gen Psychiatry* 2008; 65: 578–584.

134. Breast milk and subsequent intelligence quotient in children born preterm. *The Lancet* 1992; 339: 261–264.

135. Long-term effects of breast-feeding in a national birth cohort: educational attainment and midlife cognitive function. *Public Health Nutr* 2002; 5: 631–635.

    Breast feeding in infancy and social mobility: 60-year follow-up of the Boyd Orr cohort. *Arch Dis Child* 2007; 92: 317–321.

136. Breastfeeding and school achievement in Brazilian adolescents. *Acta Paediatr* 2005; 94: 1656–1660.

    Association between breastfeeding and intelligence, educational attainment, and income at 30 years of age: a prospective birth cohort study from Brazil. *The Lancet Global Health* 2015; 3: e199–e205.

137. The plight of nuns: hazards of null parity (2012) The Lancet; 379 (9834): 2322-2323

138. Breastfeeding and maternal health outcomes: a systematic review and meta analysis. *Acta Paediatr* 2015; 104: 96–113.

139. Statistics by cancer type. *Cancer Research UK* 2014. [Online resource accessed February 2018.]

140. Breastfeeding and maternal health outcomes: a systematic review and meta analysis. *Acta Paediatr* 2015; 104: 96–113.

141. Statistics by cancer type. *Cancer Research UK* 2014. [Online resource accessed February 2018.]

142. Breastfeeding and the maternal risk of type 2 diabetes: A systematic review and dose–response meta-analysis of cohort studies. *Nutr Metab Cardiovasc Dis* 2014; 24: 107–115.

143. Persistent effects of women's parity and breastfeeding patterns on their body mass index: results from the Million Women Study. *Int J Obes* 2013; 37: 712–717.

144. Breastfeeding and depression: a systematic review of the literature. *J Affect Disord* 2015; 171: 142–154.

145. Breastfeeding and maternal health outcomes: a systematic review and meta analysis. *Acta Paediatr* 2015; 104: 96–113.

146. The relationship between breastfeeding and postpartum weight change—a systematic review and critical evaluation. *Int J Obes* 2014; 38: 577–590.

147. Breastfeeding in the 21st century: epidemiology, mechanisms, and lifelong effect. The Lancet, 387(10017), 475–490.

148. Las dos cosas: An analysis of attitudes of Latina women on non-exclusive breastfeeding. *Breastfeed Med* 2012; 7: 19–24.

149. Infant feeding survey 2010. *Health and Social Care Information Centre* 2012. [Online resource accessed February 2018.]

150. Ibid.

151. Ibid.

152. Breastfeeding in the 21st century: epidemiology, mechanisms, and lifelong effect. *Lancet* 2016; 387: 475–490.

153. Biomechanics of milk extraction during breast-feeding. *Proc Natl Acad Sci USA* 2014; 111: 5230-35.

154. The Complete Book of Breast Care. *Fawcett* 1998

155. The effect of breastfeeding on breast aesthetics. *Aesthet Surg J* 2008; 28: 534–537.

156. Waking at night: the effect of early feeding experience. *Child Care Health Dev* 1983; 9: 309–319.

     Sleep/wake patterns of breast-fed infants in the first 2 years of life. *Pediatrics* 1986; 77: 322–329.

     Interaction between feeding method and co sleeping on maternal newborn sleep. *J. Obstet. Gynecol. Neonatal Nurs* 2004; 33: 580–588.

     Breastfeeding patterns in exclusively breastfed infants: a longitudinal prospective study in Uppsala, Sweden. *Acta Paediatr* 1999; 88: 203–211.

     Breastfeeding and infant sleep patterns: an Australian population study. *J Paediatr Child Health* 2013; 49: e147–e152.

157. Infant sleep and night feeding patterns during later infancy: Association with breastfeeding frequency, daytime complementary food intake, and infant weight. *Breastfeed Med* 2015; 10: 246–252.

158. Breast feeding increases sleep duration of new parents. *J Perinat Neonatal Nurs* 2007; 21: 200–206.

     Behavioral sleep interventions in the first six months of life do not improve outcomes for mothers or infants: a systematic review. *J Dev Behav Pediatr* 2013; 34: 497–507.

     Infant feeding methods and maternal sleep and daytime functioning. *Pediatrics* 2010; 126: e1562–e1568.

159. The effect of feeding method on sleep duration, maternal well-being, and postpartum depression. *Clin Lact* 2011; 2: 22–26.

160. Infant sleep and night feeding patterns during later infancy: Association with breastfeeding frequency, daytime complementary food intake, and infant weight. *Breastfeed Med* 2015; 10: 246–252.

161. Breastmilk and breastfeeding: A simple guide. *First Steps Nutrition Trust* 2014. [Online resource accessed February 2018.]

162. Is the macronutrient intake of formula-fed infants greater than breast-fed infants in early infancy?. *J Nutr Metab* 2012; 891201.

163. How breastfeeding works. *J Midwifery Womens Health* 2007, 52:564–570

164. Mechanisms underlying the association between breastfeeding and obesity. *Pediatr Obes* 2009; 4:, 196–204.

    Programming of appetite control during breastfeeding as a preventative strategy against the obesity epidemic. *J Hum Lact* 2014; 30: 136–142.

165. Ghrelin, leptin and IGF I levels in breast fed and formula fed infants in the first years of life. *Acta Paediatr* 2005; 94: 531–537.

    Update on breast milk hormones: leptin, ghrelin and adiponectin. *Clin Nutr ESPEN* 2008; 27: 42–47.

    Presence of obestatin in breast milk: relationship among obestatin, ghrelin, and leptin in lactating women. *Nutrition* 2008; 24: 689–693.

166. Leptin is not present in infant formulas. J *Endocrinol Invest* 2003; 26: 490.

167. Programming of appetite control during breastfeeding as a preventative strategy against the obesity epidemic. *J Hum Lact* 2014; 30: 136–142.

168. Ibid.

169. Prenatal and postnatal flavor learning by human infants. *Pediatrics* 2001; 107: e88.

170. Understanding the basic biology underlying the flavor world of children. *Curr Zool* 2010; 56: 834–841.

171. Demographic, familial and trait predictors of fruit and vegetable consumption by pre-school children. *Public Health Nutr* 2004; 7: 295-302.

    Infant nutrition in relation to eating behaviour and fruit and vegetable intake at age 5 years. *Br J Nutr* 2013; 109: 564-571

    Predictors and consequences of food neophobia and pickiness in young girls. *J Am Diet Assoc* 2003; 104: 692-698

172. Ibid.

173. Infant feeding survey 2010. *Health and Social Care Information Centre.* 2012. [Online resource accessed February 2018.]

174. Infant sleep and night feeding patterns during later infancy: Association with breastfeeding frequency, daytime complementary food intake, and infant weight. *Breastfeed Med* 2015; 10: 246–252.

175. Infant milks in the UK: a practical guide for health professionals – December 2017. *First Steps Nutrition Trust* 2017. [Online resource accessed February 2018.]

176. Essential composition of infant and follow-on formulae. *EFSA Journal* 2014; 12: 3760.

177. Infant milks in the UK: a practical guide for health professionals – December

2017. *First Steps Nutrition Trust* 2017. [Online resource accessed February 2018.]

178. Costs of infant milks marketed in the UK. *First Steps Nutrition Trust* 2017. [Online resource accessed February].

179. Suitability of goat milk protein as a source of protein in infant formulae and in follow-on formulae. *ESFA Journal* 2012; 10: 2603

180. Infant milks: a simple guide to infant formula, follow-on formula and other infant milks. *First Steps Nutrition Trust* 2017. [Online resource accessed February].

181. Infant milks in the UK: a practical guide for health professionals – December 2017. *First Steps Nutrition Trust* 2017. [Online resource accessed February 2018.]

182. Ibid.

183. Hydrolysed formula and risk of allergic or autoimmune disease: systematic review and meta-analysis. *BMJ* 2016; 352: i974.

184. Should partial hydrolysates be used as starter infant formula? A working group consensus. *J Pediatr Gastroenterol Nutr* 2016; 62: 22–35.

185. Report on phytoestrogens and health. *Committee on Toxicity of Chemicals in Food, Consumer Products and the Environment* 2003.

186. CMO's Update 37: A communication to all doctors from the Chief Medical Officer. *Department of Health* 2004. [Online resource accessed February 2018.]

187. Soy protein infant formulae and follow-on formulae: a commentary by the ESPGHAN Committee on Nutrition. *J Pediatr Gastroenterol Nutr* 2006; 42: 352–361.

188. Infant milks: a simple guide to infant formula, follow-on formula and other infant milks. *First Steps Nutrition Trust* 2017. [Online resource accessed February 2018.]

189. Guide to bottle-feeding: how to prepare infant formula and sterilise feeding equipment to minimise the risks to your baby. NHS 2015 [Online resources accessed February 2018].

190. Infant feeding survey 2010. *Health and Social Care Information Centre* 2012. [Online resource accessed February 2018.]

191. Infant milks: a simple guide to infant formula, follow-on formula and other infant milks. *First Steps Nutrition Trust* 2017. [Online resource accessed February 2018.]

192. Appetite and growth: a longitudinal sibling analysis. *JAMA Pediatr* 2014; 168: 345–350.

193. Nature and nurture in infant appetite: analysis of the Gemini twin birth cohort. *Am J Clin Nutr* 2010; 91: 1172–1179.

194. Is the macronutrient intake of formula-fed infants greater than breast-fed infants in early infancy?. *J Nutr Metab* 2012; 891201.

195. Breastfeeding and Human Lactation (4th edn). *Jones & Bartlett Publishers* 2014.

196. Infant feeding behavior: development in patterns and motivation. *Dev Psychobiol* 1996; 29: 563–576.

197. Do infants fed directly from the breast have improved appetite regulation and slower growth during early childhood compared with infants fed from a bottle? *Int J Behav Nutr Phys Act* 2011; 8: 89.

198. Risk of bottle-feeding for rapid weight gain during the first year of life. *Arch Pediatr Adolesc Med* 2012; 166: 431–436.

199. Infants fed from bottles lack self-regulation of milk intake compared with directly breastfed infants? *Pediatrics* 2010; 125: e1386–e1393.

200. Infant self regulation of breast milk intake. *Acta Paediatr* 1986; 75: 893–898.

201. Association between bottle size and formula intake in 2-month-old infants. *Academic Pediatrics* 2016; 16: 254–259.

202. Bottle size and weight gain in formula-fed infants. *Pediatrics* 2016; 138: e20154538.

203. Plate size and children's appetite: effects of larger dishware on self-served portions and intake. *Pediatrics* 2013; 131: e1451–e1458.

204. A pilot study comparing opaque, weighted bottles with conventional, clear bottles for infant feeding. *Appetite* 2015; 85: 178–184.

205. Educational intervention to modify bottle-feeding behaviors among formula-feeding mothers in the WIC program: impact on infant formula intake and weight gain. *J Nutr Educ Behav* 2008; 40: 244–250.

Maternal perceptions of infant hunger, satiety and pressuring feeding styles in an urban Latina WIC population. *Acad Pediatr* 2010; 10: 29–35.

Association of breastfeeding intensity and bottle-emptying behaviors at early infancy with infants' risk for excess weight at late infancy. *Pediatrics* 2008; 122(Suppl. 2): S77–S84.

206. Associations between breastfeeding and maternal responsiveness: a systematic review of the literature. *Adv Nutr* 2017; 8: 495–510.

207. Bottle-feeding practices during early infancy and eating behaviors at 6 years of age. *Pediatrics* 2014; 134(Suppl. 1): S70–S77.

208. Your pregnancy and baby guide: Your breastfeeding questions answered. *NHS Choices* 2017. [Online resource accessed February 2018.]

209. Complementary feeding: a position paper by the European Society for Paediatric Gastroenterology, Hepatology, and Nutrition (ESPGHAN) committee on nutrition. *J Pediatr Gastroenterol Nutr* 2017; 64: 119–132.

210. Intervention Nurses Start Infants Growing on Healthy Trajectories (INSIGHT) study. *BMC Pediatrics* 2014; 14: 184.

Effect of the INSIGHT responsive parenting intervention on rapid infant weight gain and overweight status at age 1 year: a randomized clinical trial. *JAMA Pediatr* 2016; 170: 742–749.

211. Infant eating behaviors and risk for overweight. *JAMA* 2016; 316: 2036–2037.

212. Parental control over feeding in infancy. Influence of infant weight, appetite and feeding method. *Appetite* 2015; 91: 101–106.

213. Maternal feeding practices and fussy eating in toddlerhood: a discordant twin analysis. *Int J Behav Nutr Phys Act* 2016; 13: 81.

214. Food neophobia and 'picky/fussy'eating in children: a review. *Appetite* 2008; 50: 181–193.

Feeding and eating disorders in childhood. *Int J Eat Disord* 2010; 43: 98–111.

215. Communicating hunger and satiation in the first 2 years of life: a systematic review. *Matern Child Nutr* 2016; 12: 205–228.

Development of the responsiveness to child feeding cues scale. *Appetite* 2013; 65: 210–219.

216. Responding to infants' hunger and satiety cues. *Health Promotion Agency* 2014.

217. Communicating hunger and satiation in the first 2 years of life: a systematic review. *Matern Child Nutr* 2016; 12: 205–228.

Development of the responsiveness to child feeding cues scale. *Appetite* 2013; 65: 210–219.

218. Managing infants who cry excessively in the first few months of life. *BMJ* 2011; 343: d7772.

219. Communicating hunger and satiation in the first 2 years of life: a systematic review. *Matern Child Nutr* 2016; 12: 205–228.

Development of the responsiveness to child feeding cues scale. *Appetite* 2013; 65: 210–219.

220. Infant crying and sleeping: helping parents to prevent and manage problems. *Prim Care* 2008; 35: 547–567.

221. Systematic review and meta-analysis: fussing and crying durations and prevalence of colic in infants. *J Pediatr* 2017; 185: 55-61.

222. The normal crying curve: what do we really know?. *Dev Med Child Neurol* 1990; 32: 356–362.

Systematic review and meta-analysis: fussing and crying durations and prevalence of colic in infants. *J Pediatr* 2017; 185: 55-61.

Excessive crying. In Handbook of developmental psychopathology (327–350). *Springer* 2000.

223. What is the period of PURPLE crying?. *The Period of PURPLE Crying.* [Online resource accessed February 2018.]

224. Managing infants who cry excessively in the first few months of life. *BMJ* 2011; 343:d7772

225. SIDS and other sleep-related infant deaths: evidence base for 2016 updated recommendations for a safe infant sleeping environment. *Pediatrics* 2016; 138: e20162940.

226. Rattling the plate—reasons and rationales for early weaning. *Health Educ Res* 2001; 16: 471–479.

227. Adult perception of emotion intensity in human infant cries: Effects of infant age and cry acoustics. *Child Dev* 1996; 67: 3238–3249.

   Decoding of baby calls: can adult humans identify the eliciting situation from emotional vocalizations of preverbal infants? *PloS One* 2015; 10: e0124317.

228. SIDS and other sleep-related infant deaths: evidence base for 2016 updated recommendations for a safe infant feeding environment. *Pediatrics* 2016; 138: e20162940.

229. Do pacifiers reduce the risk of sudden infant death syndrome? A meta-analysis. *Pediatrics* 2005; 116: e716-e723.

230. Pacifiers and breastfeeding: a systematic review. *Arch Pediatr Adolesc Med* 2009; 163: 378–382.

231. Swaddling baby is back in fashion. *Reuters* 2011. [Online resource accessed February 2018.]

232. Swaddling: a systematic review. *Pediatrics* 2007; 120: e1097–e1106.

233. Swaddling and the risk of Sudden Infant Death Syndrome: a meta-analysis. *Pediatrics* 2016; 137: e20153275.

234. SIDS and other sleep-related infant deaths: evidence base for 2016 Updated Recommendations for a safe infant sleeping environment. *Pediatrics* 2016; 138: e20162940.

235. Ibid.

236. Early skin-to-skin contact for mothers and their healthy newborn infants. *The Cochrane Database Syst Rev* 2012; 5: CD3519.

   Increased carrying reduces infant crying: a randomized controlled trial. *Pediatrics* 1986; 77: 641–648.

237. Managing infants who cry excessively in the first few months of life. *BMJ* 2011; 343: d7772.

238. Common features and principles of soothing. *The Period of PURPLE Crying.* [Online resource accessed February 2018.]

239. Infant crying and sleeping: helping parents to prevent and manage problems: *Prim Care* 2008; 35:547–567.

240. Colic, overfeeding and the symptoms of lactose malabsorption in the breastfed baby: a possible artefact of feed management. *The Lancet* 1988; 332: 382–384.

Managing infants who cry excessively in the first few months of life. *BMJ* 2011; 343: d7772.

Diagnosing gastro oesophageal reflux disease or lactose intolerance in babies who cry alot in the first few months overlooks feeding problems. *J Paediatr Child Health* 2013; 49: e252–e256.

241. Diagnosing gastro oesophageal reflux disease or lactose intolerance in babies who cry a lot in the first few months overlooks feeding problems. *J Paediatr Child Health* 2013; 49: e252-e256.

242. Effect of the method of breast feeding on breast engorgement, mastitis and infantile colic. *Acta Paediatr* 1995; 84: 849–852.

Diagnosing gastro oesophageal reflux disease or lactose intolerance in babies who cry alot in the first few months overlooks feeding problems. *J Paediatr Child Health* 2013; 49: e252–e256.

243. Diagnosing gastro oesophageal reflux disease or lactose intolerance in babies who cry alot in the first few months overlooks feeding problems. *J Paediatr Child Health* 2013; 49: e252–e256.

244. Lactose overload in babies. *Australian Breastfeeding Association* 2016. [Online resource accessed February 2018.]

245. Volume and frequency of breastfeedings and fat content of breast milk throughout the day. *Pediatrics* 2006; 117: e387–e395.

246. Infant milks in the UK: a practical guide for health professionals – December 2017. *First Steps Nutrition Trust* 2017. [Online resource accessed February 2018.]

247. How much milk is needed by infants and young children. First Steps Nutrition Trust. [Online resource accessed February 2018.]

248. Ibid.

249. Iron requirements of infants and toddlers. *J Pediatr Gastroenterol Nutr* 2014; 58:119–129

250. Infant feeding survey 2010. *Health and Social Care Information Centre* 2012. [Online resource accessed February 2018.]

251. Ibid.

252. Adequacy of milk intake during exclusive breastfeeding: a longitudinal study. *Pediatrics* 2011; 128: e907–e914.

253. Complementary feeding: a position paper by the European Society for Paediatric Gastroenterology, Hepatology, and Nutrition (ESPGHAN) committee on nutrition. *J Pediatr Gastroenterol Nutr* 2017; 64: 119–132.

254. Optimal duration of exclusive breastfeeding: what is the evidence to support current recommendations?. *Am J Clin Nutr* 2007; 85: 635S–638S.

255. Age of introduction of first complementary feeding for infants: a systematic review. *BMC Pediatrics* 2015; 15: 107.

256. Complementary feeding: a position paper by the European Society for Paediatric Gastroenterology, Hepatology, and Nutrition (ESPGHAN) committee on nutrition. *J Pediatr Gastroenterol Nutr* 2017; 64: 119–132.

257. Are There Sensitive Periods for Food Acceptance in Infancy?. *Curr Nutr Rep* 2017; 6: 190–196.

258. Exposure to vegetable variety in infants weaned at different ages. *Appetite* 2014; 78: 89–94.

259. Draft Feeding in the First Year of Life Report. Scientific Consultation: 19 July to 13 September. *Scientific Advisory Committee on Nutrition* 2017. [Online resource accessed February 2018.]

260. Delayed introduction of lumpy foods to children during the complementary feeding period affects child's food acceptance and feeding at 7 years of age. *Matern Child Nutr* 2009; 5: 75–85.

261. Association of early life risk factors with infant sleep duration. *Acad Pediatr* 2010; 10: 187-193.

   Infant sleep and bedtime cereal. *Am J Dis Child* 1989; 143: 1066-1068.

   Age at introduction of solid foods to infants in Manitoba. *J Can Diet Assoc* 1981; 42: 72-78

262. Infant feeding survey 2010. *Health and Social Care Information Centre* 2012. [Online resource accessed February 2018].

263. A baby-led approach to eating solids as risk of choking. *Pediatrics* 2016; 138: e20160772

264. A descriptive study investigating the use and nature of baby-led weaning in a UK sample of mothers. *Matern Child Nutr* 2011; 7: 34-47.

265. Effect of a baby-led approach to complementary feeding on infant growth and overweight: a randomized clinical trial. *JAMA Pediatr* 2017; 171: 838–846.

266. Baby-led weaning—safe and effective but not preventive of obesity. *JAMA Pediatr* 2017; 171: 832–833.

267. Complementary feeding: a position paper by the European Society for Paediatric Gastroenterology, Hepatology, and Nutrition (ESPGHAN) committee on nutrition. *J Pediatr Gastroenterol Nutr* 2017; 64: 119–132.

268. Global strategy for infant and young child feeding. *World Health Organization* 2003. [Online resource accessed February 2018.]

269. Your pregnancy and baby guide: Your baby's first solid foods. *NHS Choices* 2018. [Online resource accessed February 2018.]

270. Parenting styles, feeding styles, feeding practices, and weight status in 4–12 year-old children: a systematic review of the literature. *Front Psychol* 2015; 6: 1849.

    The role of responsive feeding in overweight during infancy and toddlerhood: a systematic review. *Int J Obes* 2011; 35: 480–492.

271. Food neophobia and 'picky/fussy'eating in children: a review. *Appetite* 2008; 50: 181–193.

272. Controlling feeding practices: cause or consequence of early child weight?. *Pediatrics* 2008; 121: e164–e169.

    Feeding practices and child weight: is the association bidirectional in preschool children?. *Am J Clin Nutr* 2014; 100: 1329–1336.

    Bidirectional association between parental child-feeding practices and body mass index at 4 and 7 y of age. *Am J Clin Nutr* 2016; 103: 861–867.

    Bi-directional associations between child fussy eating and parents' pressure to eat: Who influences whom?. *Physiol Behav* 2017; 176: 101–106.

    'Finish your soup': counterproductive effects of pressuring children to eat on intake and affect. *Appetite* 2006; 46: 318–323.

273. Feeding practices and child weight: is the association bidirectional in preschool children?. *Am J Clin Nutr* 2014; 100: 1329–1336.

    Bidirectional association between parental child-feeding practices and body mass index at 4 and 7 y of age. *Am J Clin Nutr* 2016; 103: 861–867.

    Child adiposity and maternal feeding practices: a longitudinal analysis. *Am J Clin Nutr* 2010; 92: 1423–1328.

    Controlling feeding practices: cause or consequence of early child weight?. *Pediatrics* 2008; 121:, e164–e169.

    Bi-directional associations between child fussy eating and parents' pressure to eat: Who influences whom?. *Physiol Behav* 2017; 176: 101–106.

274. Parental use of restrictive feeding practices and child BMI z-score. A 3-year prospective cohort study. *Appetite* 2010; 55: 84-88.

275. Child adiposity and maternal feeding practices: a longitudinal analysis. *Am J Clin Nutr* 2010; 92: 1423–1328.

    Feeding practices and child weight: is the association bidirectional in preschool children?. *Am J Clin Nutr* 2014; 100: 1329–1336.

    Bidirectional association between parental child-feeding practices and body mass index at 4 and 7 y of age. *Am J Clin Nutr* 2016; 103: 861–867.

    Testing the direction of effects between child body composition and restrictive feeding practices: results from a population-based cohort. *Am J Clin Nutr* 2017; 106: 783–790.

276. Restricting access to palatable foods affects children's behavioral response, food selection, and intake. *Am J Clin Nutr* 1999; 69: 1264–1272.

277. The home environment shapes emotional eating in childhood. *Child Dev* 2017; In Press.

278. Emotional feeding and emotional eating – reciprocal processes and the influence of negative affectivity. *Child Dev* 2017; In Press.

279. Eating as the 'means' activity in a contingency: effects on young children's food preference. *Child Dev* 1984; 55: 431–439.

    Effect of a means-end contingency on young children's food preferences. *J Exp Child Psychol* 1992; 64: 200–216.

280. Development of the responsiveness to child feeding cues scale. *Appetite* 2013; 65: 210–219.

281. Whole cow's milk in infancy. *Paediatr Child Health (Oxford)* 2003; 8: 419–421.

282. How much milk is needed by infants and young children. First Steps Nutrition Trust. [Online resource accessed February 2018.]

283. Information concerning the use and marketing of follow-up formula. *World Health Organisation* 2013. [Online resource accessed February 2018].

284. Infant milk in the UK: a practical guide for health professionals – December 2017. *First Steps Nutrition Trust* 2017. [Online resource accessed February 2018].

285. Ibid.

286. The importance of exposure for healthy eating in childhood: a review. *J Hum Nutr Diet* 2007; 20: 294–301.

    Early influences on the development of food preferences. *Curr Biol* 2013; 23: R401–R408.

287. Age and gender differences in children's food preferences. *Br J Nutr* 2005; 93: 741–746.

288. Effects of starting weaning exclusively with vegetables on vegetable intake at the age of 12 and 23 months. *Appetite* 2014; 81: 193–199.

    Effects of repeated exposure to either vegetables or fruits on infant's vegetable and fruit acceptance at the beginning of weaning. *Food Qual Prefer* 2013; 29: 157–165.

    Breastfeeding and experience with variety early in weaning increase infants' acceptance of new foods for up to two months. *Clin Nutr ESPEN* 2008; 27: 849–857.

289. An exploratory trial of parental advice for increasing vegetable acceptance in infancy. *Br J Nutr* 2015; 114: 328–336.

290. Infant feeding survey 2010. *Health and Social Care Information Centre* 2012.

291. Development of healthy eating habits early in life. Review of recent evidence and selected guidelines. *Appetite* 2011; 57: 796–807.

Children's acceptance of new foods at weaning. Role of practices of weaning and of food sensory properties. *Appetite* 2011; 57: 812–815.

Impacts of in utero and early infant taste experiences on later taste acceptance: a systematic review. *J Nutr* 2015; 145: 1271–1279.

292. The Composition of Foods (7th Edition). *Public Health England* 2014.

293. SACN Carbohydrates and health. *The Stationery Office* 2015. [Online resource accessed February 2018.]

294. Your pregnancy and baby guide: Drinks and cups for babies and toddlers. *NHS Choices* 2015. [Online resource accessed February 2018.]

295. Diet and Nutrition Survey of Infants and Young Children, 2011. *Department of Health and Social Care* 2013. [Online resource accessed February 2018.]

296. Baby foods in the UK: a review of commercially produced jars and pouches of baby foods marketed in the UK. *First Steps Nutrition Trust* 2017. [Online resource accessed February 2018.]

297. Complementary feeding: a position paper by the European Society for Paediatric Gastroenterology, Hepatology, and Nutrition (ESPGHAN) committee on nutrition. *J Pediatr Gastroenterol Nutr* 2017; 64: 119–132.

298. Draft Feeding in the First Year of Life Report. Scientific Consultation: 19 July to 13 September. *Scientific Advisory Committee on Nutrition* 2017. [Online resource accessed February 2018.]

299. Complementary feeding: a position paper by the European Society for Paediatric Gastroenterology, Hepatology, and Nutrition (ESPGHAN) committee on nutrition. *J Pediatr Gastroenterol Nutr* 2017; 64: 119–132.

300. SACN Salt and health. *The Stationery Office* 2003. [Online resource accessed February 2018.]

301. The development of salty taste acceptance is related to dietary experience in human infants: a prospective study. *Am J Clin Nutr* 2012; 95: 123–129.

302. Energy and nutrient intakes of young children in the UK: findings from the Gemini twin cohort. *Br J Nutr* 2016; 115: 1843-1850.

303. National Diet and Nutrition Survey: Results from Years 1-4 (combined) of the Rolling Programme (2008/2009-2011/12). Executive Summary. *Public Health England* 2014. [Online resource accessed February 2018.

304. Dietary reference values for food energy and nutrients for the United Kingdom: Report of the Panel on Dietary Reference Values of the Committee on Medical Aspects of Food Policy. *The Stationery Office* 1991.

305. How to get vitamin D from sunlight. *NHS Choices* 2015. [Online resource accessed February 2018.]

306. Resurrection of vitamin D deficiency and rickets. *J Clin Invest* 2006; 116: 2062-2072.

307. Vitamin D effects on musculoskeletal health, immunity, autoimmunity, cardio-vascular disease, cancer, fertility, pregnancy, dementia and mortality – a review of recent evidence. *Autoimmun Rev* 2013; 12: 976-989

308. SACN Vitamin D and health report. London: *The Stationery Office* 2016. [Online resource accessed February 2018.]

309. Vitamin A. *NHS Choices* 2017. [Online resource accessed February 2018]

310. Prevalence of Vitamin A deficiency in populations at risk 1995-2005: WHO global database on Vitamin A deficiency. *World Health Organisation* 2009. [Online resource accessed February 2018]

311. Vitamin C and immune function. *Nutrients* 2017; 9: 1211

312. Your pregnancy and baby guide. Your baby's first solid foods: From 6 months – vitamins for babies and children. *NHS Choices* 2018. [Online resource accessed February 2018]

313. Tolerable upper intake levels for vitamins and minerals. *European Food Safety Authority* 2006. [Online resource accessed February 2018]

314. Iron deficiency anemia. *Med Clin North Am* 2017; 101: 319-332

315. The importance of exposure for healthy eating in childhood: a review. *J Hum Nutr Diet* 2007; 20: 294–301.

316. Effects of repeated exposure on acceptance of initially disliked vegetables in 7-month old infants. *Food Qual Prefer* 2007; 18: 1023–1032.

317. Complementary feeding: vegetables first, frequently and in variety. *Nutr Bull* 2016; 41: 142–146.

318. Draft Feeding in the First Year of Life Report. Scientific Consultation: 19 July to 13 September. *Scientific Advisory Committee on Nutrition* 2017. [Online resource accessed February 2018.]

319. SACN Advice on fish consumption: benefits and risks. *The Stationery Office* 2004. [Online resource accessed February 2018.].

320. Health Survey for England, 2015. *NHS Digital* 2016. [Online resource accessed February 2018.]

321. National Child Measurement Programme – England, 2016–17. *NHS Digital* 2017. [Online resource accessed February 2018.]

322. Changes in the weight status of children between the first and final years of primary school. *Public Health England* 2017. [Online resource accessed February 2018.]

323. Predicting adult obesity from childhood obesity: a systematic review and meta analysis. *Obes Rev* 2016; 17: 95–107.

324. Psychological consequences of childhood obesity: psychiatric comorbidity and prevention. *Adolesc Health Med Ther* 2016; 7: 125–146.

325. Childhood obesity as a predictor of morbidity in adulthood: a systematic review and meta analysis. *Obes Rev* 2016; 17: 56–67.

326. Energy and nutrient intakes of young children in the UK: findings from the Gemini twin cohort. *Br J Nutr* 2016; 115: 1843–1850.

327. SACN Dietary reference values for energy. *The Stationery Office* 2011. [Online resource accessed February 2018.]

328. Dietary reference values for food energy and nutrients for the United Kingdom: Report on Health and Social Subjects no. 41. *Committee on Medical Aspects of Food Policy* 1991.

329. Protein intake during the period of complementary feeding and early childhood and the association with body mass index and percentage body fat at 7 y of age. *Am J Clin Nutr* 2007; 85: 1626–1633.

330. High protein intake in young children and increased weight gain and obesity risk. *Am J Clin Nutr* 2016; 103: 303–304.

331. Dietary protein intake is associated with body mass index and weight up to 5 y of age in a prospective cohort of twins. *Am J Clin Nutr* 2016; 103: 389–397.

332. Dairy protein in the post-weaning phase is positively associated with BMI and weight up to five years of age. *Appetite* 2015; 87: 398.

333. Dietary intake of young twins: nature or nurture?. *Am J Clin Nutr* 2013; 98: 1326–1334.
  Energy and nutrient intakes of young children in the UK: findings from the Gemini twin cohort. Br J Nutr 2016; 115:1843–1850.

334. SACN Carbohydrates and health. *The Stationary Office* 2015. [Online resource accessed February 2018.]

335. Ibid.

336. The Composition of Foods (7th Edition). *Public Health England* 2014.

337. Dairy and alternatives in your diet: Dairy intake for babies and children under five. *NHS Choices* 2018. [Online resource accessed February 2018.]

338. Effects of saturated fatty acids on serum lipids and lipoproteins: a systematic review and regression analysis. *World Health Organisation* 2016. [Online resource accessed February 2018.]

339. SACN Carbohydrates and health. *The Stationary Office* 2015. [Online resource accessed February 2018.]

340. Energy and nutrient intakes of young children in the UK: findings from the Gemini twin cohort. *Br J Nutr* 2016; 115: 1843–1850.

341. Fibre and prevention of chronic diseases. *BMJ* 2011; 343: 1075.

342. SACN Vitamin D and health report. London: *The Stationery Office* 2016. [Online resource accessed February 2018.]

343. Energy and nutrient intakes of young children in the UK: findings from the Gemini twin cohort. *Br J Nutr* 2016; 115: 1843–1850.

344. Dietary reference values for food energy and nutrients for the United Kingdom:

Report on Health and Social Subjects no. 41. *Committee on Medical Aspects of Food Policy* 1991.

345. Diet in a group of 18 month old children in South West England, and comparison with the results of a national survey. *J Hum Nutr Diet* 2000; 20: 254–267.

346. A qualitative study of uptake of free vitamins in England. *Arch Dis Child* 2013; 98: 587–91.

347. SACN Salt and health. *The Stationery Office* 2003. [Online resource accessed February 2018.]

348. Nutrition requirements. *British Nutrition Foundation* 2016. [Online resource accessed February 2018.]

349. Salt intakes around the world: implications for public health. *Int. J. of Epidemiol* 2009; 38: 791-813.

350. The development of salty taste acceptance is related to dietary experience in human infants: a prospective study. *Am J Clin Nutr* 2012; 95: 123–129.

351. National Diet and Nutrition Survey: Results from Years 1-4 (combined) of the Rolling Programme (2008/2009-2011/12). Executive Summary. *Public Health England* 2014. [Online resource accessed February 2018.]

     Energy and nutrient intakes of young children in the UK: findings from the Gemini twin cohort. Br J Nutr 2016; 115:1843–1850.

352. About Change4Life. *Change4life.* [Online resource accessed February 2018.]

353. Eatwell guide. *Public Health England* 2016. [Online resource accessed February 2018.]

354. Good food choices and portion sizes for 1-4 year olds. *First Steps Nutrition Trust* 2016. [Online resource accessed February 2018.]

355. Determinants of fruit and vegetable consumption among children and adolescents: a review of the literature. Part I: quantitative studies. *Int J Behav Nutr Phys Act* 2006; 3: 22.

356. Portion sizes for children aged 1–4 years. *Infant & Toddler Forum* 2015. [Online resource accessed February 2018.]

357. Example menus for early years settings in England. Part 1: Guidance. *Public Health England* 2017. [Online resource accessed February 2018.]

     Example menus for early years settings in England. Part 2: Recipes. *Public Health England* 2017. [Online resource accessed February 2018.]

358. #rethinktoddlerportionsizes. Infant & Toddler Forum. [Online resource accessed February 2018.]

359. Children eat what they are served: the imprecise regulation of energy intake. *Appetite* 2005; 44: 273–282.

360. Children's bite size and intake of an entrée are greater with large portions than with age-appropriate or self-selected portions. *Am J Clin Nutr* 2003; 77: 1164 – 1170.

361. Children eat what they are served: the imprecise regulation of energy intake. *Appetite* 2005; 44: 273–282.

362. Infant self regulation of breast milk intake. *Acta Paediatr* 1986; 75: 893–898.

363. Portion, package or tableware size for changing selection and consumption of food, alcohol and tobacco. *Cochrane Database Syst Rev* 2015; 15: CD011045.

364. Overweight very young children consume larger meals. *European Association for the Study of Obesity (conference abstract for the 2016 European Obesity Summit)* 2016.

365. Meal size is a critical driver of weight gain in early childhood. *Sci Rep* 2016; 6: 28368.

366. Portion sizes for children aged 1–4 years. *Infant & Toddler Forum* 2015. [Online resource accessed February 2018.]

367. Good food choices and portion sizes for 1-4 year olds. *First Steps Nutrition Trust* 2016. [Online resource accessed February 2018.]

368. A systematic review of responsive feeding and child obesity in high-income countries. *J Nutr* 2011; 141: 495–501.

    The role of responsive feeding in overweight during infancy and toddlerhood: a systematic review. *Int J Obes* 2011; 35: 480-492.

369. Systematic review of randomised controlled trials of interventions that aim to reduce the risk, either directly or indirectly, of overweight and obesity in infancy and early childhood. *Matern Child Nutr* 2016; 12: 24–38.

370. The NOURISH randomised control trial: positive feeding practices and food preferences in early childhood-a primary prevention program for childhood obesity. *BMC Public Health* 2009; 9: 387.

371. Child eating behavior outcomes of an early feeding intervention to reduce risk indicators for child obesity: the NOURISH RCT. *Pediatr Obes* 2014; 22: e104–e111.

372. Child dietary and eating behavior outcomes up to 3.5 years after an early feeding intervention: The NOURISH RCT. *Pediatr Obes* 2016; 24: 1537–1545.

373. Outcomes of an early feeding practices intervention to prevent childhood obesity. *Pediatrics* 2013; 132: e109–e118.

374. A perspective on family meals. Do they matter? *Nutr Today* 2005; 40: 261-266.

375. Is frequency of shared family meals related to the nutritional health of children and adolescents? *Pediatrics* 2011; 127: e1565–e1574.

376. Characteristics of family mealtimes affecting children's vegetable consumption and liking. *J Acad Nutr Diet* 2011; 111: 269–273.

377. A systematic review of the effect of breakfast on the cognitive performance of children and adolescents. *Nutr Res Rev* 2009; 22: 220–243.

378. Systematic review demonstrating that breakfast consumption influences body weight outcomes in children and adolescents in Europe. *Crit Rev Food Sci Nutr* 2010; 50: 113–119.

379. Appetite and growth: a longitudinal sibling analysis. *JAMA Pediatr* 2014; 168: 345–350.

    Prospective associations of appetitive traits at 3 and 12 months of age with body mass ndex and weight gain in the first 2 years of life. *BMC Pediatr* 2015; 15: 153.

    Do maternal ratings of appetite in infants predict later Child Eating Behaviour Questionnaire scores and body mass index?. *Appetite* 2010; 54: 186–190.

380. Appetitive traits and food intake patterns in early life. *Am J Clin Nutr* 2016; 103: 231–235.

381. Hormonal regulators of appetite. *Int J Pediatr Endocrinol* 2009; 141753.

382. A systematic review and meta-analysis examining the effect of eating rate on energy intake and hunger. *Am J Clin Nutr* 2014; 100: 123–151.

383. Glycaemic response to foods: impact on satiety and long-term weight regulation. *Appetite* 2007; 49: 535–553.

    Glycaemic index, appetite and body weight. *Proc Nutr Soc* 2010; 69: 199–203.

384. The non-advertising effects of screen-based sedentary activities on acute eating behaviours in children, adolescents, and young adults. A systematic review. *Appetite* 2013; 71: 259–273.

385. Effect of television advertisements for foods on food consumption in children. *Appetite* 2004; 42: 221–225.

    Children's food preferences: Effects of weight status, food type, branding and television food advertisements (commercials). *Pediatr Obes* 2008; 3: 31–38.

    Beyond-brand effect of television (TV) food advertisements/commercials on caloric intake and food choice of 5–7-year-old children. *Appetite* 2007; 49: 263–267.

    Beyond-brand effect of television food advertisements on food choice in children: the effects of weight status. *Public Health Nutr* 2008; 11: 897–904.

386. Improving preschoolers' self-regulation of energy intake. *Pediatrics* 2000; 106: 1429–1435.

387. Appetitive traits and food intake patterns in early life. *Am J Clin Nutr* 2016; 103: 231–235.

388. Restricting access to palatable foods affects children's behavioral response, food selection, and intake. *Am J Clin Nutr* 1999; 69: 1264–1272.

389. Parenting styles, feeding styles, feeding practices, and weight status in 4–12

year-old children: a systematic review of the literature. *Front Psychol* 2015; 6: 1849.

390. Picky/fussy eating in children: review of definitions, assessment, prevalence and dietary intakes. *Appetite* 2015; 95: 349–359.

391. Prevalence of picky eaters among infants and toddlers and their caregivers' decisions about offering a new food. *J Acad Nutr Diet* 2004; 104: S57–S64.

392. Associations between children's appetitive traits and maternal feeding practices. *J Acad Nutr Diet* 2010; 110: 1718–1722.

    Maternal feeding practices and fussy eating in toddlerhood: a discordant twin analysis. *Int J Behav Nutr Phys Act* 2016; 13: 81.

393. The role of infant appetite in extended formula feeding. *Arch Dis Child* 2015; 100: 758.

394. Increasing food acceptance in the home setting: a randomized controlled trial of parent-administered taste exposure with incentives. *Am J Clin Nutr* 2012; 95: 72–77.

395. Parent-administered exposure to increase children's vegetable acceptance: a randomized controlled trial. *J Acad Nutr Diet* 2014; 114: 881–888.

396. SACN Dietary reference values for energy. *The Stationery Office* 2011. [Online resource accessed February 2018.]

397. Ibid.

398. Portion sizes for children aged 1–4 years. *Infant & Toddler Forum* 2015 (online resource accessed February 2018).

Index

books to help you live a good life

Join the conversation and tell
us how you live a #goodlife

🐦 @yellowkitebooks
📘 YellowKiteBooks
📌 Yellow Kite Books
📷 YellowKiteBooks